# *Writing about Music*

FOURTH
EDITION

# *Writing*
# *about*
# *Music*

## AN INTRODUCTORY GUIDE

## Richard J. Wingell
*University of Southern California*

PEARSON
Prentice
Hall

Upper Saddle River, New Jersey 07458

**Library of Congress Cataloging-in-Publication Data**

Wingell, Richard
  Writing about music : an introductory guide / Richard J. Wingell. — 4th ed.
      p. cm.
  Includes bibliographical references and index.
  ISBN 0-13-615778-5 (alk. paper)
  1. Music—Historiography. 2. Musical criticism—Authorship. 3. Academic
writing. I. Title.
  ML3797.W54 2007
  808'.06678—dc22

                                                                    2007038557

Executive Editor: *Richard Carlin*
Editor in Chief: *Sarah Touborg*
Editorial Assistant: *Emma Gibbons*
Marketing Manager: *Sasha Anderson-Smith*
Senior Managing Editor: *Mary Rottino*
Production Liaison: *Fran Russello*
Sr. Operations Supervisor: *Brian Mackey*
Cover Design: *Bruce Kenselaar*
Manager, Cover Visual Research & Permissions: *Karen Sanatar*
Composition/Full-Service Project Management: *ICC Macmillan Inc.*
Printer/Binder: *RR Donnelley & Sons Company*

Pearson Education Ltd., London
Pearson Education Singapore, Pte. Ltd
Pearson Education, Canada, Ltd
Pearson Education–Japan
Pearson Education Australia PTY, Limited

Pearson Education North Asia Ltd
Pearson Educación de Mexico, S.A. de C.V.
Pearson Education Malaysia, Pte. Ltd
Pearson Education, Upper Saddle River,
   New Jersey

10 9 8 7 6 5 4 3 2 1

ISBN (10): 0-13-615778-5
ISBN (13): 978-0-13-615778-6

# Contents

**3    Getting Started: Research    24**

**4    Writing a Research Paper    47**

# Preface

Since it was first published in 1990, this writing guide for undergraduate music majors has proved useful in music departments and schools of music around the country. It has been used in academic courses by both music majors and nonmajors. A second edition in 1997 attempted to improve on the content and tone of the first edition, as well as updating the listings of resources useful for research and writing. A third edition in 2002 made further improvements, changing the organization of the material, expanding several sections, and adding a new sample paper. Now, to keep pace with new publications and exciting developments in electronic resources for research, it is time for a newly revised edition of *Writing about Music: An Introductory Guide.*

## PURPOSE OF THE FOURTH EDITION

Resources for research and the ways we use them have changed greatly in just a few years. Many important new print resources have appeared since the last edition, and there are new developments in electronic research. The Internet continues to be the major repository for information of all sorts; since the last edition of this guide was published, several important resources have appeared on the Web. In addition, in the sections on writing, the frequent citations of writing guides such as *The Chicago Manual of Style* and Turabian's manual needed updating to correspond to the most recent editions of these works.

Finally, there is clearly a greater need than ever for a manual like this. First of all, despite the fact that all students now use either their own computers or the sophisticated equipment colleges and universities provide for their use, many students still hand in papers that are actually preliminary drafts in desperate need of revision and proofreading. It is so much easier to revise and edit on a computer than it was in the old days of typewriters and correction tape. I will not launch into a diatribe about how difficult things were when I was a student, but those who use computers should be aware of all the things they can do to help you produce a first-class paper.

I have noticed another interesting phenomenon about papers and computers: In my last few undergraduate classes, there were always one or two students with a flair for graphics who handed in papers with wonderful illustrations on the title page. Unfortunately, that creativity and skill did not always extend to the papers inside. In every class, there are also some students who have finely honed writing skills, who can argue complex ideas clearly and skillfully, and who produce prose that is a pleasure to read. In today's expanding college population, the gap in skills such as critical thinking and persuasive writing between the students in any class is staggering. Instructors constantly try to improve the organization of their courses so that they continue to challenge the best students while still making it possible for the people who do not do as well to succeed. My hope is that this manual will be of use to all undergraduate students. Students who are already skillful writers can use it for review, and students who somehow entered college without basic writing skills can also learn useful things from it. In addition, this guide may continue to be useful for new graduate students who have not had a strong writing course in their undergraduate years or for whom English is a second language.

Another reason for producing a fourth edition of this guide is that the language is still under assault all around us. We are bombarded daily by language that is imprecise and careless. On television broadcasts of football games, we hear coaches at halftime babbling about their hopes for a better second half—"We made too many mental errors in the first half. We're gonna have to suck it up, find some people who can step up and go out there and make something happen!" The words sound resolute, but what exactly do they mean? Newscasters continue to offer observations such as "Hopefully, the rain will end by the weekend" and "Not one of the jury members were inclined to be lenient." Even leading newspapers, probably relying too heavily on their computers' spell-checking programs, print errors such as "waiting with baited breath," "pouring over the records," and "tow the line." If you don't see anything wrong with these examples, you may find this guide quite useful—or you might want to check your dictionary.

Since the last edition of this book, new cliches have sprouted up, taking over the language like crabgrass. Everywhere we hear English spoken, we hear "at the end of the day" used in the sense of "when the dust settles" or "when all is said and done." That last expression, come to think of it, never made much sense either. Some people can't speak two sentences without inserting the ubiquitous "that begs the question ... ," "raising the bar," "been there, done that," or the strange-sounding "24/7," as in "That guy must practice 24/7!" Stroll across any campus, and you will hear a primitive kind of English filled with all-purpose, meaningless fillers— "like," "totally," and "y'know"—and sentences like "I was all 'no way' and he was all 'Yeah, dude, she is so like over him."

The point of complaining about the way English is abused all around us is not that we should try to hold back the tide or freeze English into an unchanging, unspoken language like Latin. English has thrived on constant change in its long and tangled history and has absorbed new words from every language around it; it also has a long history of wildly colorful slang. But when writing an academic paper, you are expected to have control over the language and the skill to choose appropriate words and expressions with clarity and precision, so that you can communicate your ideas effectively to an academic audience. That doesn't mean adopting a stiff, pretentious tone; good writing has a grace and rhythm to it and makes the ideas it communicates clear and appealing. It is a satisfying experience to rebuild a sentence that starts as a tangled snarl of awkward expressions until you get it shaped and ordered and rearranged so that it conveys exactly what you want it to mean, with power and persuasion. My fondest hope is that this book will help students in their efforts to write clear, convincing, persuasive prose on musical topics.

## CHANGES IN THE FOURTH EDITION

We already mentioned the necessity to update several sections, such as the discussions of new areas of musicological research and new resources for research, both print and electronic publications. All citations of the reference works such as Turabian's guide and *The Chicago Manual of Style* have been updated to correspond to the latest editions. The section on electronic resources for research is completely new; the section on print resources has also been revised extensively and updated. There are new sections on critical thinking and using the ideas of others. An example of electronic music has been added to the section in Chapter 2 about using specific musical works to create research topics, both analytical topics and broader cultural topics. Chapter 5 on format includes a new section on the author-date system of citation. Finally, every sentence of every chapter has been revised, and editorial changes— some of them extensive—have improved the coherence and flow of the text. My hope, as before, is that an already useful book has been improved.

## OTHER RESOURCES

As we mentioned, this manual is directed primarily to undergraduate students. There are several published guides to research and writing designed for graduate music students that deserve mention here; they may be helpful to undergraduate students as well. Some of these guides deal with issues that are not immediately relevant to undergraduate students, such as special formats for theses and dissertations, but many of the questions they address are helpful to students at any level. Among the resources designed for students at the graduate level are the following texts:

Duckles, Vincent H., and Ida Reed. *Music Reference and Research Materials: An Annotated Bibliography.* 5th ed. New York: Schirmer Books, 1997.
Radice, Mark A. *Irvine's Writing about Music.* 3rd ed. Portland, OR: Amadeus Press, 1999.
Wingell, Richard, and Silvia Herzog. *Introduction to Research in Music.* Upper Saddle River, NJ: Prentice Hall, 2001.

A word about these resources is in order. The Duckles and Reed book, as the title indicates, is an annotated bibliography—a vast list of bibliographical and other resources for research into musical topics. Your music library undoubtedly has a copy on reference; browse through it to get an idea of the astounding variety of musical topics and resources for research into them. Mark Radice's book is a sweeping revision of Demar Irvine's *Writing about Music,* a classic text on writing designed not only for students, but also for anyone writing about music for publication. Finally, the Wingell and Herzog book is a textbook for the courses on bibliography and research required of new graduate music majors. It includes both a lengthy discussion of resources for research and a detailed guide to designing and writing a research paper at the graduate level.

There are also several standard guides to writing style. Although these works do not always discuss the special problems involved in writing about music at the level of detail we would like, they provide useful information in matters of appropriate style and format for college papers, as well as for publishing. Among the best-known guides are the following:

*The Chicago Manual of Style.* 15th ed. Chicago and London: University of Chicago Press, 2003.
Strunk, William, Jr., and E. B. White. *The Elements of Style.* 4th ed. New York, NY: Allyn & Bacon, 2000.
Troyka, Lynn Quitman, and Douglas Hesse. *Simon & Schuster Handbook for Writers.* 7th ed. Upper Saddle River, NJ: Prentice Hall, 2004.
Turabian, Kate L. *A Manual for Writers of Term Papers, Theses, and Dissertations.* 6th ed. Chicago and London: University of Chicago Press, 1996.

Turabian's manual is a standard reference work, recommended in many college and university courses. Although Turabian includes a few brief sections on the special problems of writing about music, her book is most useful as a general guide to writing graduate research papers. Recent editions of Turabian have been revised by the editors of *The Chicago Manual of Style,* the large standard reference work for writers, editors, proofreaders, and publishers.

The sixth edition of Turabian was revised to correspond to the fourteenth edition of the *Chicago Manual;* a seventh edition, revised to correspond with the fifteenth edition of the *Chicago Manual,* appeared in April, 2007, too late for inclusion in this edition.

The *Chicago Manual* is the bible of the publishing world; the size of the book and the number of editions testify to its importance. On issues of style in this guide, I have generally used the *Chicago Manual* as the final word. Like all disciplines, musicology has its own conventions in matters of style, such as uppercase letters for style periods (Baroque, Classical, Romantic); when those conventions disagree with the recommendations of the *Chicago Manual,* I have made a note to that effect. The *Chicago Manual* is now available online by subscription, and the Web site includes a helpful section on "Frequently Asked Questions." The book by Strunk and White is a thin paperback, a classic guide to effective writing style; recent editions have revised the text to make the examples more up-to-date. The *Simon & Schuster Handbook* is a useful compendium of the details of correct grammar and writing style, one of a long list of writing guides that cover what would be included in a college course on writing. Consult a Web site entitled *Research, Writing, and Style Guides* at http://www.aresearchguide.com/styleguides.html to see a long list of writing guides. Finally, students should be aware that their instructors or institutions may have chosen a particular manual as the official style guide; thus, the recommendations contained in this handbook may not be appropriate in all details for all classes on music.

## HOW TO USE THIS BOOK

This guide is not intended to be read cover to cover. It offers practical advice in several areas, including doing research on musical topics, writing a research paper, writing style, general writing problems, and the special challenges of writing about music. Although it is aimed primarily at the undergraduate music major, some beginning graduate students may find it useful to review the process of writing a paper or the chapters on effective writing. Although some students will find some comments and suggestions too elementary, all the questions discussed—even the most basic ones—are included because experience shows that they continue to cause problems for some students. Familiarize yourself with the book's organization, study the table of contents, and skim through the whole book so that you are aware of the areas that are covered. In the future, when you are involved in a writing project, you will then be able to locate the material that may be helpful to you.

The chapters in the fourth edition of this book are grouped into four large sections. Chapters 1 and 2 discuss the issue of writing about music. Chapters 3, 4, and 5 cover every stage of the process of writing a research paper, from choosing a topic through research, outlining, writing the draft, and editing and revising, as well as questions of format. Chapter 6 discusses other kinds of writing about music that you may be involved in—seminar presentations, concert reports, program notes, and essay examinations. Chapters 7 and 8 treat writing in general—principles of style, effective writing, and common problems. The concluding section offers some last words of advice. In the Appendix is a sample paper that you can use as a model, and some questions to aid you in your analysis of the paper. Skip around the book and use what you need. My hope is that all students will find helpful information somewhere in this book. If not, it should at least direct them to other resources where they can find the help they seek.

## CONCLUSION

This book is intended to serve as a practical introductory guide. It does not pretend to present the last word on all issues involved in writing about music. Rather, it is intended to be helpful in a few important areas, especially to the undergraduate student facing the task of writing a paper on a musical topic. If the book helps students to produce papers that are stronger, clearer, and more convincing, it will have justified its existence.

Finally, I should again thank some people who supplied ideas and material for this book. First, I am indebted to several editors at Prentice Hall: Norwell F. Therien, Jr., former Acquisitions Editor in Humanities, who conceived the idea for this book and supervised the production of the first edition; his successor, Christopher Johnson, who fulfilled the same function for the second and third editions; and Richard Carlin, Executive Editor for Music, in charge of this fourth edition. I am also indebted to several reviewers who offered thoughtful criticism of the second and third editions and suggestions for revisions. Next, I thank my former colleagues in Musicology at the University of Southern California; over the years, we constantly discussed student papers, writing problems, and ways to help students write better. For help on this fourth edition, particularly on the matter of electronic resources for research, I am indebted to Prof. Silvia Carruthers of Wichita State University. Finally, I must thank the hundreds of students whose papers I have read and criticized and who have contributed to this book, directly and indirectly. I hope it will prove useful to future generations of music majors.

*Richard J. Wingell*
Maui, 2007

# CHAPTER 1

# Writing about Music

## WHY WE WRITE ABOUT MUSIC

During the course of your academic career as a music major, you will certainly face the challenging task of writing about music. You will be expected to produce writing projects of various sorts—analysis projects, research papers, program notes for your recitals, essay questions in music history examinations, perhaps a presentation in a seminar or a senior thesis. If you choose to go on to graduate work in music, the writing demands will increase exponentially, including many more research papers and perhaps a lecture-recital, a thesis, or a culminating written project of some kind. Writing about music does not cease when you leave school; working musicians write program notes for concerts and recordings, articles in periodicals of various sorts, reviews of concerts or recordings, and who knows what else—perhaps writing for a performing group's Web site. Writing about music is not something you can avoid forever; you will spend considerable time both now and later working at this complex task. It therefore makes sense to begin this guide with some thoughts about the special challenges of writing about music.

Throughout the history of music, there have been those who are opposed to the whole idea of writing about music—people who feel that the task is impossible or at least incapable of accomplishing anything worthwhile. These people claim that music speaks for itself and that words are inadequate to describe musical events. Even in the nineteenth century, the age of artistic manifestos, heated arguments about the directions music should take, and endless discussions of music's capacity to tell stories, stir feelings, or express lofty philosophical ideas, there were still those who insisted that music must speak for itself and that writing about it is pointless. In our own day, many composers resist the attempts of commentators to explain their music, preferring to let the music speak for them. Why would someone go to

1

the effort of writing about this complex and difficult art? What purpose is served by crafting clear prose about music?

Sometimes the purpose of writing about music is clear and straightforward. If you are writing program notes, for example, the obvious goal is to help the audience members understand the music better and thus increase their enjoyment of the performance. Sometimes one writes about music in order to establish one's credentials as a knowledgeable musician. It seems obvious that a performer who can speak intelligently of the historical background and style of a piece of music is a more competent musician than a performer who can play the notes but cannot say anything about the music beyond "I like it," "I don't like it," or "It's hard." Further, one might write about a piece of music in order to explain one's analytic understanding of how the work is put together and what gives it coherence, logic, and syntax. One may also write about music to show how a musical work is connected to a particular culture and its concerns, or how it furthers the aims of some powerful group. Or one might want to show the connection between a musical work and the art and literature that flourished in the culture at the same time.

One important reason for writing projects is that they force students to engage in *critical thinking*. As you are no doubt aware, there is a growing national concern about standards in higher education, including attempts to find ways to evaluate higher education and measure its success at achieving its goals. Critics and government agencies want to be sure that colleges and universities teach students how to think—not just fill their minds with information. There is great discussion of "higher-order thinking"—the ability to apply newly acquired concepts and criteria to new material, and to do it independently. One standard example of critical thinking is the ability to read a number of editorials on a particular issue, sort out the various points of view, and finally choose your own position on the issue and defend that choice.

Universities, departments, and instructors are under pressure to show that in their courses they challenge students to engage in critical thinking. Instructors therefore assign writing projects to encourage students to apply the ideas discussed in class to unfamiliar musical works, a more thoughtful and demanding task than simply absorbing the professor's pronouncements and repeating them back in an examination. You may be asked to use your critical judgment to evaluate a musical work, place it in its proper historical context, and compare it with similar works.

These days, musicological research, as we shall see, is concerned with a number of broad areas beyond the music itself. Research also includes studies in biography, cultural background, connections with the other arts, performance practice issues, the way different cultures and different eras think of music from the past (what the Germans call *Rezeptionsgeschichte* or "reception history"), and critical approaches borrowed from literary theory.

Writing is obviously the only way to communicate the results of this broader kind of research; it is the only medium we have for communicating any ideas or conclusions we have come to in any sort of research.

## THE SPECIAL CHALLENGES OF WRITING ABOUT MUSIC

It is not easy to write convincingly about music. Music is a nonverbal art; it often seems to speak directly to feelings and associations deep within us that are difficult to put into words. For that reason, music has always been a crucial part of religious rituals, patriotic ceremonies, and solemn occasions of all sorts, civic or private. It is not easy, however, to express in words the powerful effect that music can have. Even when music is joined to a text, as in art song or opera, we find it difficult to express exactly what the music "says" beyond what the text says, or what the music adds to the words. We assume that the music communicates something beyond the text; unless the composer has something to add to what the poet has already said in the text, there is little point in setting a text to music in the first place. Often we feel that a musical setting captures the various levels of meaning of a text with remarkable exactness, that in some way it is exactly right for that text, but it is difficult to explain that conviction in prose. The very nature of music resists attempts to verbalize about it. On the other hand, when we finally arrive at a clear understanding of a work, or when we have strong ideas about a work's uniqueness or historical importance or its power as a cultural statement, we want to communicate our ideas, insights, and opinions. Words are the only means we have to communicate what we want to say about the music we love.

Besides the inherent difficulty of writing about music, there are extrinsic factors that make it more difficult. Some performers seem to approach all music simply as a challenge to their technique, as if the only significant music consisted of solos for their particular instrument. Their attitude seems to be, "Spare me the lectures—just give me the score, and I'll take it home and learn it." Perhaps they learned that attitude from a studio teacher; unfortunately, there still are teachers who concentrate almost entirely on technical issues, without much attention to analytic or stylistic understanding.

Outside the specialized world of musicians, society's attitudes toward music also affect us. Our culture tends to think of music as comforting background noise, an atmosphere one creates for oneself, a sort of sonic wallpaper. In this view, no one has any right to question anyone else's musical taste: Like one's style of dress or religious or political convictions, musical taste is a personal matter and not something one discusses or argues about. Qualitative judgments are not welcome in this atmosphere. The fan of heavy metal, country music, alternative rock, or rap, for example, does not welcome opinions that one sort of music is "better" or "more worthwhile" than another; questions of quality are regarded as oppressive, offensive, and unacceptable. Many people cannot imagine that there can be any thoughtful discussion of a musical experience beyond rudimentary approval or disapproval. In this atmosphere, it is difficult to argue logically and convincingly about issues of musical style or quality.

## INAPPROPRIATE WAYS TO WRITE ABOUT MUSIC

Because it is difficult to write about music, some writers fill their pages with irrelevant discussions, perhaps resorting to diversionary tactics in order to avoid the challenge of actually discussing the music. We have all read examples of these approaches to writing about music. Please note that the following examples of bad writing are not direct quotations but paraphrases of prose I have read.

Sometimes, especially in program notes and record liner notes, one finds overly precious descriptions of musical events, sentences like the following.

> The violas insist on interrupting with their own little theme, but the woodwinds are not impressed and continue chattering among themselves. Finally, the brasses put a stop to the argument by drowning out everyone else and restoring order.

> The introduction has no thematic connection to the movement proper, but provides a delightful aperitif to what follows.

These fanciful metaphors tell us little about the music.

Sometimes, sentimental or overly picturesque descriptions take the place of serious discussion. Returning themes "dispel the gloom and chaos of the preceding section," or "The light of hope finally dawns as we approach the triumphant final section." Themes "babble," "chatter," "argue," "soar," or "shout." Such picturesque rhetoric provides little of substance to the reader who wants to understand the music better.

Another tendency is to treat all music as programmatic, regardless of the style in question or the composer's intent. It is perfectly all right to let one's imagination wander and conjure up colorful pictures or scenes as one listens to music, even absolute or abstract music. It would be fascinating (or perhaps alarming) if we could magically project on a screen the images that pass through the minds of a concert audience during a performance. But sharing one's fantasies hardly fulfills the writer's responsibility to discuss musical matters in a serious paper. One student, in a paper analyzing a *concerto grosso*, mentioned that Baroque music always conjures up images of royal processions in her mind. That bit of shared information is not much help to a discussion of the music.

There is a nineteenth-century description of the opening of Brahms's First Symphony that goes on at some length about "the cosmic questions posed by the philosophic C." The opening of that symphony is certainly one of the most dramatic opening gestures in the symphonic literature, but "cosmic questions"? If you want to convey the power of that opening, you have to say something about what actually happens in the music. Whatever words you might choose, the important elements are the relentless pounding of the pedal C and the contrary motion between the upper instruments as they move away in chromatic steps from their initial unison C. Take a moment and try to describe that opening in your own words; you will find that mention of the crucial musical events is the only way to keep the statement from lapsing into Romantic dreaming or programmatic nonsense.

Related to the programmatic tendency is the approach that tries to explain all music through events in the composer's life. Beethoven's deafness, for example, occupies altogether too much space in discussions of his later music; it is easier to write about his affliction than to discuss the puzzling, fragmented style of his late works. There is a published discussion of Mozart's Piano Concerto in B-flat, K. 595, that relates this final concerto to Mozart's supposed feelings as he neared the end of his short life. The writer describes the serene slow movement as "suffused with the soft glow of evening," or words to that effect, and hears resignation and a longing for death in every note. Connecting this particular movement to Mozart's alleged feelings in his last days is hard to justify, since one can easily find several earlier slow movements that are equally serene. Besides, from what we know of Mozart, he hardly seems the sort of person who would approach his untimely death with an "evening glow" of resignation. Nineteenth-century writers loved to picture Mozart as a tragic Romantic hero cut down in his prime, but the emphasis on the tragic side of his life tells us little about Mozart's real genius, his compositional style, or his music.

Sometimes details of a composer's life, such as an important friendship or love affair, a new position, or connections with artists or writers can shed helpful light on his or her evolving musical style. One must always bear in mind, however, that unhappy composers can write happy music, and composers whose lives are dull can write turbulent, passionate music. Bartók's *Concerto for Orchestra,* for example, is an exuberant, exciting work; it hardly sounds like the work of a composer who at the time was dying of leukemia in an American hospital, exiled from war-torn Europe, impoverished, discouraged, and depressed. Richard Strauss in his private life was, we are told, a henpecked, middle-class German, but his tone poems embody all the sweep, grandeur, and ardent heroism of late Romanticism.

The lives of composers and their interaction with the culture around them are of course endlessly fascinating to us and worthy material for research and writing. Biographical studies are one of the traditional areas of musicological research. Currently there is great interest in studying the relationship between societies such as Nazi Germany and the Soviet Union and the composers who lived, willingly or unwillingly, under these repressive regimes. What we are saying, however, is that composer's lives, or particular events in them, do not necessarily tell us all we want to know about their music.

On the other hand, it is not necessarily enough to confine your writing to describing what happens in the music. Some students think they have said all there is to say about a piece of music when they have reported the musical events in the order in which they occur. You surely have read—perhaps written—prose like the following.

> The first sixteen measures of the development section are based on the first theme, and gradually reduce the musical idea to the first phrase, and finally to just the opening flourish, which moves through several key areas. The next thirty-two measures continue the modulatory process, after which a dominant pedal prepares for the recapitulation.

Let us assume that these observations are accurate. This "one-thing-after-another" approach appears to be neutral, objective, and scientific, but it is not real analysis, as we shall see later. Unless the music happens to be organized as a series of otherwise unrelated events, as in some twentieth-century styles, merely compiling a list of events avoids taking a position on what is important in the music, what unifies the work and gives it coherence, and what makes it different from other works in the same style or genre. The listing of musical events is certainly a vast improvement over gushing prose about babbling brooks, chattering woodwinds, the imagined feelings of the composer at the time, or the fevered dreams of the listener's imagination. It is only a beginning, however, and does not complete the task of describing the music.

Some great music is the result of enormously complicated compositional processes. When working with genres such as isorhythmic motets, eighteenth-century fugues, or serial and pan-serial compositions, the first step in understanding the music is the sometimes arduous task of identifying and listing all the elements of the compositional process—permutations of the *talea* and *color,* appearances of the fugue subject in all its different versions, or occurrences of the row in all its permutations. Taking the composition apart in this way is often a fascinating challenge, and it may be a necessary first step, but explaining the compositional process of a piece of music is not the same as making a statement about its style. The complex web of events and design elements is important but does not really explain the style of the work, as a few examples will illustrate. Schoenberg's serial works are quite different from Webern's; many serial works by Schoenberg, as you listen to them, are actually organized in nontonal versions of standard classical forms. In the same way, a trained ear can distinguish between a cantus firmus Mass by Dufay and one by Josquin des Prez, or between a sonata-allegro movement by Haydn and one by Mozart, even though the compositional process in both cases may be the same. Dufay's style is different from Josquin's; Haydn's is different from Mozart's. Explaining those differences is real critical thinking, and could be the basis of a fine paper. Zeroing in on the unique qualities or the individual essence of a great musical work and then clearly expressing that insight is perhaps the most challenging part of writing about music.

Another error is anachronistic analysis—trying to understand or describe music of one era by using the analytic tools and categories appropriate to music from a different era altogether, or forcing a piece of music into the wrong stylistic mold. The concepts of structure and key areas that work perfectly well for analyzing Classical symphonies will not be of much use in analyzing a motet by Machaut, a song by Charles Ives, or aleatoric music by John Cage. Students often try to analyze early music by using their newly acquired vocabulary of analytic terms appropriate for tonal music from the eighteenth and nineteenth centuries. When grappling with music that does not have antecedent and consequent phrases, clear key areas, dominant-tonic cadences, or familiar classical forms, they sometimes try to force the music to fit the wrong style. Clearly, each musical work has to be judged on its own terms, against the background of the cultural and stylistic norms of its own day.

It is important to realize that stylistic analysis is not an exact science, with quantifiable issues and definite answers. Nor is it a permanently fixed, unchanging methodology; several new approaches to analysis emerged in the twentieth century, each with its own contribution to the understanding of music, its organization, and its meaning. On one side are the analytic systems of Heinrich Schenker, Paul Hindemith, and Allen Forte. These methods of analysis emphasize the structure of a work and its materials and methods; further, they seek to approach a single system that will work for all styles of music. Musicologists, on the other hand, generally approach music from a wider perspective, emphasizing stylistic evolution and connections to the broader culture.

## MUSICOLOGICAL RESEARCH AND WRITING

Some musicologists continue to work in research areas that have been popular since the discipline began. Analytical research focuses on the music and places it in the larger picture of evolving genres and styles. Archival research searches for information about the musical life of a particular place and time, such as the venues in which music was performed and the forces that were available to perform the music. Biographical research uncovers information about the lives of composers and performers, shedding light on why and how they produced their music. Cultural research connects music with the historical and artistic trends at work in the surrounding culture.

In recent decades, musicological research has greatly widened its sphere of activity. Cultural studies have expanded to include areas such as reception history, which studies the ways in which cultures have understood and responded to particular works, either works from the past or contemporary works, or how societies have used works from the past in the pursuit of their own aims. In addition, some scholars have adopted the concept of "deconstruction" from literary theory and take as their starting point the idea that any work of art, programmatic or absolute, makes a statement about the power structure or culture from which it comes. Armed with new methodologies, we can learn to "read" those statements. This concept has also led to such specialized types of research as feminist criticism, queer studies, and colonial and postcolonial studies. The modernist/postmodernist debate goes on in music as well as in the other arts, sometimes leading to ringing manifestos and heated debates. All these new approaches have produced thoughtful and provocative studies that broaden and add to the traditional methods of musical analysis and research.

Some undergraduate students may be asked to do these new kinds of research in their classes; choosing one of these new approaches for a research project will certainly be an option for those who choose to go on to graduate studies. In the next chapter, we will illustrate different kinds of research as they might be applied to selected musical works—stylistic analysis first, as that is presumably the main sort of research undergraduates will be asked to do, and then suggestions about other directions one might pursue, taking those works as a starting point. The important thing to realize is that, whatever focus one chooses, any sound research on a musical topic must always start from an understanding of the music itself. Stylistic analysis and an understanding of changing musical styles is the essential starting point for any serious research. Otherwise, we are back in the world of fanciful imagination or personal reaction, not something one can argue logically or intellectually.

We move on, then, to a discussion of some striking musical works from different eras and the ways in which these individual works suggest possible avenues for research and topics for papers.

# CHAPTER 2

# Analysis and Research

This chapter continues our discussion of stylistic analysis of music, as musicologists use the term, and illustrates the concept through brief discussion of some well-known musical works. In addition, for each of these works we will try to show how the researcher might develop directions and ideas for research, moving outward in concentric circles from a single piece of music. We begin with a discussion of stylistic analysis.

## ANALYSIS

In theory courses, the term *analysis* usually refers either to harmonic and structural analysis of pieces from the so-called standard-practice period, from 1750 to 1900, or to new systems of analysis developed in the twentieth century. Music historians, on the other hand, generally use the term to mean stylistic analysis, and they study musical works in the broader context of changing historical styles. All composers work within a stylistic context; they either accept the stylistic assumptions and conventions of their time or consciously depart from those conventions, creating new musical styles. Meaningful analysis should be based on a clear understanding of the stylistic developments that form the context in which a particular work appeared. We cannot appreciate the unique aspects of a particular work until we understand the principles that guide the music of the period. Therefore, musicological research often concentrates on defining the principles of a particular style.

No matter how one defines analysis, it certainly involves more than mere description, chord counting, or making a list of events. An approach based on "first this happens, then that happens, then something else happens" is not true analysis. Analysis implies insight into how the music is conceived and organized as a unit. To reach that insight, one may have to start with list-making activities as described in the last chapter. These activities, however, are only the preliminaries to analysis; after events are identified and sorted out, the real work of analysis begins. One must decide which events are significant, which are not, and how the work relates to a more general historical style—only then can one decide which elements of the work are standard practice for the time and which are innovative. In other words, analysis is not really an objective, scientific activity; it involves a creative mind, critical thinking, and artistic judgment, as well as the ability to create an analytic hypothesis and the appropriate means to test that hypothesis. Note also that analysis should include among its tools the ear as well as the eye. If an analysis arrives at a clear idea of the basic elements that hold a work together and give it unity, presumably that view of the work ought to be audible. Music is, after all, a sonic art, not a visual one, and the marks on a page of score are only representations of the sounds the composer chose and the way they are organized.

In a similar vein, analysis of a musical work, as we said in the last chapter, is more than understanding the compositional process involved. Discovering all the permutations of a fugue subject or deciphering every chord and complex modulation in a highly chromatic tone poem is not the same as understanding the style of the work. Even the laborious task of locating all the permutations of the row in a twelve-tone work is different from stylistic analysis. Schoenberg's serial works are stylistically quite distinct from those of Berg, Webern, or Boulez. The issue of compositional process may even be peripheral to the question of style, since the structure and coherence of a work often result from entirely different considerations. Many of Schoenberg's twelve-tone works, for example, are organized in recognizable versions of classical structures such as sonata-allegro or rondo. Even the seams between sections are usually articulated through familiar classical means, such as melodic and rhythmic cadence, change of texture, or change of instrumentation, which have little to do with row permutations. Knowledge of the compositional process can certainly shed light on the organization of a work; Schoenberg viewed the serial process as the fundamental source of the work's unity and coherence. Still, the task of analysis involves more than awareness of compositional process.

Analysis, then, is something other than harmonic and structural analysis of works from the standard-practice period, making lists, or understanding the compositional process. Most historians define analysis as insight into how a work is organized, what gives it logic and coherence, and how it relates to the important stylistic developments of its time.

## QUESTIONS TO CONSIDER

To begin the process of musical analysis, one should consider several basic questions. Is this particular work organized as a coherent unit? If so, what is the basis of its coherence? What makes this work a unified whole? Is it based on one of the traditional structural patterns, such as sonata-allegro, minuet and trio, or theme and variations, or does it have some other form? We can always assume that musical works are based on some principle of organization, standard or not; unless at some level we sense some logic and coherence in a work, we dismiss it as random, inartistic, and a waste of our time and attention. Identifying the musical means by which the composer has built in unity and coherence is a fundamental step in analysis.

Another basic question in stylistic analysis is how a particular work relates to the stylistic developments of its time. Is it a venture into completely new territory, or does it build on established styles? Is it a further refinement of a style in which the composer has worked previously, or is the composer experimenting with new stylistic ideas? In what way has the composer worked out his own individual version of an established style? For example, when Stravinsky and Copland venture into twelve-tone writing, do they create unique, personal versions of the style? Can you still hear their personal style in these works, or do their twelve-tone works sound just like other composers' twelve-tone works?

A related issue is the question of whether the composer was influenced by another composer. Sometimes the line of influence is obvious: We know that the shadow of Beethoven inspired Brahms but also daunted him; he hesitated for years before allowing his First Symphony to be performed, knowing that it would be compared to the symphonies of Beethoven. On the other hand, claims of another composer's influence are sometimes difficult to support. Similarity of style is not enough in itself to justify such a claim, since there are several other possible explanations for such similarity. The line of influence might run in the opposite direction, or both might have been influenced by a third composer or a pervasive style of the period. It is difficult to prove influence from the music alone, unless we have the composer's own words or some other historical evidence that establishes a connection. Within these limits, however, the question of influence and the other general questions listed earlier can be helpful ways to approach the crucial issue of where a work fits in the overall history of a style.

Another possible direction to pursue when beginning an analysis project is relating a particular work to the surrounding culture and contemporary developments in the other arts. At some times in history, the connections between music and the other arts are particularly obvious. French art songs of the late nineteenth and early twentieth centuries, for example, cannot be understood without reference to the symbolist literary movement, the source of the evocative texts that attracted composers, determined their musical choices, and led them to create a new musical style. Likewise, the songs of Schoenberg and Berg cannot be understood without some understanding of the expressionist movement in German art and literature. We often use terms borrowed from the world of the literary and visual arts, such as impressionism and expressionism, to describe musical styles; we cannot discuss impressionism or expressionism in music without first understanding what the terms mean in their original context. In addition, it is obvious that programmatic music cannot be analyzed without some reference to the story or picture the music depicts.

The question of cultural context affects all music, not just those musical styles obviously influenced by the visual or literary arts. The physical setting in which music was performed, the audience for whom it was intended, the context that called for a performance, and the way a particular society viewed the roles of composer and performer—all these issues have an influence on issues of style. Understanding a musical work may involve research into these broader questions. We need to be aware of musical life in earlier ages, the performing forces composers had at their disposal, and the context in which music was performed. In order to understand the cantatas of Bach, for example, we must understand that they were not created to be concert pieces; they were intended to be performed in a small church as part of a four-hour Sunday service. In addition, we cannot understand this music without some sense of the religious movement known as Pietism and its effect on religious ideas and approaches to worship in the Lutheran Church of Bach's day. The better we understand the original purpose of a musical work, the audience for whom it was intended, and the circumstances of its first performance, the better prepared we are to make sense of the music.

Another fundamental question to raise in the early stages of an analysis project is the composer's intent. Composers write music for many different reasons, and understanding their motivation may very well be the key to understanding the music they produce.

Sometimes when a composer writes music for a particular occasion, that special purpose determines the style of the music. A famous example of music for a special occasion is "Nuper rosarum flores," a motet by Guillaume Dufay, one of the masterpieces of the early Renaissance. The piece is remarkably complex. Not only does it utilize the fourteenth-century compositional process of isorhythm; it further complicates the process by utilizing two isorhythmic tenors that move in canon at the fifth. Further, the large sections of the piece are organized in different rhythmic proportions—another process used by earlier composers, but utilized here in a more complicated way. Of course one could analyze the motet from the score alone, but it makes more sense to see the work in its historical context. The motet was commissioned in 1436 for the dedication of Brunelleschi's new dome for the cathedral in Florence. This ceremony was an important occasion in Renaissance Italy; the Pope was in attendance, and the fact that Dufay was asked to write special music for this ceremony was a sign of the high regard in which he was held. Recent scholarship has made a convincing argument that the double-tenor structure of Dufay's piece was intended to mirror in music the mathematical elements of Brunelleschi's bold design for the large unsupported dome. The proportions of the sections may also have been based on the proportions of the finished basilica or the proportions of Solomon's Temple as described in the Bible. In other words, the circumstances explain the complex structure of the music, and it would be a mistake to treat this piece as if it were an ordinary motet.

Composers have often written music for particular performers, and that circumstance should help us understand those works. Compositional choices may be based on the particular talents of the performers for whom the works are intended, and the question of expanded instrumental idiom may be a central question to raise in the analytical process.

Sometimes the composer's main purpose is to experiment with new materials or structures. In much of the modernist music composed in the second half of the twentieth century, composers are intent on creating new styles, sometimes with each new work. George Crumb, for example, often combines in his music ideas borrowed from Eastern music, astronomy, ritual, and drama, and one should take these ideas into account in approaching his works. If a composer has organized a particular work around mathematical structures, has ordered all the elements serially, or has integrated musical ideas from other cultures into Western structures, we cannot analyze or appreciate the work except in those terms.

Sometimes, on the other hand, a composer may be refining an established style, and one must view the work against the background of that established style. That is the case with much of the music from the standard-practice period. When we approach a Mozart symphony, we know how to proceed, armed with our understanding of the principles of classical structure. When a composer moves from one style to another, as Stravinsky did in his later years, we have to be aware of that change; it would make no sense to analyze his serial works using the same criteria we would use to analyze his neoclassical works.

Finally, if a composer has written a programmatic work, we must judge the music in those terms; we cannot adequately appreciate the music without some understanding of the program. The same holds true for text setting in song and opera; the complex relationship between text and music is one of the major questions to consider in the process of analysis.

In short, we should judge musical works against the background of what the composer was trying to do. To ignore available information about the composer's intent is to deprive ourselves of useful information about the directions the analysis should take. In some cases, we may have to begin our analysis by study of the composer's ideas and aims, so that we can approach the music as he or she approached it and use criteria that are appropriate for this specific work.

We now look at some specific works and analytical approaches that are appropriate for studying them, as well as further directions for research that these works suggest.

## EXAMPLES OF WORKS AND RESEARCH DIRECTIONS

The following works are readily available in standard anthologies of music and certainly can be found in any music library. It would be helpful to have the scores and recordings at hand as you read this section, so that you can follow the discussion and decide for yourself which approaches seem most fruitful.

### Carlo Gesualdo: "Moro, lasso"

This famous madrigal is an example of Gesualdo's idiosyncratic style. As you glance at the score, several aspects of the musical style will strike you immediately. The first is the strange chromaticism in the setting of certain phrases—"Moro, lasso," "ahi, che m'ancide," "O dolorosa sorte," and "ahi, mi dà morte." We start from our awareness of what sixteenth-century madrigal composers were trying to accomplish and the idea of *musical rhetoric*— that is, finding appropriate musical ways to depict the striking words and feelings of the texts. The way to approach this piece is from the point of view of text setting, starting with the Italian text and focusing on word painting. The words "Moro, lasso," for example, are set to a chromatically descending phrase in the low range; the music seems particularly apt for the words "I die, I languish." Starting the piece with this disorienting chromaticism jars the listener and captures his or her attention. There are several chordal, chromatic sections that resemble the opening phrase; the texts in those sections always focus on pain and death. Alternating with them are polyphonic sections in diatonic style, which set the more hopeful lines such as "e chi mi può dar vita" ("and she who could give me life").

You might also focus on the details of the chromatic passages—for example, the composer's choice to combine parallel chromatic descent in the outer voices with what later theory would label root movement by thirds. The chromatic passages can be discussed as violations or extensions of the modal theory of the time. One might also focus on the question of overall structure, here formed by the regular alternation of the two different styles and repetition of contrasting passages. Because of this pattern of alternating sections in contrasting styles, one might argue that the style lacks overall unity and coherence. Whatever direction you follow, the question of text setting and "madrigalisms" would certainly be one of the first questions to pursue.

It is easy to use this piece as a starting point for research topics that are not exclusively analytical. One interesting question is who performed these works. We know from contemporary accounts that these difficult works were sung with one voice on each part, and that the soprano and perhaps the alto parts were sung by women, not by the professional choirboys who sang in the court chapels. Where these women came from and how they achieved this virtuoso level of vocal training is an important question; suddenly, professional women singers were in great demand in the Italian courts. One could also pursue the question of Gesualdo's texts. Gesualdo chose not to set the beautiful and subtle texts by the poets favored by his contemporaries—Petrarch, Guarini, Tasso, and Marino. His madrigals therefore tip the balance in favor of music over text and do not achieve the same delicate equilibrium between text and music that we see in most of the madrigals by composers such as Marenzio and Monteverdi. The contexts for performance of madrigals and the constitution of the audience would be another interesting area to investigate. How the audience reacted to the texts and music of these pieces with their constant harping on the "sweet pain" of love is another interesting cultural question.

### J. S. Bach: Opening Chorus of Cantata No. 80, *Ein' feste Burg ist unser Gott*

The obvious first step in an analytical study of this chorus, as in all the choruses of Bach's chorale cantatas, is to compare the source melody of the traditional chorale with the complex counterpoint that Bach constructed from it. Analysis must begin with the chorale tune with which Bach began; the unadorned tune is usually found in the soprano line of the final number of the cantata. The key to the structure of this chorus is that Bach uses the chorale tune in two different ways at the same time. First, the choral parts constitute a *chorale motet*—that is, Bach uses each phrase of the chorale tune, modified but still recognizable, as a subject for imitative entries in all the voices. Each phrase in turn is treated this way. This is an old technique associated with the motets and paraphrase Masses of Josquin des Prez and his contemporaries. The melody is not quoted literally, but given new rhythmic shape and amplified by added notes, just as Renaissance composers paraphrased chant melodies when they used them as imitative subjects in their motets.

At the end of each imitative section, the orchestra presents the same phrase of the chorale in a different way—in literal form, in long notes, called *cantus firmus* style. In addition, these quotations of the chorale phrases are set canonically between the upper and lower instruments of the orchestra at a rhythmic distance of one measure. Once one grasps the two ways Bach uses each phrase of the chorale, one understands the whole chorus, since these two processes continue throughout the chorus. Read through the music and follow the progress of the chorale motet; the orchestra's quotations of the chorale phrases in cantus firmus style clearly mark the end of each imitative section. In addition, the structure of the chorus duplicates the AAB structure of the chorale. Other questions one might consider are the relationship of this huge first chorus to the other movements and the overall structure of the cantata. One might also compare this chorus to an opening chorus organized differently, such as the first chorus of Cantata No. 140, *Wachet auf, ruft uns die Stimme.*

It is easy to imagine different directions of research suggested by this work. One interesting question is the editorial one. The copies and parts that serve as the basis for editions of this work exist in two different versions. One uses oboes and the bass strings to announce the chorale phrases in cantus firmus style and in canon at the end of each choral section. The other version, produced after Bach's lifetime, uses trumpets rather than oboes, and adds the kettledrums that usually accompany trumpets in the Baroque orchestra. In the nineteenth century, when the editors of the *Bach-Gesellschaft-Ausgabe* prepared an edition of this work, they combined these two versions; the chorale phrases are played by both oboes and trumpets. The more recent edition in the *Neue-Bach-Ausgabe* includes only the oboes. Tracing the origin of the version that adds trumpets and drums and the reasons for the addition would be an interesting project.

Cultural issues surround this work as well. One could study the Pietist movement and its effect on Bach's career as a church musician. It is interesting to note, for instance, that extreme Pietists were opposed to all liturgy and ritual and believed that they did not need pastors or ceremonies to tell them how to interpret the Gospels. In that version of Pietism, Bach's elaborate church music would have no place at all. On the other hand, had the ideas of Pietism not shaped to some extent the worship of the churches where Bach worked, his deeply personal responses to the Gospel readings, the main reason why we still find his church music appealing, would not have been welcome. Another interesting area is the question of reception history; this cantata, based on a chorale ascribed to Luther himself and performed on Reformation Sunday, came to be associated with a militant spirit that was not the primary sentiment that inspired Bach to compose it. Finally, the question of performance practice is a fruitful area for investigation; many modern scholars are convinced from contemporary evidence that these cantatas—in fact, all of Bach's sacred music—were performed with one voice on each part, a far cry from the giant choral-orchestral performances and recordings we are familiar with.

### W.A. Mozart: Concerto for Piano and Orchestra in C Minor, K. 491, First Movement

In this work, the researcher is on the familiar ground of standard-practice analysis, dealing with familiar elements such as key areas, thematic repetition, the development process, and classical structures. What this particular movement illustrates is the variety possible within standard classical forms. Structural analysis shows that this movement does not follow the double-exposition version of sonata-allegro structure described in some textbooks as the model for the first movement of a classical concerto. Most commentators view this movement as an example of *ritornello form* rather than a sonata-allegro structure. Look through the whole movement. Does the solo piano ever play the first theme? Should that theme be viewed as an orchestral ritornello? Do the key areas work out as you would expect in a classical sonata-allegro movement in the minor mode? Structural issues would certainly seem to be the main focus for an analysis of this movement. In addition, some commentators view this particular concerto as an example of Mozart's darker, Beethovenian side, in contrast to the sunnier, gentler spirit of some of his other piano concertos. A comparative analysis contrasting this concerto with another one, perhaps the Concerto in A Major, K. 488, would be an interesting project.

Related to structural analysis are two other areas worthy of study—instrumental idiom and orchestration. As you know, Mozart used the piano not only as a solo instrument, but also as a sort of third choir added to the classical orchestra of strings and winds. Thus, for example, the piano sometimes plays an accompanimental role while the solo winds pass around the themes, and over the course of the movement, piano, strings, and winds are deployed in every possible combination of roles. One could also study the pianos Mozart would have played and the effect their particular sound and color would have on the performance. One might investigate the occasions, venues, and audiences for performances of concertos as opposed to symphonic music. Modern scholarship suggests that improvisation played more of a role in concerto performances than we think—not just in the cadenza prolonging the final cadence of the movement, but in an improvised introduction and other places as well. This idea would make another area for investigation. One might also study connections and differences between the idea of the concerto in the Classical and Romantic periods.

### Giuseppe Verdi: *Otello,* Act I, Scene 3

The love duet between Otello and Desdemona at the end of Act I of Verdi's *Otello* is stunning music and effective theater, a moving finale to the first act. The opera opens with a famous storm scene, followed by Otello's triumphant return from a victory over the Turks. A celebration follows, during which Iago sets the plot in motion by getting Cassio drunk and goading him into a fight so that Otello will punish him with imprisonment. Then everyone else leaves the stage, and Desdemona welcomes home her triumphant warrior. The extended love scene that closes the act is one of the high points of the opera and can be studied from several points of view. The musical style is richer and more complex than the style we associate with Verdi's earlier operas. We are immediately struck by the delicately beautiful orchestration, filled with careful and unusual effects. The harmonic idiom, marked by frequent modulations and enharmonic shifts, is strikingly different from Verdi's earlier works. Although some commentators see the structure of a traditional *scena* in this duet, the music is more continuous and flowing than in Verdi's earlier works. The climax of the scene is the "un bacio" motive, which will return at the tragic close of the opera. Besides analysis of these musical details, one might undertake a comparative analysis. There is a clear shift in style between Verdi's earlier operas and his late works, *Otello* and *Falstaff*. One might try to identify common stylistic traits in these two late works and then contrast them with earlier works.

Moving to nonanalytical topics, one fascinating issue is the way the plot and the characters change because of the cuts Boito made in the process of transforming Shakespeare's play into a libretto. One obvious example is the character of Desdemona. Because Boito cut the entire first act of Shakespeare's play, which establishes Desdemona's strength and independence, in the opera she appears as a typical nineteenth-century heroine, victimized and helpless. The issue of changes in the characters is not just a question of text, because characterization is delineated through musical means as well. Iago, for example, is presented differently in his frightening "Credo" number than he is in the play, where his motivation for destroying Othello is subtler and more puzzling. When Boito and Verdi adapted the play, which has its own shape and flow, into another medium, change was inevitable; music has its own rules of structure and flow. You might also compare this adaptation with Verdi's other adaptations of Shakespeare's plays—*Macbeth* and *Falstaff*. Other areas that would be interesting to study would include the issue of reception. The audience was quite familiar with Verdi's earlier singer-centered style, made up of separate numbers, each with its climactic high notes and triumphant cadences. I wonder how the first audience reacted to this new and somewhat Wagnerian style, in which the singers' lines weave through a complex orchestral fabric, and the music is not usually divided into separate numbers that have clear starting points and obvious cadences with their built-in pauses for applause. Finally, the sociological question of racism and Othello's position as an outsider, a representative of an attractive but dangerous foreign culture, is always inextricably linked with this great tragedy.

### Franz Liszt: "Faust" Symphony, First Movement

The "Faust" Symphony of Liszt is a masterpiece of Romantic program music and a fascinating work to analyze. The three movements represent the three main characters of the Faust legend—Faust, Gretchen, and Mephistopheles. Added to the final movement is an apotheosis, during which a tenor soloist and male chorus sing the last few lines of Goethe's *Faust*.

The most important element in this work is the technique of thematic transformation. All the themes of the long first movement are derived from a few melodic cells or motives; as these basic cells are given different musical shape, they are transformed into distinct themes or leitmotifs representing the different sides of the hero—mystery, heroism, passion, tender love, and so on. One analytic approach might focus on the cells and the different thematic shape they take on. Another analysis might focus on the question of structure. The first movement is long and somewhat rambling; the question of underlying structure in a Romantic movement of this size is always an interesting one to pursue. Is the form derived from the program, or is there some intrinsically musical form that guides the organization of this sprawling movement? Another interesting study might compare the first and third movements, since nearly all the themes representing Mephistopheles are parodies of the Faust themes. In other words, the melodic cells that are manipulated and transformed in the first movement are further transformed in the final movement to depict completely different ideas and feelings. Other important elements for analysis include the rich harmonic language of late Romanticism and Liszt's effective use of the large orchestral forces.

This work suggests a rich variety of potential topics in the area of cultural studies. Although the Faust legend began in the Renaissance and the best-known version of the story by Goethe has elements of Enlightenment thinking, we know that this story was a favorite of the Romantic era. There are many musical settings derived from the story; it would be interesting, for example, to compare Liszt's symphony to parts of Mahler's Eighth Symphony, which use some of the same material from Goethe's *Faust*. The question of musical characterization in Liszt's work is fascinating. Gretchen is presented in the second movement as innocent and pure, a quiet center of serenity and love in the whirlwind of Faust's endless quest, exactly the sort of nineteenth-century depiction of woman—"das ewig Weibliche," woman on a pedestal, a beacon and inspiration for the hero—that feminists justly object to. Another interesting issue is the philosophical statement the music makes about Faust and Mephistopheles. The demon is presented musically not as a separate being, an external source of evil, but as the dark side of the hero, since the music that depicts Mephistopheles is made up largely of grotesque, mocking variations of the Faust themes from the first movement. The autobiographical side of the work might be interesting to pursue as well. Liszt was fascinated with the satanic and grotesque, as seen in compositions such as the "Mephisto" Waltz and *Totentanz,* and Faust's redemption through religion and the love of an innocent woman may represent the way Liszt viewed his own life, or the life of any artist. This complex work sometimes puts people off because of its moments of bombast and overreaching, but it illustrates perfectly both the Romantic spirit and the rich possibilities for research, both analytical and cultural, that such works suggest.

### Igor Stravinsky: *The Rite of Spring,* Opening Sections

Although *The Rite of Spring* is by now a classic of the early twentieth century, it calls for analytical methods different from those appropriate for music of the eighteenth and nineteenth centuries. In this landmark work, Stravinsky deconstructed and rearranged the elements of music and their relative importance in order to create a style appropriate to the story and the ballet. In the opening section, rhythm is all-important, melody less so; the few tunes in this section, some borrowed from Russian folk music, are fragmentary, narrow-range motives that repeat obsessively. Ostinato techniques and increasing thickness of texture take the place of traditional development. Instruments are used in new ways; the whole orchestra is sometimes used as a giant percussion instrument. Form is articulated through rhythm and orchestration as much as through melodic material or harmonic cadences. Analysis of this work must begin by understanding the succession of musical events rather than by looking for traditional forms. The historical importance of this work lies in its innovative qualities: While its purpose is a nineteenth-century one—it is, after all, program music to accompany a ballet—its musical language is in many ways new.

You might focus an analytic study of this work on either the new elements or the traditional aspects of the work. It would also be fruitful to compare this work to its immediate predecessors, *Firebird* and *Petrushka*, in order to isolate the new elements in this work. One might also compare the orchestral score to Stravinsky's later arrangement for two pianos. In any case, *The Rite of Spring i*s certainly a work that demands to be analyzed on its own terms.

There are several obvious broader research topics suggested by this work. It is generally described as an example of primitivism, an important artistic movement of the early twentieth century, which held that European culture had become stodgy and effete; the only way new vitality could be injected into the culture was to borrow ideas from other, more vital cultures. Thus, Picasso and other visual artists turned to African masks for inspiration, and one group of rebel painters christened themselves "Les Fauves" ("The Savages"). The notion that the musics of other cultures, or music from other levels of one's own culture, such as jazz and popular music, should be co-opted in order to breathe new life and vibrancy into "high culture" crops up frequently in the history of Western music and is a fascinating concept to pursue. Another cultural issue is the one of reception. Richard Taruskin, a noted Stravinsky scholar, has written that the premiere of *The Rite of Spring* was not the wild riot that we are used to reading about, and that the catcalls were provoked by the choreography, not the music. Concert performances of the music shortly after the premiere were not marked by civil disorder of any kind. Another area of research suggested by this work is the connection between dance and music in the twentieth century; we sometimes forget that composers as diverse as Debussy, Stravinsky, Copland, and Cage spent much of their careers collaborating with dance companies.

### Karlheinz Stockhausen: *Gesang der Jünglinge*

Like *The Rite of Spring*, *Gesang der Jünglinge* ("Song of the Youths"), a famous example of electronic music composed by Karlheinz Stockhausen in 1956, calls for new analytical methods. As is the case with most modernist music, the researcher must begin with the composer's intent, the materials he used to create this work, and the ways in which he used them.

Although the compositional process in this case is modernist, the composer's intent in this work is to give expression to religious ideas and feelings, an aim as old as Gregorian chant and the Masses and motets of the Renaissance. The work is a musical impression of the story in the Book of Daniel of the three young men thrown by the Babylonian king into a fiery furnace for refusing to worship the gods of Babylon. According to the story, the boys, protected by the God of the Hebrews, emerged unharmed and sang a hymn of praise. A recording of that hymn of praise, recited in German by a boy, along with various electronically generated sounds, are the materials used in this composition.

The ways in which these two kinds of material are manipulated give this piece its organization and dramatic effect. The composer broke down the recorded words spoken by the boy into syllables, then phonemes (individual sounds), and still further into tiny sound events such as attacks. In this way, the composer blurred the materials: Some manipulations of the vocal materials are indistinguishable from the electronically generated sounds. The vocal material is also overdubbed to create the effect of a group of voices. Overdubbing of the vocal material creates passages of increasingly complex group sounds; the tension thus created is resolved by slower, calmer passages.

A critically important gesture the composer utilizes is occasionally allowing a single word or phrase, such as "preiset den Herrn" ("praise the Lord"), to emerge in intelligible form after a passage of electronic sounds or unintelligible vocal material. These suddenly intelligible words strike our ears as important dramatic events; the effect is similar to that of a chordal passage following a long passage of complex imitation in a Handel oratorio chorus.

The various electronically generated sounds constitute the second source of material. Well into the piece, for example, a new electronic sound is introduced—a sound like the rattle of a snake. It is striking because we have not heard it earlier, and, as we hear it alternating with the vocal sounds, it seems evil and menacing. As the electronic sounds get faster and faster, a sense of tension or danger is created. Just as with the vocal material, tension is dissipated and a feeling of cadence is created when the sounds slow down and thin out.

One possible topic for analysis is the spatial effects the composer wrote into the work. Unfortunately, this effect cannot be captured in a stereo recording of the piece. At the first performance, the audience was surrounded by five groups of speakers, and the sounds swooped around the audience at various speeds, heightening the drama of the piece. Many other electronic pieces utilized similar spatial effects. It might be interesting to connect electronic music's use of spatial effects to earlier uses of spatial effects, as in Venetian polychoral music.

Another obvious area for research is the form and organization of this work. There is no real sense of melody or harmony in this piece, but, since it lasts for thirteen minutes, the listener naturally tries to identify sections, related events, and periodic cadences of some sort. Repeated listening reveals that the composer has created clear structures in several different ways. The piece starts and ends with rapid jumbles of electronic sounds that frame a series of vocal and electronic sections. Within sections, new events are delineated by changes in the timbre, speed, or complication of the electronic sounds, as well as by sudden bursts of group passages or intelligible words in the vocal material. Silence also delineates the structure—sometimes there are significant pauses between syllables or words, and pauses in the electronic sounds as well. Taking into account all these techniques, commentators suggest that the overall form is a series of three related but varied sections framed within the electronic introduction and coda. One might argue for other patterns as well, based on the arrangement of sound events and relationships between them.

Research topics that study this piece from the broader perspective of cultural studies come readily to mind. One issue is the question of reception. Among the general music audience, this work is probably the best-known example of electronic music, unquestionably one of the more accessible works in that medium. One can argue that the combination of modernist and traditional materials and means of organization, as well as the dramatic story, give the work its universal appeal. One might also search for other works, both live and electronic, that play with the threshold of intelligibility and compare the effects they create to this work. One might also find other electronic works based on religious themes and try to assess the effectiveness of electronic music to deal with large themes such as religion. Finally, there is the philosophical question of whether this work is really modernist. The creative techniques and some of the materials are thoroughly modernist, but some of the materials and the ways they are organized are close to traditional, and the purpose of the work is not really modernist. Some researchers might even use this fascinating piece as an opening into the larger issue of modernism and postmodernism.

In conclusion, note that these brief comments do not pretend to be exhaustive lists of research areas suggested by these works, but preliminary indications of directions you might take to develop analytical topics or other kinds of research connected with these pieces. If you plan to do analytical research, remember that each work must be studied in ways that illuminate its particular organization. In one sense, stylistic analysis is a circular process. Its goal is the understanding of a musical style, but one cannot begin the analysis unless one knows enough about the style to be able to choose appropriate methods of analysis. At the start of an analytic project, you may need to put the specific work aside for a while and first develop an awareness of the stylistic context from which it came.

Finally, we emphasize again that not every research paper for a class in music must be analytical in design and purpose. The ideas above about the nonanalytical research projects these works might suggest do not pretend to be any more exhaustive than the suggestions about analytical approaches. The purpose has been to show that any piece of music suggests areas for research, both analytical and cultural, if we brainstorm for a moment. One final reminder: Whatever direction your research might take, anything you say about music must be based on a solid understanding of the style and organization of the work you are discussing—what holds it together as a unified work of art and what makes it unique.

The next chapter moves into a discussion of the nature of research, some basic resources for research, both print and electronic, and research methodologies.

# CHAPTER 3

# Getting Started: Research

This chapter discusses the first phase of the process of producing a paper on a musical topic—research. Naturally, the process will vary greatly, depending on the topic; each project calls for its own resources and research strategies. In this chapter we will discuss basic resources and places to start, rather than the resources for highly specialized research. For further information on specialized resources, consult the texts designed for graduate researchers listed in the Preface, especially the Duckles/Reed bibliography and the Wingell/Herzog book. Here we are more concerned with the process of research and how to get started on an undergraduate research project.

## CHOOSING A TOPIC

In some undergraduate classes, the instructor may assign a single topic for the whole class, or perhaps a list of topics from which the students are to choose one. At other times, the choice of a topic may be entirely up to you. When the choice is yours, the following considerations may be helpful.

When the project is first discussed, you need to have a clear idea of the kind of paper the professor has in mind. Pay close attention to the handout explaining the assignment and the explanation in class, so that you clearly understand the instructor's expectations, lest you waste time dreaming up projects that will not be acceptable. The time to ask questions about the range of acceptable topics is when the assignment is first discussed.

Once you understand what sort of topic is expected, you need to choose a general research area and then narrow that area down to a specific topic. One way to begin selecting a topic is to survey the range of genres within the historical period specified by the assignment. If the class covers Baroque music, for example, you should first decide whether you want to work with instrumental or vocal music. If you choose the vocal area, the next step is to select from the various genres—for example, opera, cantata, sacred concerto, oratorio, etc. If you decide on opera, then you will need to choose from the various styles—Florentine, Venetian, Neapolitan, French, German, and English. Next, you might want to choose a specific time period, composer, or work. Another way to select a topic is to start with a particular time period or geographical area and find a suitable topic related to that time and place. There are many ways to choose a topic; the important thing is to begin making that decision early, long before the project is due.

During this early stage, you will need to do some preliminary browsing in the music library and on the Internet to see what scores and recordings are available and what the secondary literature has to say. By *secondary literature,* we mean reference books, histories, biographies, articles, or anything else published by later generations of scholars, as opposed to *primary sources,* the manuscripts, early prints, and similar materials that come from the period you are studying. There is little point in getting excited about a topic if there are no scores available and nothing has been written about the topic in the secondary sources. If it becomes clear that investigating a topic would involve sending for microfilms of unpublished materials from a European library, spending three months in an archive somewhere, or traveling across the country to interview a living composer, you might want to choose another topic. If it turns out that you need facility in an unfamiliar language, knowledge in some completely new area, or training in a new methodology to investigate a topic, then that topic clearly does not make sense for a semester or term project.

Once you have decided on a topic, clear your idea with the instructor before going much further with your research. Do not waste valuable time working on a topic that may not be acceptable or one that the instructor knows will not be suitable for an undergraduate project. If you really want to work on a project that the instructor is not sure about, you may be able to convince him or her that you have the skills and motivation to work with an unusual topic. It still might be worth having a backup plan in mind if your instructor is not convinced or if the topic turns out to be impossible once you get into it.

The main goal in choosing a topic is to select something of the right scope. Topics should be specific enough to be realistic as a topic for a paper, without getting so specific that you have problems with availability of materials or find yourself moving into levels of research for which you are not qualified. "The Symphonies of Haydn" or "Schoenberg and Twelve-Tone Music," for example, are obviously not appropriate topics for a term paper—they are much too broad and better suited for book-length or multivolume studies. On the other hand, the topic should not be so narrow that it involves highly technical research problems better left to experienced scholars. There is a wide range of possibilities between these two extremes. In the area of Haydn symphonies, you might choose to compare an early symphony with a later one, trying to determine through comparative analysis how Haydn's style changed over the course of his career. You might focus on a few first movements, comparing different versions of the sonata-allegro process; you might concentrate on the question of structure in a few slow movements. You might also compare a symphony by Haydn with one by Mozart, in an attempt to isolate the subtle differences between the two composers. Moving beyond analytical topics, you might focus on performance practice issues or the circumstances in which these works were first performed. You might also concentrate on reception history—how these works were regarded in their time or by later ages. There are hundreds of viable topics within the general area of Haydn symphonies; it takes some thought and some preliminary work with the scores and secondary sources to find a topic that will work for you. Since you will spend considerable time working on the topic you settle on, be sure that is a topic you like, one you are qualified to tackle, and one that you can carry through to a successful conclusion.

## KINDS OF TOPICS

Most undergraduate research papers fall into a few standard types. One type focuses on analysis of a single work. Assigned topics often fall into this classification; the instructor, knowing that a particular work is an especially fruitful topic for analysis or a useful example of an important style, directs the students to analyze that work and report their conclusions. A paper on a single work typically begins with a review of the background of the work and a summary of what has been written about the work in secondary sources. The main body of the paper would be the student's analysis of the work, followed by a short conclusion and a bibliography.

Another type of topic is a comparative analysis; an example would be a topic we mentioned already, a comparison of early and late symphonies by Haydn. Analysis of similar works by different composers can be very instructive as well. A project that has worked well in classes on Renaissance music, for example, is a comparison of Dufay's *L'Homme armé* Mass with one of Josquin's Masses on the same cantus firmus. Because both works utilize the same source material, compositional process, and basic style, the comparison isolates and sheds light on the differences in personal style between the two composers and the way musical style evolved over time. In designing a comparative analysis project, it is important that the works be closely related stylistically. A study comparing a Schoenberg twelve-tone piece to a neoclassical work by Stravinsky would obviously conclude that the two works are fundamentally different—hardly a world-shaking discovery. On the other hand, it would be interesting to compare twelve-tone works by Schoenberg and Berg or Webern, since that study would uncover individual stylistic differences within the same compositional process.

Sometimes it is useful to survey a larger group of related works in the same style. The danger in dealing with a large body of literature is that the student may end up producing a glorified list, dull to assemble and boring to read. That sort of project is useful only when such surveys do not already exist and the student has some reason to produce such a list, such as compiling a graded and annotated repertory of pieces for teaching purposes. That project, however, would be more suitable for a music education class than a music history class.

There is also a world of biographical and cultural topics that do not focus directly on analysis of specific works. Such projects might study, for example, a Renaissance court and its musical life, or the musical situation in turn-of-the-century Vienna. A biographical study of an important performer of the Baroque era, such as the castrato Farinelli or Gottfried Reiche, Bach's trumpeter at Leipzig, would shed light on the question of the role of performers in the evolution of musical style, as well as the ways in which musical careers in that era differed from careers now. There are some potential problems connected with historical, biographical, or sociological topics. First, topics of this sort can sometimes result in summaries of material already readily available in standard sources, in which case they are largely pointless busy-work. Any research paper should have something new to offer—if not new information, then an original thesis, a fresh approach, or a thought-provoking conclusion. Secondly, students sometimes propose nonanalytic topics that seem too broad-ranging, either because of the large repertory of works they wish to cover or the combination of disciplines and research skills needed to do the sort of work they propose. In choosing a topic, it is good to be curious and adventurous; it is also good to be practical and choose topics that are realistic and within your competence to complete by the assigned deadline.

You can now understand why professors sometimes assign specific topics, require students to choose from a prepared list of topics, or insist on approving topics early in the semester. Some proposed topics are promising, some are not, and some would take years to cover adequately. Trust your professor's judgment about topics; as we said earlier, if you are intent on pursuing an offbeat topic, most instructors will try to help you pursue that interest and still produce a successful paper.

## WHAT RESEARCH MEANS

Once you have a workable topic, the next step is gathering information about that topic through the process called research. Research means more than just locating a group of relevant quotations and stringing them together in a paper, even if the writer includes the necessary quotation marks and footnotes. Reporting what authorities have said about a topic is one standard way to begin a paper, but this step does not fulfill the researcher's responsibility. Research in any field must also have a creative, personal side, especially in the arts, where we study the products of human creativity and artistic vision. Even research in the natural sciences involves more than merely measuring and quantifying phenomena. It takes a creative mind to make the leap necessary to create a hypothesis to explain puzzling phenomena and the appropriate means to test that hypothesis. Research in the arts is not just gathering information, any more than musical analysis consists of listing and counting musical events. Facts by themselves are useless unless they lead to ideas. The writer must have a thesis and a conclusion; after the writer has quoted this authority and that authority, the reader expects to be told what the writer thinks. A paper that consists of a review of the literature without then moving to the writer's own ideas is a book report, not a research project.

At some point as you are gathering information, all your observations and the ideas you read should begin to coalesce around one central point which will lead to the main thesis of your paper. The next chapter will discuss the thesis in more detail. Here it will suffice to say that the reader wants to know what you think. Do you agree with the secondary sources? Does your view of the work differ from the view reported in the standard literature? Does your analysis of the music, or the other kinds of research you have done, lead you to side with one opinion rather than another or to disagree with them all?

Your hypothesis and conclusion need not be world-shaking. The reader of undergraduate papers does not expect to see conclusions such as "This alleged Bach cantata could not possibly have been written by Bach," or "The Mendelssohn Violin Concerto is actually based on a concealed twelve-tone row." The reader does expect, however, to see your informed opinion, based on the research you have done. Too many papers stop abruptly after reporting on the secondary literature and the analysis process, as if the last few pages of the project were somehow lost. As a scholar and musician, even if you regard yourself as an apprentice in one or both fields, you have a responsibility to follow the research process to its conclusion, to risk taking a position, and to communicate your informed ideas and opinions about your topic.

## GATHERING MATERIALS

Once you have a workable topic and approach, the next step is to gather the materials you need. Start by assembling a bibliography on the topic. It is crucial to be thorough and systematic right from the beginning of your search. Set aside a large block of time for this step, take careful notes on what you find, and keep your information in some organized fashion—in a file on

your computer, in a notebook or folder, on file cards, or in some other convenient way. Whatever system you use for gathering and storing information, it is important to be thorough, consistent, and systematic. There is
nothing worse than discovering at the last minute, with the deadline press-
ing, that your notes are incomplete or no longer make sense to you. Each
entry should include complete bibliographic information, so that you do
not have to return to each book or Web site to find the author's full name,
the date of publication, the page on which the material you want to quote
appears, and other such details. The more complete and consistent your
note-taking system is, the easier it will be to use the material when you get
to the writing stage.

## PLACES TO START: PRINT RESOURCES

As you begin the search for information on your topic, start with the standard kinds of resources. The first thing to be aware of is that bibliographies
on many topics have already been assembled and are published in several
places. Rather than reinventing the wheel, start with these existing bibliographies; you will not only save considerable time and effort, but you are
much less likely to overlook important sources. Extensive lists of published
bibliographies appear in the guides for graduate students; here are some
basic resources, with some advice on how to use them.

### Library Catalogs

The first place to begin your search for information is the catalog of a
good music library. Library catalogs have standard ways of dividing subjects
into large headings and subheadings; a new researcher should spend some
time browsing through a card catalog (if your library still has one) to get a
sense of these patterns and the standard headings they use. College and university library catalogs are generally available online. Try searching for various topics in the standard ways, by "author" (meaning "composer" in the
case of musical works), title, or key word. Experiment with different key
words to see how the results vary, and don't be satisfied with the standard
search. Most catalogs have "advanced search" options that facilitate more
sophisticated searches. The better you know how to use your institution's
online catalog efficiently, the easier and more productive your search for
information will be. In addition, all library catalogs use the same system for
matters such as spelling and alphabetizing composers' names and transliterating composers' names from foreign alphabets. The more experience you
have with the way catalogs work, the easier it will be to find what you are
looking for. The researcher also needs to be patient and resourceful; you may
not find what you are looking for in the first place you look. Don't give up

quickly. Look for cross-references, try a different spelling or a different key word, start from the name of an author who you know has written about the subject, or design some other path to find what you are looking for.

### Dictionaries and Encyclopedias

Another good strategy in the early stages of a research project is to consult musical dictionaries and encyclopedias. The following are some of the standard musical reference works.

*Baker's Biographical Dictionary of Musicians*. Centennial ed. New York: Schirmer, 2000.
Randel, Don Michael, ed. *The Harvard Biographical Dictionary of Music*. Cambridge,
    MA: Belknap Press of Harvard University Press, 1996.
————, ed. *The Harvard Dictionary of Music*. 4th ed. Cambridge, MA: Belknap Press of
    Harvard University Press, 2003.
*Die Musik in Geschichte und Gegenwart*. 2nd ed. Kassel: Bärenreiter, 1994–.
Sadie, Stanley, and John Tyrrell, eds. *The New Grove Dictionary of Music and Musicians*.
    2nd ed. London: Macmillan, 2001.

We need to add some commentary about these important works. *Baker's Biographical Dictionary of Musicians* existed for years as a standard one-volume reference work edited by Nicolas Slonimsky. It went through several editions in this form, the last being the eighth edition in 1992. In 2000, Schirmer published the centennial edition, a greatly expanded, six-volume work under the same title. This edition, also called the ninth edition, includes all the articles by Slonimsky from the eighth edition, plus a large number of additional articles, some on musicians from outside the world of classical music.

Note that *Baker's* and *The Harvard Biographical Dictionary* are *biographical dictionaries*—that is, they contain entries on composers, performers, and theorists and include worklists and selective bibliographies; they do not contain articles on terms, instruments, genres, or periods. *The Harvard Biographical Dictionary* is the new standard one-volume biographical dictionary. For some time, many researchers of all levels have kept a one-volume biographical dictionary on their shelves, along with a standard music dictionary, for quick reference.

*The Harvard Dictionary of Music* replaced an earlier work edited by Willi Apel. It is a one-volume dictionary of terms, with many longer articles and useful selective bibliographies. It is constantly being updated; as you see, in 2003 it was in its fourth edition.

We turn now to two giant encyclopedias of music. *Die Musik in Geschichte und Gegenwart,* known familiarly as MGG, is an important German music lexicon, with sizeable articles written by experts, complete worklists, and extensive bibliographies. The first edition, in twenty-one volumes, nine organized by subject and twelve volumes of biographical entries, was eventually also made available online. A second edition of this work began to appear in 1994; it is divided into ten volumes of information organized by subject, all of which have already been published, and seventeen volumes of biographical entries, sixteen of which were published by 2007. The print version of the second edition is therefore nearly complete; there is no notice on the MGG Web site that any parts of the second edition are available on-line. Students sometimes dismiss the MGG because it is in German, but it is a magnificent, beautifully produced reference work, and the lavish illustrations, worklists, and bibliographies require no knowledge of German—the bibliographies, however, are filled with German abbreviations that you might have to get used to. If you have never opened a volume of this impressive reference work, look up a few of your favorite topics in it and see for yourself how useful it can be for your research.

The *New Grove,* as it is familiarly called, is the most important encyclopedia of music in English. Like MGG, it contains signed articles by an international body of scholars, complete worklists, and extensive bibliographies. It is obviously the best place to start your search for bibliographical information. The first edition of the *New Grove,* which replaced an older British series, was published in twenty volumes in 1980. The second edition, which appeared on library shelves in March 2001, consists of twenty-nine volumes, including an index volume. Each article was written by an expert in that particular field; some articles are the length of monographs or small books, and all contain complete worklists and bibliographies that were up-to-date at the time of publication. All music libraries have this basic resource on their reference shelves; it can be found in many public libraries as well. Always check the *New Grove* when you are starting on a project, and use some imagination as you search for information—the material you seek might be located in an article on the composer or in the articles on genres, instruments, terms, or historical eras. The second edition is available online as well as in print, and additions and revisions are being added constantly. We will have more to say about the online version in the section on electronic resources.

The *New Grove* series also includes supplementary encyclopedias that deal with specialized areas; obviously these are the best places to start research for topics in those areas. The dictionaries of jazz and opera are available online, along with the main dictionary.

Sadie, Stanley, and H. Wiley Hitchcock, eds. *The New Grove Dictionary of American Music.* 4 vols. New York: Grove Dictionaries, 1986.
Kernfeld, Barry, ed. *The New Grove Dictionary of Jazz.* 2nd ed., 3 vols. New York: Grove Dictionaries, 2001.
Sadie, Stanley, ed. *The New Grove Dictionary of Musical Instruments.* 3 vols. London: Macmillan, 1984.
Sadie, Stanley, ed. *The New Grove Dictionary of Opera.* 4 vols. New York: Grove Dictionaries, 1992.

There are many other dictionaries and encyclopedias of music; the handful listed above are the standard sources for most topics. One issue to consider in using these resources is how to locate the most up-to-date bibliographical listings, realizing that any published bibliography is at least slightly out of date by the time it is published. Clearly, the most recent bibliographical information on musical topics will be found in the constantly updated *Grove Music Online,* unless MGG becomes available in a regularly updated online version.

### Histories of Music

Most histories of music include bibliographical notes, located either at the end of each chapter or at the back of the book. These bibliographies are another fine place to start your research, once you locate the appropriate chapter in the book or series that deals with the area you are researching. The following are the current standard one-volume music history textbooks, listed alphabetically by author.

Bonds, Mark Evan. *A History of Music in Western Culture.* 2nd ed. Upper Saddle River, NJ: Prentice Hall, 2006.
Burkholder, J. Peter, Donald J. Grout, and Claude V. Palisca. *A History of Western Music.* 7th ed. New York: Norton, 2005.
Rosenstiel, Leonie, general editor. *Schirmer History of Music.* New York: Schirmer, 1982.
Stolba, K. Marie. *The Development of Western Music: A History.* 3rd ed. Boston: McGraw-Hill, 1998.
Wright, Craig, and Bryan Simms. *Music in Western Civilization.* New York: Schirmer, 2005.

There is also an important multivolume history of music by a single author.

Taruskin, Richard. *Oxford History of Western Music.* 6 vols. New York: Oxford University Press, 2005.

The multivolume series of books on music history also contain useful selective bibliographies. Among the standard music history series are the following publications.

*The New Oxford History of Music.* London, New York: Oxford, 1954–90. Ten volumes, each covering a different period and consisting of a collection of essays by different writers, rather than a continuous narrative. Consult the Oxford University Press Web site for titles, editors, and details.

Norton Introduction to Music History Series. New York: Norton, 1978–. Intended to supplement the older History of Music Series. Each volume has a companion anthology of scores. Extensive bibliographies, organized by chapter, appear at the back of each volume.

Hoppin, Richard. *Medieval Music.* 1978.
Atlas, Alan. *Renaissance Music: Music in Western Europe, 1400–1600.* 1998.

Hill, John Walter. *Baroque Music: Music in Western Europe, 1580–1750.* 2005.
Downs, Philip G. *Classical Music: The Era of Haydn, Mozart, and Beethoven.* 1992.
Plantinga, Leon. *Romantic Music.* 1985.
Morgan, Robert P. *Twentieth-Century Music.* 1991.

The Prentice Hall History of Music Series. Englewood Cliffs (later Upper Saddle River), NJ: Prentice Hall, 1965–. The volumes in this series focus on the various periods of Western music; there are also several volumes on American music and world musics. Bibliographical notes appear at the conclusion of each chapter. Many of these volumes have gone through several editions; a few are apparently out of print at this time, but are still available in libraries.

Yudkin, Jeremy. *Music in Medieval Europe.* 1989. Replaced Albert Seay, *Music in the Medieval World,* 1965; 2nd ed., 1975.
Brown, Howard, and Louise K. Stein. *Music in the Renaissance,* 2nd ed., 1999.
Palisca, Claude V. *Baroque Music.* 3rd ed., 1991.
Pauly, Reinhard G. *Music in the Classic Period.* 4th ed., 2000.
Longyear, Rey M. *Nineteenth-Century Romanticism in Music.* 3rd ed., 1988.
Salzman, Eric. *Twentieth-Century Music: An Introduction.* 4th ed., 2002.
Nettl, Bruno. *Folk and Traditional Music of the Western Continents.* 3rd ed., revised and edited by Valerie Woodring Goertzen, 1990.
Malm, William P. *Music Cultures of the Pacific, the Near East, and Asia.* 2nd ed., 1996.
Hitchcock, H. Wiley. *Music in the United States: A Historical Introduction.* 4th ed., 2000.
Béhague, Gérard. *Music in Latin America: An Introduction.* 1979.

Music and Society Series. A series of ten books, edited by Stanley Sadie and published by Prentice Hall, designed to present music "in a broad context of socio-political, economic, intellectual, and religious life." Each volume is a collection of articles by various authors on the changing cultural background during a particular historical era. The first two volumes to appear, on the Renaissance and the Classical era, were published under the series title *Man and Music;* the other eight were published as the *Music and Society* series. At this writing this useful series is out of print and is not listed in the publisher's online catalogue; the volumes may still be found in music libraries.

McKinnon, James, ed. *Antiquity and the Middle Ages: From Ancient Greece to the 15th Century.* 1991.
Fenlon, Iain, ed. *The Renaissance: From the 1470s to the End of the 16th Century.* 1989.
Price, Curtis, ed. *The Early Baroque Era: From the Late 16th Century to the 1660s.* 1994.
Buelow, George, ed. *The Late Baroque Era: From the 1680s to 1740.* 1994.
Zaslaw, Neal, ed. *The Classical Era: From the 1740s to the End of the 18th Century.* 1989.
Ringer, Alexander, ed. *The Early Romantic Era: Between Revolutions, 1789 and 1848.* 1991.
Samson, Jim, ed. *The Late Romantic Era: From the Mid-19th Century to World War I.* 1991.
Morgan, Robert, ed. *Modern Times: From World War I to the Present.* 1994.

Cambridge Companions to Music Series. The Cambridge University Press publishes several series of handbooks about musical topics. The press's Web site currently lists sixty-eight "Companions to Music," which are monographs on composers, genres, and instruments, as well as twenty "Lives" of composers and thirty "Studies" of composers. There are also ninety-one handbooks on individual orchestral and choral works, thirty-one handbooks on individual operas, and fifteen monographs on cultural studies related to opera. In addition, there are series on musical texts, music literature, twentieth-century music, studies in performance and reception, and new perspectives in music history and criticism. Browse the Web site (go to Cambridge University Press Series, then click on "Academic" and "Music") to see the amazing number and variety of these handbooks. If "Companions" or other handbooks dealing with the composer or work you are researching are available, they would be well worth consulting, since all these handbooks are written by experts but designed to be read by students and interested amateurs, and each provides an informative and engaging study of the topic and a list of the important source materials. Keep an eye out for volumes in these series; they are not all lined up in a row in libraries, but located in the appropriate sections—biography, analysis, etc.

### Biographies

If there is a published biography of the composer you are interested in, it will probably be very helpful for your project, particularly if it is a "life and works," including description and analysis of the composer's works. Biographies are classified in the Library of Congress system under the number ML (for Music Literature) 410; within that section, books are shelved alphabetically by subject, so that one browses for biographies by looking under the composer's name. In the Dewey Decimal System, all biographies are shelved together under the classification 92 (shorthand for 920), then alphabetically by subject; thus, biographies of composers are mixed in with all the other biographies.

Not all biographies of composers and performers are serious research studies; later in this chapter, we will discuss how the researcher can judge whether a book is a serious study or not. Serious scholarly biographies are extremely useful for research.

### Thematic Catalogs

Thematic catalogs can be useful tools in many ways for the researcher. A *thematic catalog* (the German term is *Verzeichnis*) is a listing of every work of a composer, with information about the forces required, the background and history of the work, surviving manuscripts, early editions, current editions, etc. The most famous thematic catalogs are Schmieder's *Bach-Werke-Verzeichnis,* which is organized by genre, and the Köchel catalog of the works of Mozart, which is organized chronologically. These are only the best-known examples; a random sampling of composers whose works have been systematically cataloged includes composers as diverse as Beethoven, Brahms, Busoni, Clementi, Haydn, Lully, Schoenberg, Schubert, Shostakovich, Strauss, Stravinsky, Vivaldi, Wagner, and Walton. A list of thematic catalogs may be found in

Barry S. Brook, *Thematic Catalogues in Music: An Annotated Bibliography* (Stuyvesant, NY: Pendragon Press, 1972; revised ed. with Richard Viano, 1997). Catalogs published after that date are indexed in *The International Repertory of Music Literature,* which will be discussed later. One important advantage of using these resources is that the entry for each work generally includes a bibliography limited to that specific work. In the Bach catalog, for instance, the entry for each cantata lists articles on that particular cantata as well as the pages in general books where that work is discussed. Obviously, the efficient researcher will want to take advantage of these helpful resources.

### Articles

An enormous body of recent research has not yet found its way into the standard histories and is available only in musicological journals such as *The Journal of the American Musicological Society, The Journal of Musicology, Musical Quarterly, Acta Musicologica, Music Review,* and similar scholarly publications. Articles are the only source of substantial information on some topics—the standard one-volume histories can hardly stay abreast of recent research on all musical subjects. The best way to acquaint yourself with the journals and get some idea of the sort of research they publish is to browse through the current issues of periodicals in the music library.

Locating articles on your research topic among the scores of scholarly journals may seem to be an intimidating task, but there are resources designed to help researchers locate articles on specific topics. Many journals publish cumulative listings of the articles they have published. There are also two general guides that list articles published in the musical journals. The first is the *Music Index,* a collection of titles and authors of articles published in selected music periodicals. The *Music Index* began publication in 1949; it is published monthly, and cumulative listings are published annually. The quickest way to locate articles in the print version is to search first through the annual cumulative listings and then consult the monthly issues for listings of the articles that look promising. It takes time to go through all the annual listings, but it is an excellent way to locate articles related to your topic.

Another important resource is the *International Repertory of Music Literature,* known as "RILM" from the initials of its title in French. This index contains abstracts of articles, dissertations, and other publications, and is published several times a year. Cumulative listings are published every five years. Using RILM can save considerable time because of the inclusiveness of its coverage. Articles in collections that are not regularly indexed or included in card catalogs are indexed in RILM; it can be very helpful indeed. Both *Music Index* and RILM are now available in searchable versions on the Internet; see the section on electronic resources. Internet search engines can also help you locate articles and point you to sites where the full texts of articles can be found; again, see the section on electronic resources.

### Dissertations

Doctoral dissertations can be very helpful to the researcher, since they are usually thorough scholarly studies that utilize primary resources and include complete bibliographies. Reference libraries contain published lists of dissertations accepted in American and European universities and abstracts of dissertations published by University Microfilms of Ann Arbor, Michigan. Music libraries frequently order copies of dissertations; actually, anyone can order a copy of a dissertation from University Microfilms. If you find a listing of a dissertation you would like to consult but are worried about the cost or about getting a copy in time, talk to your instructor; he or she might want to request that the library order a copy. Titles and abstracts of dissertations are now available also in electronic formats; see the section on electronic resources.

### Scores and Recordings

The researcher should be aware that there are many different kinds of scores, some more reliable than others for scholarly research. *Primary sources,* such as manuscripts and first editions, are of course the most reliable, but they may be difficult for a nonspecialist to locate or read. *Scholarly editions* constitute the next level; they attempt to present a version of the music that represents as exactly as possible what the composer actually wrote, based on surviving autograph materials and the earliest surviving manuscript and printed editions. Then there are *performing scores,* some of them quite reliable and others heavily edited. Pianists and organists are familiar with the old performing editions of Bach's keyboard works, cluttered with fingerings, slurs, dynamic markings, and other editorial additions that nearly obscure the notes that Bach wrote. These markings of course may be helpful for a young student first learning the piece; scholarly work, however, should be based not on these heavily edited versions, but on a clean scholarly edition. It is better to find a reliable scholarly edition in the collected sets or the collected works of a composer and photocopy that score to use as your working copy than it is to base your work on a more accessible performing edition that may or may not represent what the composer actually wrote. Collected sets of scores are assigned M2 and M3 numbers in the Library of Congress system and shelved in the library's noncirculating score section. Collections in the M2 category are organized by countries or genres; the M3 section contains the collected works of individual composers, organized alphabetically by composer's last name. The Dewey system groups these editions similarly and has special numbers for each type of collection. Browse through the M2 and M3 sections of your music library to get a sense of the wealth of scholarly editions available to you.

In order to assist the researcher in finding specific pieces within these large collections, there are published guides that list the contents of each volume of each set; they are also equipped with extensive indexes. These guides are shelved in the reference sections of music libraries. There is also an online database of collections and their contents based on the Hill and Stephens guide; we will discuss that database later.

Heyer, Anna, comp. *Historical Sets, Collected Editions, and Monuments of Music*. 2 vols., 3rd ed. Chicago: American Library Assoc., 1980.
Hill, George R., and Norris L. Stephens. *Collected Editions, Historical Sets, and Monuments of Music: A Bibliography*. Berkeley, CA: Fallen Leaf Press, 1997.

Recordings may be part of your research for a project; the same critical judgment must be applied to recordings as to scores, perhaps especially in the case of early music. Although we know more about historically informed performance practice than we did some years ago, many questions remain hotly contested issues. Still, if you have a choice of recordings to use for your project, it makes sense to use one that takes historical authenticity as one of its goals. Check to see whether historical instruments were used, how the edition was arrived at, and whether the performing group specializes in old music.

Critical judgment should be applied not only to the recorded performance but also to the notes that accompany the recording. Sometimes these notes are written by well-known experts and based on scholarly research. At other times, the limited space is devoted to biographies of the performers or advertisements for other recordings, with perhaps a paragraph or two of cursory discussion of the music. Serious liner notes, especially if they are signed by a recognized scholar, or extensive discussions in the booklets included with multidisc albums, are certainly appropriate to cite in a paper. Brief, unsigned comments, on the other hand, are not likely to provide the sort of material that you would want to cite.

## PLACES TO START: ELECTRONIC RESOURCES

The pace of recent developments in the area of electronic research is one of the main reasons for updating this guide. Exciting new resources are available, and some of the resources listed in earlier editions are no longer available or have been supplanted by new developments in the field. The main trend we noted in earlier editions—using the Internet as the main channel for information—has continued and eclipsed some of the electronic resources that were important earlier. Researchers studying musical topics now have access on the Internet to important databases that used to be available only on CD-ROM, full texts of articles in scholarly journals, updated articles in *Grove Music Online*—even downloadable scores in collections such as the one available on the Indiana University Web site, among others. In addition, new, specialized search engines have been created to help researchers find their way through the masses of information available on the Internet. This section will review the current situation in electronic research and discuss some of the important and useful resources now available.

Whenever the Internet is discussed as a resource for research, the discussion always begins with the need to exercise critical judgment about materials on the Internet. As you know, the Internet is democratic—anyone can put up a Web site. Sites range from serious scholarly discussions to blogs about the latest gossip in some middle school. There are commercial sites where one can buy almost anything, ranging from Amazon.com, a wonderful source for books and recordings, to eBay, a giant electronic rummage sale where one can buy whatever someone else wants to unload.

In view of the bewildering variety of information on the Internet, obviously the researcher must exercise critical judgment about Web sites. When the Internet was new, this warning was issued with a sense of urgency. Now we realize that the necessity of critical judgment is nothing new; we exercise the same critical judgment when evaluating print resources—books, articles, or anything else. It is obvious that so-called "refereed" or "peer-reviewed" articles in scholarly journals are more trustworthy than someone's opinion found in a letter to the editor or a blog. Even on the Internet, the spirit of democracy sometimes runs afoul of questions of authority and reliability. It has been interesting, for example, to watch the evolution of Wikipedia, the democratically produced Internet encyclopedia. The guiding principle was that articles were not edited in advance; if any reader felt that a particular article was wrong or incomplete, he or she was free to submit a supplementary article. Then events forced some rethinking of this basic philosophy. Questions arose about corporations hiring writers to submit articles written from the corporation's point of view in order to counteract existing articles critical of them. In some cases, authors on opposite sides of some contentious subjects kept submitting arguments and counter-arguments, defending conflicting points of view rather than discussing factual information, and the people who run the site eventually suspended editing privileges on some articles. As I understand the situation, there now is some review done before articles are published on the site. The idea of a democratically produced encyclopedia never made sense to me in the first place. If I need to know more about the life of Stravinsky or the War of 1812, I want to consult an authority, not someone whose only qualification is a burning desire to write about the topic. In the same way, if I needed an emergency appendectomy, I would want someone with credentials and experience to perform the surgery—enthusiasm and a consuming desire to cut people open would not be enough. In any case, I now sense a commonsense approach to this question—we need to be just as critical of online resources as we are of print resources and seek out writings by experts in the field in peer-reviewed journals and collections.

Next we will discuss some of the important electronic resources and how to make use of them in doing research for your papers. For some of you, this discussion will be a review; our aim is to provide basic information that should help with any project.

### Search Engines

As you know, search engines are a natural place to start any kind of research. You type in a topic, and in a matter of seconds the search engine produces a list of Web sites that deal with that topic and links to those sites. It is probably fair to say that Google is the best known of these search engines— it has even given us a new verb, "to google" someone or something, as in "I googled my history professor and discovered that she's written five books and a ton of articles."

The speed and wide range of search engines is astounding. Their amazing efficiency, however, is also in one sense a disadvantage, at least for some kinds of research. Let us say that you are interested in information about the history, background, and analysis of Brahms's Symphony No. 4. I typed "Brahms Symphony No. 4" (without the quotation marks) into the topic line on Google and within a few seconds got a list of 1,250,000 hits, or sites containing those words. The most diligent researcher would be daunted by the task of reading through that entire list. There are ways, of course, to narrow a search; if you put quotation marks around the topic, the search engine includes in the list only sites that include all those elements. Even with the quotation marks, there were 74,400 hits—still a fairly daunting number.

The problem, of course, is that search engines do not differentiate between various types of sites. On the first page of the list of sites about the Fourth Symphony were several listings of recordings available from Amazon.com and other sites. I'm sure if I checked a few more pages, I would find listings of performances and reviews of recordings and performances. A researcher might also find comments on the work that some writer included in a personal Web site or a blog. Articles in scholarly journals would be listed too, mixed in with the more numerous commercial and personal sites.

There are ways to restrict searches to particular kinds of sites—for example, you can exclude sites that deal with recordings or performances. You can read about these restricting techniques in the "advanced search" instructions that all search engines include on their sites. More important, now we have Google Scholar, a new search engine that restricts its searches to theses, books, and peer-reviewed articles in scholarly journals and collections published by academic publishers, scholarly societies, and universities. At the moment, Google Scholar is listed as a "beta resource," meaning that it is still in the process of development and modification. The occasional glitches that come with the beta phase are a small price to pay for a search engine dedicated solely to scholarly research. For the sake of comparison, I typed "Brahms Symphony No. 4" in the topic line on Google Scholar, first without quotation marks and then with them. In contrast to the results from the main Google site, when I typed the topic without quotation marks, Google Scholar listed 4,270 hits; with the quotation marks, there were 41 hits. You can see how dramatically a specialized search engine narrows the list. By the way, even those 41 hits included some sites about recordings; there are ways to eliminate them from the list.

One final word. Clicking on the sites listed by a search engine, even Google Scholar, will not necessarily lead you to exactly what you are looking for. If a search engine lists an article in *Grove Music Online* or the JSTOR archive (both discussed later in this section), you can go straight to those sites but not directly to full texts of the articles; both are subscription sites. If your university library subscribes to these sites, you can get to the full text of the article through your library's Web site; we will have more to say about that later.

In summary, search engines are amazing resources and can quickly inform you about what has been written about a topic, but you need to develop the skills to navigate them efficiently to get to the information you seek.

### Databases

There are several databases on the Internet that are essential for research on musical topics. These resources have existed in print versions for years; some were also published in CD-ROM format. In recent years, these databases have moved to the Internet, where they are available by subscription. University libraries usually subscribe to these sites, and students have access to the sites through their library accounts. Browse these Web sites; the home pages explain their purpose, coverage, and how to use them. Specialized databases exist for all sorts of specific topics, such as early music, jazz, choral music, etc. Here we will discuss general databases useful for all musical topics.

***RILM Abstracts of Music Literature***     RILM (the acronym stands for the title in French; the English title is *International Repertory of Music Literature*) publishes abstracts of books, dissertations, and articles in journals and collections; the official title of the print database and the Web site is *RILM Abstracts of Music Literature*. We discussed the print version earlier. This important resource is now available online. It is most useful in the early stages of research, since it directs researchers to materials already published on their topics. In addition, each abstract, written by the author of the book or article, summarizes the thesis and argument of the publication, making clear to the researcher whether a particular publication is important to his or her research. Note that databases do not provide the full text of the publication; *RILM Abstracts*, however, provides enough information to let the researcher know whether it is important to track down the full text. The range of materials covered by *RILM Abstracts* is important as well; note that it includes not only journal articles but also books, dissertations, and articles in collections. Browse the *RILM Abstracts* Web site and read its mission statement and the explanation of its coverage.

*Music Index* We discussed the print version of *Music Index* earlier; now *Music Index* is also available online, again by subscription. Browse through the Web site; it is useful to compare the coverage of RILM and *Music Index* to get a sense of areas of overlap and difference. In general, *Music Index* lists only journal articles, not dissertations or books, and it includes only titles and authors, not abstracts. On the other hand, it covers a somewhat wider range of journals than RILM, and, especially for topics beyond traditional classical music, such as jazz, musical comedy, or pop music, *Music Index* is a useful supplement to RILM.

*Dissertation Abstracts* As we mentioned earlier, dissertations can be rich sources of information for researchers, and they generally include exhaustive bibliographies. To find out whether there is a dissertation on a particular topic, the researcher consults this database, which lists completed dissertations by title, author, and granting institution, and includes abstracts written by the authors. This database, like others, existed for years in print, then was available on a series of CD-ROMs that libraries purchased, and is now available online. The Internet, with its search capability, is a perfect medium for these databases; one can rapidly ascertain whether or not there is a dissertation related to a particular topic, and, when there is, read the abstract to get an idea of the thesis and methodology of the work to decide whether or not it is essential to find a copy of the full text.

There are other online databases, such as the one we mentioned earlier based on the Hill and Stephens catalog of monuments and collected sets, useful when you want to locate a particular work in these collections. The databases discussed above, however, are the most useful for most research into musical topics.

### Lexicons

Earlier we discussed the two important music lexicons—the *New Grove* and *Die Musik in Geschichte und Gegenwart* (MGG). As of 2007, the latest edition of MGG was not yet available online; by the time this fourth edition is published, it may be. The *New Grove* is now available online, where it is called *Grove Music Online,* and, as we noted before, the online version is updated constantly—new and revised articles are added regularly. If you have not seen the *Grove Music Online* Web site, I strongly recommend that you browse through the site, where you will find information about its use, lists of recently updated articles, and the editors' recommendations about their preferred format for citing both the print and online versions, among other things.

Grove Music Online is a subscription site; your university library probably subscribes to the service. From your library Web site, your library ID and password provide access to the full text of Grove Music Online articles. It is interesting to compare the experience of reading an article online as opposed to the print version. Online, the first thing you see is the title, the author, the date (if the article has been updated), and the outline. Clicking on an item in the outline brings up the full text of that section of the article. If you want to consult just the worklist or bibliography, you can skip the text and call up just those items. It is wonderful to have this vast lexicon online and to be able to consult it whenever and wherever you are connected to the Internet; the online version, of course, also has the great advantage of the constant updates. I must confess, however, that I miss some aspects of the experience of reading the print version. For one thing, the online version does not always include all the illustrations found in the print version. In addition, it is set up so that researchers can get straight to the information they want. Fine—but I recall that often an illustration or an intriguing article would catch my eye as I paged through a volume of the print version on my way to another article. Sometimes I got so completely sidetracked that I had to return to the library later to read the article I was looking for in the first place. In addition, I always liked scanning through the whole article, rather than sections selected from the outline. Serendipity is an important part of research, and one may learn more from what one encounters accidentally along the way than from the specific information one is trying to find. On the other hand, I am sure that those who regularly consult Grove Music Online have their own ways to do the unplanned browsing that leads to wondrous new discoveries. In any case, Grove Music Online is a rich and convenient resource, the perfect place to start one's research into any musical topic.

### Online Journals

Some new journals that have begun publication in recent years are published only online and not in a print version; in addition, some journals that existed in print have now shifted to online publication. This seems to be a significant trend. As university libraries run out of money to subscribe to new journals and space to store back issues of journals, publishing a journal online makes perfect sense. Libraries can subscribe without worrying about space issues, trees are not felled to supply the paper for a print version, and researchers can consult the journals at their convenience whenever and wherever they can connect to the Internet. Generally these online journals are not subscription sites; everyone has access to the full texts of the articles. The organizers of these journals are more interested in making information available and stimulating lively discussion than they are in charging researchers for access.

There are online journals in all fields. As you can imagine, the Internet is a particularly appropriate platform for music journals. Not only can an article include score examples; now the reader can hear audio examples as well. At the present time, there are a number of online music journals. On its Web site, the Hargrove Music Library at the University of California, Berkeley, publishes a list of online music journals—that is, journals published only online, not journals available in print as well as online. The list includes the *Journal of Seventeenth-Century Music,* published by the Society for Seventeenth-Century Music; *Ethnomusicology OnLine; Music Theory Online,* published by the Society of Music Theory, which supplants its print journal, *Music Theory Spectrum;* and *Popular Musicology Online,* an international journal of research into popular music. Look up these journals and browse through a few issues to get a sense of the kinds of research questions they address. It seems safe to predict that as time goes on, more and more journals will move to publication online.

### JSTOR

JSTOR, short for "Journal Storage," is an important new site, subtitled *The Scholarly Journal Archive.* To quote from the description on its Web site, "JSTOR offers researchers the ability to retrieve high-resolution, scanned images of journal issues and pages as they were originally designed, printed, and illustrated." In other words, it is an archive of back issues of scholarly journals in many fields, created and maintained to free libraries from the responsibility of storing the back issues of scholarly journals, and to make their contents available to as wide an audience as possible.

This is another Web site worth browsing. The titles of all the journals archived thus far are listed, along with the years that are included in the archive. JSTOR does not include current issues; there is a gap of from one to five years between the latest issues in the archive and the current issues in print. One can also search through the archived journals by subject, so you can go immediately to the list of music journals if you wish. Thirty-two journals on music are included in the archive, including all the important journals in English as well as journals in several other languages. Remember that the archive contains high-resolution scans of each page of each issue of each journal, so that what you see on your screen is exactly what you see in the print version of that page, complete with musical examples, diagrams, illustrations, etc. Remember also that JSTOR archives journals in many fields. Often research on musical topics involves research into other fields such as political history, art history, literature, sociology, religion, and so forth. Now the researcher can use the same Web site to read not only music journals, but also journal articles in these related fields.

Having back runs of all the important musical journals available on this Web site, like having the complete *New Grove* online, is a remarkable advance for researchers working on musical topics. Researchers need not worry about whether or not a particular university library has a complete run of a particular journal or whether it subscribes to a particular journal. Now a music library at a small college or a brand-new campus need not immediately fill its shelves with complete runs of all the music journals. If a library subscribes to the databases listed above, *Grove Music Online,* and JSTOR, researchers who have library privileges have automatic access to these incredible Internet sites. JSTOR, like most of the other electronic resources we have mentioned, is a subscription site; your library probably subscribes to it, and you get to the archived journals through your library's Web site. Once you enter your library ID and password, you should see a way to select databases, and from there a clear path to JSTOR, then the journal you want, the issue you want, and the particular article you want to read.

A final word on electronic resources. Now that it is possible to do high-level research at your computer, there is little excuse for settling for shallow, half-hearted research. New opportunities imply new responsibilities, and one expects that the research for nearly any writing project in a music course will now include at least forays into *Grove Music Online* and JSTOR. The availability of these wondrous resources also means, of course, that the researcher must come armed with some computer skills. A student without the ability to use a computer to do research as well as write and edit a paper is at a serious disadvantage in this changing world, and whatever one can do to improve one's computer skills is time well spent.

## EVALUATING RESOURCES

It is important for the researcher to realize that he or she must exercise critical judgment when consulting published materials of any sort. Not everything you find in print or on the Internet is to be taken as gospel truth or followed blindly. Not all biographies, for example, are scholarly studies. Biographies run the gamut from serious studies, such as Robbins Landon's multivolume study of Haydn's life and works, to romanticized nineteenth-century biographies, which may be entertaining but are not very helpful for scholarly work. If one has to choose between two biographies, the more recent one or the one that shows evidence of serious scholarly research is generally more trustworthy than the earlier or more popular treatment. You know what serious scholarship looks like; books published for the scholarly community come equipped with footnotes, a bibliography, and an index. In addition, they should take account of recent research and should be free from any obvious bias that would cause you to question their reliability. Learn to trust your own judgment; reading a few pages will give you a fair idea of how serious and reliable a book is. The same comparison can be made about other kinds of resources: There are different kinds of journals, different sorts of histories, even different levels of reference works intended for different audiences, and, with experience, one can quickly tell which resources are intended for serious research and which are not.

As we said earlier, critical judgment is just as necessary when one is doing research on the Internet. Amid the jumble of commercial sites and casual blogs, there are scholarly sites that are perfect for serious research. The online journals, for instance, are refereed just like print journals—that is, articles are accepted for publication only after being vetted by experts in the field. The difference between scholarly sites and the other sites is as immediately obvious as the difference between serious books and popular fiction, or between *The Journal of the American Musicological Society* and *People* magazine. It is always the researcher's responsibility to treat information critically, no matter where it comes from, and to accept only those sources that seem trustworthy.

Sometimes the researcher finds that wrong or misleading information is repeated unchallenged from secondary source to secondary source. You are free to take issue with ideas and conclusions you find in print; in fact, you must take issue if your research indicates that those ideas are not borne out by the facts or by a careful reading of the evidence. That is precisely what the researcher's task is—to raise questions about what is written in secondary sources. Sources are not to be followed blindly, but should be judged realistically and critically. A one-volume history of music, for example, cannot be expected to include up-to-date reports of research findings on every detailed question or the latest information about every composer mentioned; that is not its purpose. On the other hand, you cannot expect a narrowly focused scholarly article to provide the long-range view that you find in a general history. Evaluation of sources, both print and electronic, is one of the major responsibilities of the researcher.

## FOREIGN-LANGUAGE RESOURCES

The responsible researcher cannot ignore important books and articles just because they happen to be written in a language other than English. It is a fact of scholarly life that many important books and articles are written in German, French, Italian, Spanish, and other languages. German is especially important for research on musical topics, because the discipline of musicology—*Musikwissenschaft* in German—was first developed in German universities, and many scholarly resources are still published in German. If you do not read German, and it becomes clear that a book or article in German is a crucial source for your topic, ask someone who knows German to translate the relevant sections for you. There are people on college campuses, both faculty and students, who can translate any language under the sun. Bear in mind, also, that illustrations, musical examples, tables, and bibliographies are exactly the same in German sources as in English ones. Students sometimes avoid using the Schmieder catalog of Bach's works, for instance, because "it's in German," when the bibliographies are exactly the same as they would be in English. The book can be useful to anyone, regardless of language experience.

## WHEN TO STOP: HOW MUCH RESEARCH IS ENOUGH?

The point at which you decide that you have gathered enough information for a paper will vary, depending on the topic and the limits set by the instructor when the paper was assigned. It is understood that the bibliography for an undergraduate project is not expected to have the same length and depth as a bibliography for a graduate paper or thesis, but it is still difficult sometimes to know when to call a halt to the research stage and move on.

There are two extremes to be avoided. Some students are satisfied with a citation or two from their music history textbooks or some all-purpose encyclopedia and never approach serious research. Others, even though their files are already bulging with citations, keep uncovering new resources that they feel obliged to include. If the research phase seems to be getting out of control, especially if the information you find seems not to support your original thesis, it may be time to arrange a conference with your instructor. You may need to negotiate some limits on your research, or you may be approaching your research in the wrong way. Perhaps your topic is too broad and needs some rethinking. It may be helpful to step back a bit from your research to see it in perspective and to decide whether what you have done is appropriate for the project.

What should happen near the end of the research phase is that all the information begins to fall into place in your mind, leading to clear ideas and opinions, and coalescing into a logical framework. The mass of information has to be shaped by you into a coherent plan. In the interests of unity and coherence, you may not be able to use every item you have uncovered in your research; one always does more research than one can actually include in a paper. The next step is to organize everything you have discovered in the research phase into a logical outline with one central idea or hypothesis, arguments in support of that central idea gathered from secondary sources and from your analysis of the materials, and a conclusion. Thoughtful and diligent research is critical, but it is only the first phase in the writing process. A mass of information is not a paper; it is only raw material that must be organized into a clear and coherent presentation.

# CHAPTER 4

# Writing a Research Paper

This chapter describes the process of writing a research paper, step by step, once the research phase is completed. Naturally, the writing process will vary, depending on the specific topic, thesis, and focus of the paper; this chapter discusses general principles and practical advice applicable to most papers.

## THE OUTLINE

The first step in writing a paper is to design a clear outline, so that when you begin to write, you will know exactly where you are going, what comes next, and which material belongs where. It is at this stage that you make the difficult decisions about what should be included, what should be left out, and how the material should be ordered. The outlining stage is critical and has at least as much impact on the quality of your paper as any other step. In the process of outlining you settle the critical questions of unity, coherence, and logical flow. Once you create a clear and logical outline, writing the paper becomes a matter of filling out the outline, putting flesh on the outline's skeleton. It is a serious mistake to settle for an outline that is incoherent or hastily thrown together.

### Topic and Thesis

The most important part of the outline is the thesis—a topic sentence that represents the main point of the paper, the central statement you wish to make about the topic, the controlling idea of the entire paper. A topic is a broad area of study; a thesis is the precise point you want to make about that topic. "Stravinsky's neoclassicism" is a topic; "Stravinsky's *Octet for Winds* is a perfect embodiment of the aesthetic aims of neoclassicism" is a thesis related to that topic. Notice that it is a sentence, not just a word or phrase; in this case, it is a statement illustrating critical thinking—a promising thesis that could be the basis for a fine paper. The difference between topic and thesis is clear: A topic is general, whereas a thesis is narrow, focused, and individual. "The history of the saxophone" (or the oboe, or the trombone) is a topic, not a thesis, and students who propose such topics generally have a difficult time choosing a thesis; these topics are too broad and do not offer much opportunity for critical thinking.

The thesis is the central statement that represents the writer's critical judgment about the topic; it also determines what should be included in the paper and what must be left out. The thesis is the key to the entire paper—every sentence in the paper must relate to it in some way or other. You may start your research with a tentative thesis (what scientists call a hypothesis) in mind; more likely, the thesis will emerge from your research, as your study of the secondary literature and your own discoveries and insights begin to coalesce around a particular idea or position, your statement about the topic. To move from research into the writing process, the first and most important requirement is a viable thesis that you are enthusiastic about. A typical paper introduces the topic and states the thesis in an introductory section; the rest of the paper presents arguments that support the thesis.

### Topic Outline Versus Sentence Outline

There are two kinds of outline: the topic outline and the sentence outline. As the names indicate, a topic outline consists of a list of single words or phrases representing areas of discussion; the sentence outline consists of the actual statements or arguments that the writer plans to develop in the paper. For a research paper, I recommend a sentence outline. Making each heading or subheading a statement forces you to plan exactly what you want to say, rather than simply listing areas to be discussed. A sentence outline will keep the paper more tightly organized and separate actual arguments from background information that may be helpful but is not really the main thrust of the paper.

### Introduction

The outline of your paper should include your plans for the introduction. The function of an introduction is to ease into your topic, put it in some perspective, and announce your thesis. Browse through some articles in the musicological journals to see how introductions work. They often start with a general idea and then move to the specific topic and thesis of the paper. It is also possible to move in the opposite direction, starting with a specific fact or a description of a specific event and progressing to a broader issue and then to the thesis.

There are two extremes to be avoided in introductions. One extreme is to write a brief sentence or two, plunging right into the body of the paper. An abrupt introduction disorients the reader. Suppose a paper began this way: "In the first measure of this violin concerto, we hear the musical ideas that Bach used as the basis for the entire movement." The reader thinks, "Wait a minute—what are we talking about? What's the time frame? Which Bach are we talking about—J. S., C. P. E., J. C., W. F., or P. D. Q.? Which work? Which movement?" The fact that the paper's title names the topic does not free the writer from the obligation to lead the reader into the topic at the beginning of the paper. An introduction should introduce the general topic, the specific area the paper will deal with, and the thesis that the paper will argue.

The other extreme is a long introduction that develops a life of its own, bringing up issues that are not germane to the main point of the paper and meandering away from the topic instead of leading the reader into it. Books on writing recommend as a general rule that an introduction should occupy no more than one-tenth of the paper's length. Some papers require a longer introduction, particularly when it is necessary to define technical terms and concepts or explain important background material. Generally, if an introduction to a paper of about fifteen pages runs beyond two pages, it is too long; the writer should hunt down and delete the extraneous material.

The introduction should include a clear idea of where the paper is going and announce the thesis that you will defend. At the outline stage, decide exactly how you will introduce your topic and thesis, and what you plan to include in the introduction.

### Body

Next, you need to outline the body of your paper, listing first the main arguments to support your thesis and then the subtopics to be included under each of the main points. It is a good idea to work out your outline in considerable detail, even to the level of individual paragraphs, so that when you begin writing you know exactly what goes where and what comes next. At this point you need to decide the order in which the material will be presented. Which argument should come first? Which deserves the strong final position? You should also include in your outline some idea of the methodology to be followed in establishing each point—where you will use quotations from secondary sources, where musical examples will be most effective, which points depend on analysis, and so forth. You should end with an outline so specific that if you were to submit just the outline, your instructor would have a very clear idea of what the final paper would look like. The more time you spend fussing with the outline, the more logical, coherent, and convincing your paper will be.

### Conclusion

Sometimes the most difficult section of a paper to write is the conclusion. The writer feels that everything has been said already and does not want to repeat what the paper has already explained. Conclusions are necessary, however, not only to reemphasize your main point, but also to wrap up the study in a tidy, memorable way. You can connect your thesis with the existing body of research on your topic, show what your research adds to critical opinion of the composer or issue in question, or point to related areas in which similar research would be appropriate. Be careful not to go overboard in your conclusion. Some student writers, relieved to finally reach the end of the paper, get carried away in their conclusions and lapse into flowery language or exaggerate the world-shaking importance of this particular topic. Provide a logical and forceful closing for the reader—then stop. As you create your outline, think about effective ways to conclude your paper.

### Revising the Outline

Once you have a tentative outline, stop and take a critical look at it. In my experience, the problems raised when a candidate defends his or her thesis or dissertation at the end of the long process of research and writing are almost always outline problems—material appears in the wrong place, the order is not logical, the emphasis is wrong, some material is not related to the project's thesis, or some necessary material is missing. It is much easier to modify the design of your paper at the outline stage than it is at the later stages of the draft or final copy. Check the outline carefully for unity, coherence, and logical flow. Experiment with a different order within the body of your paper. Would your thesis be more convincing if you changed the order of supporting arguments? Is the last argument the weakest or the strongest? Is there a weak argument that doesn't really contribute to the thesis and perhaps should be deleted? Is there anything in the outline that is not related to your thesis and therefore has no place in the paper? Is there a topic that comes up in several different places, requiring awkward cross-references? Might it make more sense to combine those discussions in one place? Tinker with your outline; try a different order; experiment. The more logical, coherent, and forceful your outline is, the more logical and convincing the paper will be. The time you devote to revising your outline will pay off in a stronger and more effective paper.

There are many ways to design an outline. Some writers were trained to jot down ideas in the form of spokes growing from a central thesis or main point, or to quickly assemble a preliminary list of possible arguments and then select the most promising ideas and arrange them into an outline. Most word-processing programs have an outline function that helps you set up headings and subheadings. Whatever system you use, the outlining phase is crucial and will have an enormous effect on the success of your paper.

## WRITING THE DRAFT

After you have designed an outline that works, with everything in its proper place, the next step is to sit down, face the blank screen, and start writing what you want to say. The goal is to get it all down, even in less-than-perfect form, with typos, grammatical errors, false starts, and awkward sentences, just to see what you have to say, and to have a preliminary version of your paper to work with. Assuming that you have sufficient time for editing and revising, your main concern in the draft stage should be to get it all written down, imperfect or not, to create the raw material that you can polish and edit. If you try starting with the introduction and can't get started, skip the introduction, write the body of the paper instead, and return later to add the introduction. The important thing is to complete the draft.

The computer is by far the most efficient way to draft a paper, provided that you can compose at a keyboard. The better your keyboard skills are and the more fluent you are in using the features of your word-processing program, the easier it is to concentrate on what you want to say, rather than worrying about the next letter or the correct command to change something. Assuming you can type fairly rapidly, you can draft large chunks of the paper in a relatively short time. The main thing to bear in mind as you write the draft is that it is only a draft, not the final version you will submit. Do not get bogged down by typographical errors, misspellings, or awkward sentences. You can always make editorial changes and revisions at a later stage, but you first need a completed draft to work with. The draft is raw material that you will refine and polish to produce the final paper.

It makes sense to draft your paper in the correct format for college papers, so that you can see how long your paper will be and more or less how it will look. The next chapter discusses details of correct format; here we are suggesting that you set up the proper margins, fonts, and spacing before you begin the draft rather than waiting until you are ready to print your final copy. Don't depend on your word-processing program to set up the format for you; the default formats that appear automatically on the screen are not necessarily correct for college papers. You might want to set up a template for papers that includes the proper format, ready to use whenever you start on a paper.

Finally, whenever you are working at a computer, whether drafting or revising, the basic rule is *save, save, save*. Set the program to save your work automatically every ten or fifteen minutes and get in the habit of saving frequently yourself. A single keystroke or click on an icon takes no time and will keep your hard work from disappearing. We have all heard horror stories about losing large amounts of work because of a power surge, an outage, or a computer glitch of some sort. The rule is simple: Save—stuff happens. If you approach your professor with a tearful tale of losing hours of work, you might get some sympathy, because we have all have suffered such losses, but your story will not really work as a valid excuse. These disasters are at least partially the writer's fault, since you could have prevented a major loss by saving more often.

### Musical Examples

While you are writing the draft, or earlier, in the outline stage, you should pick out the exact points in your paper where musical examples are necessary or appropriate and decide how you will deal with them. In analytical papers, it is helpful to include musical examples; a carefully chosen musical example may be more convincing to the reader than a page or two of descriptive prose. If you are trying to make a point about a striking cadence, an unusual modulation, or a particularly charming melodic idea, show the reader the music along with your commentary. Always consider clarity first—the examples should clearly support your arguments, not confuse the reader.

There are several ways to include musical examples in a paper. If you have the necessary computer skills, the best way is to copy the passage using one of the music-writing programs and import it into your text at the proper place. You can also photocopy a few measures or a portion of a score that will illustrate your point and insert the copy into your paper. It is difficult to extract useful musical examples from some kinds of scores: Oversize Romantic orchestral scores, for instance, are not only difficult to photocopy, but also difficult to read, and may be confusing or distracting to your reader. Some twentieth-century scores are also difficult to photocopy. It may be better in such situations to prepare a reduced score or some sort of diagram to illustrate your point. When you use photocopied examples, be sure they contain all the information the reader needs to make sense of them. If you copy measures from the middle of a line of score and there are no clefs or key signatures in your example, obviously you need to add them. If photocopied musical examples are to be included in the paper, prepare them before you print the final version of the paper, so that you can leave sufficient space for each example. Be sure that photocopied examples are securely attached to the page with double-stick tape or by some other means. A better strategy is to photocopy the pages that include musical examples after the examples are taped or glued in place. The examples then become a permanent part of the page; using those copied pages in your final copy makes your paper look cleaner and more professional. A final note: If it is necessary to include a large number of musical examples, or examples longer than a page, it may be better to put all the examples in an appendix rather than within the body of the paper.

Sometimes the best way to illustrate the point you are making is to add analytic annotations on a photocopy of a page of score. Some students have a talent for graphics and can mark a score in such a way that the reader immediately sees the point the writer is trying to make. In the hands of others, marked scores end up looking like Beethoven sketches, with the notes and the point of the example nearly obscured by unclear markings. Never rely on a marked score alone to make your point about the organization of a work; there must always be some verbal explanation as well. Finally, whenever you include musical examples, whether they appear in the text or in an appendix, each example must be clearly captioned so that the reader knows exactly what the example represents. The specific work, movement, and measure numbers must be identified for each example, and the reader must know precisely where the example fits into the text. We will discuss these details later, in the chapter on format.

### Diagrams, Graphics, and Tables

Related to the issue of musical examples is the question of designing your own diagrams or graphic representations of musical events. Particularly in questions of large-scale structure, diagrams can be extremely useful, provided that they are clear and make the point effectively. One can diagram the structure of the first movement of Bach's Brandenburg Concerto No. 5, for example, on a single page, whereas the *Bach-Gesellschaft* edition of the score occupies twenty-two pages.

Tables can be useful as well. A table might be an effective way to show how the cantus firmus is used in the various movements of a Renaissance Mass, to represent the loose or unusual structures sometimes found in Romantic symphonic works, or to depict the unusual structure of a contemporary work. The point is always clarity and effectiveness. Will this table, diagram, or graphic analysis be clear to the reader? Is this the best way to communicate the point I am trying to make? You can always test the effectiveness of a table or diagram by trying it out on a friend whose judgment you trust. If it makes the point clearly, it helps the paper enormously; if it does not, toss it—it will only detract from the effectiveness of your paper.

### Footnotes

While you are writing the draft, you must decide where footnotes are needed, insert the footnote numbers in your text, and write the notes as you write the text, so that everything matches up correctly. Do not leave the footnotes for later; the key is to be precise and systematic early in the process. We will deal with details of footnote format, along with other format issues, in Chapter 5. Here we will assume that the paper requires footnotes or endnotes, not parenthetical references, which are also discussed later. Our concern is when one should include notes and where they should be located in the finished paper.

Once you understand the purpose of footnotes, the rules about them make perfect sense. Footnotes are included in a paper in order to establish that the writer has some basis for the assertions he or she makes, and to acknowledge indebtedness to the authors and ideas discovered in the process of research. The idea is that readers can go to the sources themselves to check the information or to pursue related lines of investigation. There are two extremes to be avoided. Some writers include very few footnotes, even when they are obviously repeating information they discovered in their research. The issue of using the words and ideas of others is a complex one and brings up the important question of plagiarism; these matters are discussed in a separate section near the end of this chapter. The other extreme is to footnote nearly every sentence, a practice that is tiresome for the reader and unnecessary. Some general guidelines may help.

First, *every direct or indirect quotation calls for a footnote.* When you quote someone directly, copying the quotation word for word within quotation marks, you must include a footnote that tells exactly where that quotation appears, citing the book or article, publication information, and the page where the quoted material appears in the original source. If you cite someone's opinion indirectly, paraphrasing or putting the idea in your own words, you still need a footnote to support your claim that the earlier author actually said what you ascribe to him or her. The following sentence is an example of indirect quotation.

> Stuckenschmidt claims that Schoenberg first conceived the idea for *Pierrot Lunaire* in 1910, whereas Rufer cites a letter to Berg, dated October 1912, as the earliest indication of his intent to set these poems.

The writer states as a fact that these two scholars made these conflicting statements; incidentally, these are real scholars, but the statements are imaginary. Even though the writer has not quoted their exact words, the reader still wants to know where the writer found these statements. You cannot write a sentence such as this without adding a footnote listing the exact places in the writings of Stuckenschmidt and Rufer where they supposedly made these claims. The footnote must cite the appropriate books or articles, including information about the place and date of publication, as well as the pages on which these statements can be found. Readers, if they wish, should be able to check the sources themselves if they are not sure that the writer has correctly represented the earlier authors or if they want to pursue the matter further.

Second, *matters of common knowledge do not require footnotes.* This rule can be slippery—how exactly does one determine what fits under the rubric of "common knowledge"? At the extremes, the answer is fairly obvious.

> Beethoven composed nine symphonies.
> J. S. Bach died in 1750, after a long and productive career.

Those sentences hardly need footnotes—in fact, these sentences themselves are hardly necessary for an audience of music majors. Anyone who has the slightest smattering of knowledge about classical music knows these things already. Adding a footnote to these sentences would be naïve and would mark the writer as an inexperienced researcher. On the other hand, consider this sentence.

> Later in his life, Stravinsky regretted the fact that people associated him with his early works in late Romantic style—particularly *Firebird.*

Here you certainly need a footnote. This is certainly not common knowledge. The reader naturally wonders how the writer could possibly know what was going on in Stravinsky's mind. What's your authority for this statement? A sentence such as this needs a footnote citing the source where you came across this information.

Between these two extremes, use your common sense. It is helpful to keep in mind the audience for whom the paper is intended. Rather than trying to guess what your instructor considers common knowledge, imagine yourself presenting your paper to your classmates. What is general knowledge to a group of music majors in a music history class is different from general knowledge among the population at large or a typical concert audience. Do not footnote what would be obvious to your colleagues. When in doubt, it is probably better to err on the side of including too many footnotes rather than too few.

One helpful way to avoid obtrusive numbers of footnotes is to use a general footnote for a paragraph or section of a paper rather than attaching a footnote to each sentence. For example, if your paper includes a biographical sketch of a composer based on one or two sources, it is not necessary to include a separate footnote for each item of information—date of birth, education, positions, important works, and date of death. Instead, write a single footnote referring the reader to the sources in which you found the biographical information, and make clear that the note refers to that whole section. If an analytical section makes use of published analyses, you might list them in a single note at the beginning of the section and then footnote only direct or indirect quotations. The best way to get a sense of proper footnote use is to read articles in scholarly journals; the scholars who write them and the experts who approve them understand correct footnote practice. Note as you browse through journal articles that the footnotes tend to cluster near the beginning of the article, where authors are likely to list publications that have dealt with this topic or the primary materials on which their research is based. Footnotes appear less frequently after the first few pages, as authors move into the discussion of their own findings.

A final question is where the footnotes should be placed in the final paper. The rules for theses and dissertations used to require that the footnotes be placed, as the name indicates, at the bottom of the page, rather than grouping them as *endnotes* at the ends of chapters or at the end of the study, before the bibliography. One practical reason for that requirement was that dissertations sometimes circulate in microfilm form; if all the notes are at the end, it is a nuisance to scroll back and forth through hundreds of pages of text each time the reader wants to check a footnote. However, using endnotes rather than footnotes is usually acceptable in undergraduate papers; check with your instructor to see what his or her policy is.

Word-processing programs handle footnotes with ease and place them wherever you want—at the bottom of the page, at the end of a chapter of a longer project, or at the end of the paper. You might choose to put them at the bottom of the page in the draft stage so that it is easy to check them along with your text as you edit. You can easily move them to the end before submitting the final copy. Word-processing programs also are very good about keeping track of footnotes as you make changes during the editing process. Whenever you add, move, or delete a section of text, the program automatically adds, moves, or deletes the footnotes that go with that text, making sure that the footnotes stay with the appropriate text and changing the numbers when necessary. Without launching into a digression about how much tougher things were in the old days, let me point out that the complicated business of dealing with footnotes is one of the main reasons we should all be grateful that the computer was invented.

The central issue about footnotes is the writer's responsibility to acknowledge sources of direct and indirect quotations and cite authorities to back up important assertions. Once you understand the purpose of footnotes, questions about when to include them usually solve themselves; when in doubt, you can always check with your instructor.

### Bibliography

The last section of your draft is the bibliography. Assuming that during the research stage you kept a detailed list of all the sources you used, along with the necessary publication information, preparing the bibliography is a simple matter of listing those sources in alphabetical order by the last name of the author or authors and checking to be sure that the format is correct and consistent. Questions of bibliography format will be discussed in Chapter 5. At this point we need to discuss what should and should not be included in your bibliography.

There are different points of view on the question of what to include in a bibliography. The strictest position is that only those works actually cited in the body of the paper should be listed in the bibliography. In other words, only those publications that appear in footnotes (or endnotes) should be listed in the bibliography. A less strict position would allow the inclusion of publications that the writer actually consulted, whether or not they are cited in the footnotes. The most inclusive position would allow the listing of any sources the writer has run across, whether or not he or she actually had access to them. Check to see what your instructor's policy is about limiting the bibliography to materials you have quoted or actually seen. If one goal of the project is practice in the process of doing research and assembling a bibliography, the instructor might want you to include as many items as you can, whether or not you have actually consulted them.

A related issue has to do with secondhand references. Let's say that in the course of your research you notice that all the authors refer to one important source—let's call it book A. From the frequency and deference with which it is mentioned, it is clearly a central source, something you would certainly consult if you could. Let us further imagine that for one reason or another, book A is unavailable to you, but a section of it is quoted in book B, one of the books you were able to consult. In that case, should you list both book B and book A in your bibliography? An interesting dilemma: If you decide to list book A, are you somehow cheating, creating the impression of direct knowledge you do not have? If you don't list book A, are you leaving yourself open to the charge of being a careless researcher, unaware of an important source? In such cases, I think it is fair to list book A. If you feel uncomfortable listing a publication that you have not actually seen, one solution is to add an annotation such as "not available for this study." Then the reader knows that you are aware of this important source, but you cannot be accused of creating the false impression that you have actually used it.

One last reminder: It is a mistake to pad a bibliography with questionable items just to make it look longer. Don't list the sources you used for reports in high school, such as general-purpose encyclopedias or books written for record collectors or young students. Also, don't list your music history textbook in a bibliography; the whole point of research is to go beyond readily available sources of information. Including inappropriate items is another sure way to mark yourself as a fledgling author.

Finally, the instructor may ask you to annotate your bibliography, which means to include brief critical comments on some or all of the items. The purpose of annotations is to point out the special advantages or limits of each publication. Annotations on the order of "a definitive biography, based on newly discovered primary sources," or "particularly useful for its extended analyses of major works," or "extensive material on the composer's political views, based on newly translated correspondence" show that you are a discerning researcher and provide useful information for the reader who may want to pursue related research in those same sources. Annotated bibliographies are standard assignments in some graduate courses; they may be required at the undergraduate level also.

## REVISING AND EDITING THE DRAFT

Now you have a file containing a complete draft of your paper on your hard drive (or on a disk or flash drive, if you worked in the school computer room or on a friend's computer). The draft is an early stage of the paper, not the finished product you will hand in; as we said earlier, a draft is raw material and no doubt needs considerable editing, revising, and polishing. Allow a large block of time for editing and revising; it often takes longer to edit and polish than it did to produce the draft, particularly if you are one of those people who gets into a creative frenzy and writes drafts quickly. It is also helpful to let the draft "cool off" several times—that is, to put it aside for a while between editing sessions. When you return to a draft after a few days, it is easier to see the mistakes, awkward phrases, and questionable passages that need revising. The sentence that seemed perfectly clear and perhaps even ringing and eloquent when you drafted it at two in the morning may sound embarrassing or pretentious a few days later.

### Computers and Editing

We pointed out above that working at a computer is the ideal way to draft a paper, provided you have reasonable typing skills. Word-processing programs are even more powerful and helpful for revising and editing. It is strange that more students do not take advantage of the editing capability that word-processing programs provide; it is a waste of expensive, sophisticated equipment to use a computer to bang out a clumsy draft and then quit and hand it in as your final piece. Word-processing programs are wonderful for editing. You can move sentences or paragraphs around easily, change a word or two and then change your mind and instantly restore the original wording, and, in general, fuss with your paper until you have it just the way you want it, all without retyping. If you discover that you have misspelled an important name or technical term throughout your draft or decide that you want to replace a term with a better one, you can use the "find and replace" function to locate every appearance of the word and change them all in a flash. Learn what your word-processing program can do and put its power to work for you. If you don't have the time to master a word-processing program during the school year, take the time during a break to learn all the things it can do for you. The time you spend mastering a program will save you countless hours, raise the level and professionalism of your work, and probably improve your grades.

Finally, during the editing process, it is crucial to remember the basic rule we mentioned earlier: Save, save, save. Editing is hard work, but it is very satisfying to finally get a paragraph or section to say exactly what you want it to say after an hour or two of trying alternative wordings, moving words and phrases around, breaking up and moving sentences, and all the other work of revising. Nothing is more disheartening than watching the results of your hard work vanish because you forgot to save.

### Checking Spelling and Grammar

Word-processing programs are usually equipped with tools to check spelling and grammar. These tools can be very helpful, provided that you understand what they can and cannot do and how they work. The spell-checking tool comes with a built-in dictionary against which it checks the words it sees in your prose. If a word does not appear in its dictionary, it notifies you, suggests a few similar words you might have meant, and lets you decide. If you see that you misspelled the word, you can select one of the suggested alternatives and the corrected word pops into your sentence. If the checker does not recognize a name or a useful technical term, you can usually click on "add" and the word will be added to the dictionary; the spell-checker should recognize it the next time it appears. If the word is an unusual one that you do not want to save, you click "ignore" and go on to the next problem.

Naturally, spell-checkers cannot contain every possible word in their dictionaries. They stop, for example, on most proper names; if you think you might use a particular name again, add it to the computer's dictionary. As you would expect, technical terms and foreign words also cause the checker to stop and question you—in fact, any unusual word will stop it. My program objects to "musics," never having encountered the plural form before; it also stopped at "Eb," when I meant "E-flat," suggesting that perhaps I was trying to write the word "ebb." Note that you cannot assume that the built-in dictionary is the final authority on questionable and evolving matters such as hyphenation. I remember writing "upper-case," with a hyphen; the spell-checker flagged it and recommended "upper case," two words with no hyphen; an up-to-date dictionary listed the preferred spelling as "upper-case," a single word with no hyphen. The responsibility for final decisions is always the writer's, and you still need a good dictionary. However, it is worth the time it takes to use a spell-checker. Think of the advantages. The checker will find every typo, every case of inverted letters, single letters when doubles are correct, and vice versa, and do it quickly. New technology creates new responsibilities; now that it is easy to eliminate typos, there is no excuse for turning in a careless draft filled with misspellings.

Grammar-checkers, as you can imagine, are more complicated than spell-checkers, since the problems they are designed to identify are not as straightforward as incorrect spellings. Sometimes a grammar-checker does not make suggestions but merely points out things you might want to think about—for example, sentence fragments and sentences in the passive voice—hinting that you might want to change them. In addition, it points out other issues such as extra spaces and punctuation problems. Grammar-checkers are surprisingly helpful with small details as well as larger questions of sentence structure.

The careful writer should take advantage of these devices, aware that a spell-checker or grammar-checker cannot possibly understand all the subtleties of language, particularly technical terms and foreign terms, and that, handy as they are, such tools cannot mend everything. You cannot delegate to a machine the responsibility for turning your problematic draft into beautiful prose. But use these aids for what they can do, and in general, trust them on mechanical details; both can save you from embarrassing typos and mistakes.

### The Editing Process

As you begin editing your draft, you need to assume a different mental attitude from the one you assumed while creating the draft. At this point, your role is not creator but critical reader, questioning everything about your draft—the logic of its organization, every argument, every word, every phrase. You should be prepared to shuffle paragraphs or sections around if moving them will make your argument more effective, prepared to throw out sentences or whole paragraphs if they do not work, even ready as a last resort to delete the whole thing and start again. Better to discover and correct your own bad writing than to see it circled in red when the paper is returned to you.

When you are editing your draft, you need to criticize your work from several different points of view. Read through the draft several times, working on different issues with each pass. During the first reading, concentrate on unity, sense, and coherence, looking at the entire paper as a unit and questioning the order and effectiveness of your arguments. Have you said exactly what you wanted to say, or does your prose sometimes wander around, skirting the central issues without actually getting to the point? Are the arguments in the proper order, or does the draft ramble? Do some issues come up in several different places? Should those discussions be combined in one place? If so, where is the most effective place for the combined discussion? Would your arguments be more effective in a different order? Are there abrupt shifts from topic to topic or from argument to argument? Do you need to add some transitional material to let the reader know when you are shifting to a new subject? Try to approach your work as if you were reading it for the first time. Can you follow the train of thought as it is laid out in the draft? Are there gaps in the logical argument, assumptions that are never clearly explained? Do you know at all times where you are in the argument? Is it clear how each section fits in the overall progress of the argument?

To deal with these questions, you need to view the paper as a unit, concentrating for the moment on the big picture and ignoring problems in the wording and writing style. If you plunge immediately into the detailed work of correcting typos and misspellings or rewriting awkward sentences, you may find it difficult to keep the big picture—the thesis and argument—in your mind. Checking for overall unity and coherence should be done early in the editing process, since it is a waste of time and effort to revise and polish the wording of a paragraph that you might later decide to delete because it does not advance your thesis. Before you expend precious time and energy polishing a paragraph or section, you want to be certain that it will still be there in the final version of the paper.

On a second pass, you need to revise your draft at the level of detail, correcting typos and asking yourself whether this word, this phrase, this sentence says what you want to say or whether you need to revise it or delete it and try another way. Note the cases of weak wording, the awkward phrases, the sentences whose syntax is jumbled and unclear, and the paragraphs that need to be rewritten, and correct each problem in turn. It may take several days or evenings of hard work to polish the draft; the process is not over until you feel confident that your words say exactly what you want them to say, with the clarity and emphasis you intended.

At some point, read the paper aloud to yourself. Some mistakes, particularly jumbled syntax and pretentious or flowery language, become embarrassingly obvious when you read your prose aloud. It is true that written style and spoken style are two different things. Still, if a passage comes out wrong every time you try to read it aloud, or you cannot get through it without stumbling, you can assume there is something wrong with your writing. If you—the person who wrote it—cannot read it convincingly, the reader will not be able to make sense of it either. Jumbled syntax is often an indication that the idea is not clearly formed in your mind. When you run into a tangled and confusing sentence in your draft, back up, think about exactly what you are trying to say, and then devise a way to say it clearly and effectively. There are always other ways to say whatever you want to say; you can always back up and start again.

One final note about the editing process: Once you have finished editing on the screen, it is a good idea to print a copy of the paper and make one last pass through the hard copy. Some editing tasks are easier when working with hard copy rather than working on the screen. When you want to compare a section early in your paper with a later section, for example, it is easier to put two printed pages side by side than to scroll back and forth through several intervening pages. For some reason, it is sometimes easier to notice typos, spelling errors, and extra or missing spaces in hard copy than on the screen. If that first hard copy turns out to be perfect, you can always hand it in as your final copy.

Chapters 7 and 8 will discuss some principles of effective writing and ways to improve your wording and sentence structure during the editing process. Revising and editing are absolutely necessary and crucial to the success of your paper. Remember that nobody writes perfect drafts. The quality of your finished paper will depend to a great extent on the amount of work you put into this essential step. Brilliant ideas do not automatically transform themselves into effective papers—in fact, unless you manage to couch your ideas in clear and persuasive prose, no one will ever know how brilliant your thoughts really are. Leave enough time in the editing stage to revise, wait a day or two, then return and revise again. The more effort you put into editing, the better your paper will be. Without extensive revising and editing, your paper stands little or no chance of being a success and earning you the grade you want.

## PRINTING

After the editing stage, your computer screen should show you exactly the way your final paper will look—revised, polished, with parts moved around and reassembled, everything just the way you want it. It then should be a simple matter of pushing the print button to produce your final hard copy. The chief requirement of your printed copy is that it be clear and legible. Today's printers produce wonderful copies; the only printing problem I have seen lately is that some students do not replace their printer cartridges frequently enough, so that their papers vary in darkness and clarity from page to page. If your printer is not in the best condition, transfer the file containing your paper to a disk or a flash drive, or e-mail the file to yourself and open it up on someone else's computer to print, or take it to the school computer room and print your paper on the equipment provided by the school.

## PROOFREADING

The writing process is still not complete when the final hard copy is in your hand. There is one remaining important step—proofreading. You cannot assume that everything is perfect in your printed copy. As we mentioned above, some problems show up more easily in hard copy than on a screen. You need to give your paper one final read, just to be sure that everything is in order—the pages are all there, in the proper order and correctly numbered, the printer didn't accidentally insert an extra blank page, the musical examples are where they belong, and there were no glitches in the printing process. When students have already spent so much time on research, writing, and editing, it is hard to understand why they skip this final stage. Proofreading a paper does not take very long; correcting any mistakes you find may take more time. You will have to go back into the file, make the necessary corrections, and print the corrected page or section again. Depending on the nature and extent of the mistakes and how they affect the pagination, you might have to reprint a large section or even the whole paper. When you have the final paper in hand, you may still need to paste in photocopied musical examples, and you should check everything one last time to see that all the examples are in their proper places and clearly captioned.

Pride in your work necessitates careful attention to this final quality check. Any errors that remain in the final copy will detract from the effectiveness of your paper, no matter how much time and effort you have put into the earlier stages. A paper prepared with care at all stages, including proofreading, will represent your best work, communicate your ideas as clearly and effectively as possible, and prove that you are a competent researcher, capable of producing professional-quality work.

## KEEP YOUR FILE

Assuming you have worked hard to produce a first-class paper, you will want to keep the file or disk containing your paper. Although professors seldom lose papers, they may take a long time to return them or sometimes not return them at all. You may want a copy of your paper in the future—for example, you might need to submit examples of your work if you decide to apply for admission to graduate school. If your paper is returned to you covered with corrections and criticism, that copy is not the version you want to send off with your application. On the other hand, if it comes back with an A-plus and a paragraph of glowing praise on the title page, submit that copy to the graduate school. Even if graduate school is not in your plans at the moment, it still makes sense to save the papers that represent your best work.

## QUOTATION, PARAPHRASE, AND PLAGIARISM

In the earlier section on footnotes, we pointed out the writer's obligation to footnote direct and indirect quotations of the words and ideas of other writers. It is certainly not wrong to use the ideas of others; the first step in research is usually to search through the secondary literature to discover what has been written about your topic. It makes no sense to start from scratch, ignoring the information and insight already available. Good papers often start with a review of the scholarly literature on the particular topic, summarizing what has already been done.

When you use the ideas of another writer, however, you must always give credit to the source of those ideas and cite in a footnote the exact place where you found the words or ideas. Even when you do not use another writer's exact words but paraphrase or summarize the ideas, putting them in your own words, you are still obliged to cite the source of the ideas. Presenting the words or ideas of another writer without the proper citation creates the impression that you are presenting them as your own work—and that constitutes *plagiarism*, a serious breach of academic ethics. We need to comment on exactly what constitutes plagiarism and on the consequences that are likely to follow in the academic world when plagiarism is detected.

The definition of plagiarism is clear enough—*the use of the words and ideas of another writer without giving proper credit to the source.* Determining what actions fall under that definition, however, seems unclear to some students, perhaps because there are several ways to commit plagiarism. Some kinds of plagiarism are obvious—for example, submitting as your own work a paper you purchased from one of the shady organizations that advertise on the Internet and in campus newspapers. No student would seriously argue that buying a paper and submitting it as your own work is legal or ethical. Usually, however, cases of plagiarism are not that obvious. Sometimes part of a paper—perhaps most of it—is the student's own work, but some paragraphs or sections are copied verbatim from uncredited sources, creating the impression that the material appropriated from elsewhere is the student's own work. Such an action is plagiarism, whether or not the writer intended to claim that the copied words are his or her own work; the ethical breach is in the action itself, not the writer's intention. Further, it is possible to commit plagiarism even if you do not copy the exact words of another author. Paraphrasing an idea you find in another's work—stating it in your own words—is indirect quotation, and it is plagiarism to include an indirect quotation without citing the source. Even if the words are more or less your own, the idea was someone else's, and the original author must be credited.

In addition to what constitutes plagiarism, you need to know how seriously academic institutions regard it. Plagiarism is regarded as a serious breach of academic ethics, as serious as any other form of cheating. The usual punishment for plagiarism is a failing grade for the paper and probably for the course. In addition, most colleges and universities require that cases of plagiarism be reported to the committee on student conduct. If the committee decides that the student is guilty of plagiarism, it usually questions the student's fitness to continue in the program, and perhaps recommends academic probation or even expulsion. No matter how desperate things seem as deadlines approach near the end of a semester, there are no circumstances that could possibly justify the risk of trying to pass off someone else's words or ideas as your own. If the fraud is detected, your college career could come to a sudden and unhappy end. Students caught plagiarizing often protest that they did not intend to plagiarize, that they did not understand the rules, or that the punishment is too harsh for what they consider a minor lapse. Unfortunately, those arguments are not much help. Perhaps you are confident that you can manipulate your soft-hearted professor, or that well-timed tears will save you, but the harshest reaction will come from elsewhere, from the university committee on academic conduct. If you think academia makes too much of a fuss about plagiarism, remember that in the publishing world, plagiarism is an actionable crime resulting in lawsuits, huge settlements, and disgrace for the guilty party. Nobody takes plagiarism lightly.

You should also be aware that plagiarism is usually not that difficult to detect. In the case of papers bought from illegal paper mills, remember that your professors read those same ads and can find the same Internet sites you can. Besides, do you really think that your professor will not notice that the paper is not written in your style? In addition, I have read that most of these papers are not very impressive and certainly not worth the inflated prices. In the case of papers with sections that are plagiarized, remember that the students who are most tempted to plagiarize are often those who have difficulty writing convincing English prose. How hard do you think it is to notice the sudden break between the halting style of a student's prose and the polished and eloquent style of a published expert? Chains of subordinate clauses, complex and elegant parallel constructions, and abstruse technical terms used only by experts are not found that often in student prose. Sometimes plaigiarists give themselves away in obvious ways—for example, by copying prose from British sources, complete with telltale British spellings such as "colour" and "organise," British idioms, and British punctuation conventions. Once in a student paper I found the German word *"Durchfürung,"* an old term for what we now call "development" in sonata-allegro form. There the word sat, nestled in a patch of flowery Victorian prose. The paragraphs preceding and following this flowery section were barely literate, making the plagiarized patch stand out even more. I called the student in and asked him what the German term meant; he had no idea and admitted that he plagiarized that section. Some of these desperate ploys would be comical if they did not have such serious consequences. Forewarned is forearmed; if you have gotten yourself into such a hopeless jam that you are actually contemplating desperate measures such as plagiarism, at least you should know how serious the consequences can be.

## CONCLUSION

The process of producing a well-written, convincing paper is long, involved, and time-consuming, a far cry from the desperate scramble a day or two before the deadline or one or two frantic late nights in which some students think they can produce a decent paper. The process, including the research phase, occupies several weeks at least. Even the process of writing the draft, editing, revising, printing, and proofreading, as described in this chapter, takes more than a few evenings' work. Remember—no one writes perfect drafts, and turning a draft into a polished paper takes hard work. Provided that you have done adequate research and have thought carefully about the topic, your paper will succeed or fail in direct proportion to the time and care you devote to the process of drafting and revising. If you work hard at these steps, your finished product will be something you can be proud of, work that you know will meet the highest academic standards.

# C H A P T E R 5

# Questions of Format

## FORMAT FOR COLLEGE PAPERS

There are standard rules about the way a college paper should be formatted. These rules may seem to be archaic holdovers from the past, but whether or not they make sense to you, follow standard practice if you want to be taken seriously and demonstrate your professionalism. In another sector of the musician's world, recital etiquette has it own rules of proper dress and behavior, which may also seem archaic or pointless to you. In both cases, however, if you want to be taken seriously and judged as a professional, you should follow accepted practice.

The accepted format for a research paper is generally the same within disciplines such as the arts and humanities; other fields have their own rules for format issues. In the natural and social sciences, for example, it is customary to use a citation system known as *author-date* citation, in which works are cited by the author's last name and the date of publication in parentheses within the text, rather than in footnotes or endnotes. Both *humanities style,* which uses footnotes or endnotes and a bibliography, and the author-date style are explained in detail in both the Turabian guide and *The Chicago Manual of Style*. To complicate the situation further, the Modern Language Association has developed its own version of author-date citation, called *MLA style*. In this chapter we will discuss the standard humanities format in detail and the general principles of the author-date system, which is now being used in a wider range of disciplines. The chapter closes with a discussion of some of the unique format problems encountered in writing about music. Note at the outset that there are few absolute rules; there are often several ways to handle certain details, all within the range of correct standards.

There are two basic principles to remember about format issues. First, be consistent. If you follow Turabian's model for one footnote, then follow it for all your footnotes. Second, be logical; the purpose of footnotes and bibliographies is to be helpful to the reader. Be sure that your notes are helpful rather than confusing, and if you cannot find a model for a particular kind of citation in one of the standard style manuals, choose a logical and helpful way to handle the question. There is another principle for students: Check with your instructor to see whether you have any latitude in choosing a style guide; your instructor or institution may insist that you follow one particular style manual. When the choice of a guide is up to you, follow the rules as explained in Turabian or *The Chicago Manual of Style*. Turabian is the standard guide in most colleges, and the *Chicago Manual* is the most authoritative guide in the world of publishing. The important thing to most instructors is that you follow one of the accepted style guides and that you are consistent and logical in the way you deal with details. The worst offenses are carelessness and inconsistency.

### Paper

College papers should be printed on one side only, on plain white paper of the standard size we use in the United States, eight-and-a-half by eleven inches. Do not use legal-size paper or the paper that is standard in Britain and Europe, which is a bit longer and narrower than the paper used in this country. The rules for theses and dissertations specify paper of a particular weight, sometimes with blue lines marking the borders of the text; there is no reason to use this special paper for an undergraduate project. It seems too obvious to mention, but lined sheets ripped from a notebook, with the shredded perforations hanging off, are not acceptable. Save your colored paper for correspondence; lavender or buff paper is out of place for a research project and is regarded as an affectation, like using green or lavender ink in a business letter.

Two other kinds of paper that were common years ago are not acceptable. Lightweight "onion skin" paper is difficult to read because it is nearly transparent. Also avoid "erasable bond," a holdover from the days of typewriters, which is difficult to write comments on and annoying to read, because the letters tend to rub off on the reader's hand or sleeve; portions of your deathless prose can vanish. Any plain white typing paper will do, including paper manufactured for copy machines.

### Page Format

Papers are supposed to have standard margins. Turabian (14.2) specifies a margin of at least an inch on all four sides and notes that some institutions require larger margins, particularly on the left side. That means that nothing can extend beyond these margins; text, footnotes, and illustrations, including musical examples, must not extend beyond the top, bottom, and side margins.

There are practical reasons for standard margins. First, the reader needs some space in which to write corrections and comments. A wider margin on the left is especially useful when the paper is bound or enclosed in a cover or folder.

### Fonts

Most word-processing programs offer a wide variety of fonts and type sizes. For papers, choose a font that looks like those found in printed books (Turabian 13.27). Although the names vary somewhat from program to program, choose something with a name like Times or Times New Roman, Bookman, New Century Schoolbook, Garamond, Palatino, or anything else that looks like printing. Turabian also recommends Courier, a font that resembles work produced on a typewriter. I disagree; use one of the proportionally spaced fonts that look like print. Some writers prefer fonts such as Helvetica, called *sans-serif* fonts because they lack the *serifs* or small ornaments found on the letters in most fonts. Sans-serif fonts look clean and attractive; on the other hand, some feel that they are more difficult to read over a long period of time than the fonts with serifs. In any case, avoid idiosyncratic fonts that are unusually spaced, too light, too dark, or too weird, and certainly avoid fonts designed to look like script. The appropriate size depends on the font; most fonts look good and are quite readable in 10-, 11-, or 12-point size. Experiment with your favorite fonts to see which sizes work best. Fonts that are unusually small or cramped are difficult to read; fonts or sizes that are too big make your paper look like a children's book or else signal to the world that you are trying to make your paper look longer than it really is.

### Spacing

The text of your paper should be double-spaced (Turabian 14.5). Word-processing programs have several options for line spacing, and a page of text with one-and-a-half spaces between lines looks quite attractive. The standard practice, however, for both college papers and manuscripts for publishing, is to double-space the text. In college papers, block quotes, footnotes, and bibliography entries are usually single-spaced—that is, single-spaced within each entry, and double-spaced between entries. The practice is different in the world of publishing; publishers usually require that everything in the manuscript, including notes and bibliography, should be double-spaced. Follow the recommendations of your instructor and the style guide you use.

### Justification

Word-processing programs offer several options for justification: left-hand, center, and right-hand. The advantage of right-hand justification is that it creates a "justified" or aligned right margin and a uniform text block on each page. The disadvantages of right-hand justification are that it creates uneven and incorrect spacing within the lines of text, making the text harder to read, and sometimes it introduces incorrect hyphenation at the end of the line. For those reasons, it is now accepted practice to avoid right-hand justification (Turabian 14.3). Set your computer for left-hand justification instead; the right-hand margin will be uneven, but your spacing will be correct and you won't have to deal with problematic hyphenation.

### Page Numbers

The pages of your paper should be numbered in the following way (Turabian 14.6-9). If your paper has a separate title page, it is not numbered; nor is the optional blank sheet between the title page and the first page of text. In the case of long papers, the pages of introductory material (preface, dedication, table of contents) are numbered with lowercase roman numerals— i, ii, iii, and so forth. The reason for this different numbering system is that those sections, known collectively as *front matter,* are not part of the text proper and are often written last, after the main body of text is completed. In most undergraduate papers, the text begins immediately after the title page, without preliminary sections; the text is numbered in arabic numerals, and the first page of text is page 1. If the title appears above the first page of text, rather than on a separate title page, then that first page is counted as page 1 but not numbered, and the following page is numbered 2. Within the text, pages are numbered with arabic numerals placed at the top margin, one double-space above the top line of text, either in the upper right-hand corner or at the center of the page. Do not place numbers at the bottom of the page, where they can interfere with footnotes. Pages are numbered consecutively through the whole paper, including appendixes, endnotes, and bibliography. If the paper is divided into chapters, the numbering does not begin anew with each chapter but continues consecutively through the entire paper. If during the course of working on a project you store your paper in more than one file, be sure to set up the final copy so that it is consecutively numbered.

When your paper is complete, you may want to staple the pages together with a single staple near the upper-left-hand corner of the pages or insert the paper into one of the covers or folders sold for this purpose, so that the pages stay together and in the proper order. Remember that your instructor will probably have a large stack of papers to read. Loose pages can easily get out of order; paper clips often slip and can mix papers together. Your paper can easily get jumbled together with other people's projects. Another way to be sure that each of your pages is clearly identified is to set up a header including your name, a short version of the title if you wish, and the page number.

## FORMAT FOR QUOTATIONS

Quoting the words of recognized experts can be a very effective way to reinforce your arguments or state a point more clearly. Quotations should be used sparingly, however, and only when you decide that they are the most effective way to argue your point. A long string of quotations does not constitute a research paper, because there is no room for you to develop and express your own ideas. An excessive number of quotations makes the reader suspect that the writer is hiding behind the quotations to conceal the fact that he or she has nothing original to say.

The proper format for quotations seems to cause problems for many students. First of all, direct quotations must be clearly marked. Citing the exact words of another author without quotation marks and a footnote acknowledging your source is unethical; see the discussion of plagiarism in Chapter 4. Different kinds of quotations are handled in different ways.

### Short Quotations

Quotations are defined as short when they occupy less than three to ten full lines, depending on which guide you read; Turabian (5.4) defines short quotations as anything less than two full sentences occupying eight lines of text. Short quotations are integrated into the body of the text and placed in quotation marks. For example:

> Rosen finds the term "recapitulation" misleading. "If we use it to mean a simple repeat of the exposition with the secondary material put into the tonic, then the whole idea must be thrown out as unclassical: this type of recapitulation is the exception rather than the rule in the mature works of Haydn, Mozart, and Beethoven."[1]

Note that the material cited must be quoted exactly, with the author's spelling and punctuation intact. One could argue that Rosen should have used a semicolon rather than a colon in line 3, after "unclassical," between two independent clauses not joined by a conjunction, but when quoting another author, the writer must quote exactly. Note also the order of the punctuation marks at the end of the quotation: period, then quotation marks, then the superscript footnote number.

### Block Quotations

Long quotations—anything longer than three to ten lines, or in Turabian's view, two complete sentences occupying more than eight lines—should be set off from the body of your text. Long quotations, also called *block quotes* or *extracts,* are started on a new line, single-spaced (according to most style guides), and indented (Turabian 5.4). Style guides vary in describing how far to indent block quotations; most specify four or five spaces. If the opening of the quotation is the beginning of a new paragraph in the original source, the first line of your block quote may be indented further than the rest, just like the opening line of any paragraph. If a new paragraph begins within the block quote, indent that first line as well, but single-space between the paragraphs. When block quotations appear on the page in this special format, there is no mistaking that the quoted material is distinct from your own text. For that reason, quotation marks are not needed at the beginning and end of block quotes; the appearance of the page makes clear that these are not the writer's own words. Since there are no quotation marks around the whole citation, material that appears inside quotation marks within the cited material is put inside double quotation marks, not the single quotation marks one would normally use for a quotation within a quotation. Although it is possible to introduce a long quotation with an incomplete sentence, such as "As Rosen says," and then start the block quote on a new line, that method sometimes seems awkward. It is easier to introduce the quotation with a complete sentence. If the first line of text after a block quote continues the paragraph that preceded the quote, it begins at the left margin; if it starts a new paragraph, it is indented as usual.

Whenever you are contemplating including a long quotation in your paper, stop and think about its effectiveness. It is generally possible to achieve the same effect in other ways, such as paraphrasing or summarizing the content of most of the quotation, and selecting one particularly strong sentence or phrase to quote. On the other hand, the long quotation may be the best way to make your point. As is true in so many matters, moderation is the rule. If you use too many long quotations, you create the impression that you are simply stringing together apt quotations that you found, rather than formulating your own ideas and writing your own prose.

### Ellipsis and Editorial Additions

If you omit some words from a direct quotation, either a short quotation or a block quote, honesty and accuracy demand that you signal that omission, called an *ellipsis,* by the use of three spaced periods to show where material was left out (Turabian 5.18-23). If the material preceding the ellipsis ends with a period or the following material starts a new sentence, use four spaced periods. Most word-processing programs produce a special character consisting of three spaced dots rather than three separate periods.

> As Rosen says, "If we use it to mean a simple repeat of the exposition . . . then the whole idea must be thrown out as unclassical."

Be careful in your use of ellipses. The preceding example is not a legitimate use of an ellipsis, since it misrepresents what Rosen said; obviously, he did not mean to define recapitulation as a simple repeat of the exposition. The omitted qualifying phrase, "with the secondary material put into the tonic," is essential if the quotation is to make sense. Even when use of an ellipsis does not misrepresent what the original author wrote, it can be confusing to the reader and can raise questions about your argument. The reader naturally wonders what was left out, why it was left out, and how the omitted material might change the force of the quotation.

If you feel required to add something to a quotation for the sake of clarity, you must make clear to the reader that you are doing so by putting the editorial comment in *square brackets*—not parentheses (Turabian 5.35). Such interpolations may be necessary to supply contextual material that is not clear in the sentence cited, such as the antecedent for a pronoun that appears in the quoted section. Square brackets are a universal sign of editorial additions. Without them, you are technically misquoting the cited author by creating the impression that the insertion is part of the direct quotation. If you wish to clarify what Rosen means by "it" in the above quotation, for example, you must enclose the added antecedent in brackets.

> **Incorrect:** If we use it—the term recapitulation—to mean a simple repeat of the exposition . . .
>
> **Incorrect:** If we use it (recapitulation) to mean a simple repeat of the exposition . . .
>
> **Correct:** If we use it [recapitulation] to mean a simple repeat of the exposition . . .

### [*sic*]

There is a special editorial comment one can insert within quotations to let the reader know that the writer is quoting the source exactly, and that mistakes that appear in the text are the responsibility of the cited author, not the writer. The Latin word *sic* ("thus") is inserted in square brackets after an apparent error (Turabian 5.36), meaning "This is the way it appears in the source." Since *sic* is a foreign word, it is set in italics; since it is a complete word, not an abbreviation, it is not followed by a period.

> Thomas Morley, in *A Plaine and Easie Introduction to Practicall Musicke* [*sic*], takes a somewhat different approach.

In this case the use of *sic* is not necessary. Since anyone with any knowledge of Elizabethan English is aware that spelling at that time was erratic, the [*sic*] seems overly cautious or pretentious. There are situations, however, in which this device is useful. When you are sure, for example, that a date in a quotation is wrong, you can use *sic* or insert the correct date in brackets so that the reader understands that you are aware of the error. Some experts would set *sic* in standard type, rather than in italics; Turabian (2:25) and the *Chicago Manual* (7.56) recommend italics.

## BIBLIOGRAPHY AND FOOTNOTE FORM: HUMANITIES STYLE

The following section is a summary of the detailed guidelines for formatting bibliographies and footnotes as given in the Turabian manual and *The Chicago Manual of Style,* and is adapted from the analogous section in Wingell and Herzog, *Introduction to Research in Music.* Note that the various guides do not always agree on every detail of a particular kind of citation, although the general principles are clear; a guide may also list more than one way of dealing with a particular issue. In these cases, you are free to follow any format found in one of the accepted guides, unless your instructor or institution insists that you follow one particular guide or format for school projects. In both bibliography and footnote references, you must be both clear and consistent; if you choose one option for listing volume and page number of a periodical early in your bibliography, you must follow that format all the way through.

Note that this section treats format issues for bibliographies and footnotes together, going through each type of resource (books, articles, etc.) in order. The main difference between bibliography and footnote format is that bibliography entries are written as a series of separate "sentences," each bit of information starting with an uppercase letter and ending with a period. Footnotes, on the other hand, are written as single "sentences," with commas rather than periods in between the various items of information and parentheses enclosing the publication information. Note also that the footnote format listed here is for the first reference in a paper; see additional note 9 under the **Books** section for ways to refer to the same items later in the paper, after the complete information has been listed in an earlier footnote.

### Books

**Bibliography—basic form**    Author, last name first. *Title: Subtitle,* in italics. City: publisher, year. Bibliography entries are *out-dented*—that is, the first line of each entry is flush with the left margin, and subsequent lines are indented one tab stop. This technique is sometimes referred to as a *hanging indent.*

Smith, John. *The Music of John Cage: An Analytic Guide.* New York: W. W. Norton, 1982.

**Footnote—basic form**    Author, first name first, title and subtitle, in italics (city: publisher, year), and page numbers, if you wish to cite a particular passage. Footnotes are *indented*—that is, the reference number and first line of the entry are indented one tab stop, and subsequent lines are flush with the left margin (Turabian 14.13). Footnotes begin with the reference number—either a superscript number or a standard numeral followed by a period. Footnotes, unlike bibliography entries, frequently end with page numbers referring to a particular passage relevant to the issue under discussion. To refer to a single page, type the letter "p" followed by a period, a space, and the number. To refer to several pages, "pp. 24–29" is clearer than the alternative "pp. 24 ff." signifying "page 24 and the following pages." Some guides allow the omission of "p." if there is no possibility of confusion. All footnotes end with a period.

[1]John Smith, *The Music of John Cage: An Analytic Guide* (New York: W. W. Norton, 1982), pp. 132–45. **Or:** . . . (New York: W. W. Norton, 1982), 132–45.

### Additional Notes for Both Bibliography Entries and Footnotes

1. In a bibliography, if there are multiple authors, the name of the first listed author appears last name first; the names of subsequent authors are usually listed in normal order, but may also be listed with the last name first. In footnotes, the names of all authors are listed in normal order.

**Bibliography**
Smith, John, Walter Brown, and William Jones, *Joachim Raff, Neglected Genius*. New York: W. W. Norton, 1939.

OR

Smith, John, Brown, Walter, and Jones, William, *Joachim Raff, Neglected Genius*. New York: W. W. Norton, 1939.

**Footnote**
[1]John Smith, Walter Brown, and William Jones, *Joachim Raff, Neglected Genius* (New York: W. W. Norton, 1939), pp. 37–43.

2. In the bibliography, if there are multiple entries by the same author, it is not necessary to type out the author's name each time. After the first entry by the author, instead of the name enter a long dash—Turabian (9.27) specifies an eight-space dash, and Chicago (16.84-85) says a three-em dash—followed by a period and the title. If there is a second author, the dash is followed by a comma and the name of the joint author. Entries under the single author's name should be alphabetized by the first word (excluding articles) of the title; the entries by multiple authors come after all the entries by the single author, and, if there are several such entries, they too should be alphabetized by first word of the title.

Smith, John. *John Cage Remembered.* Bloomington: Indiana University Press, 1994.

————. *The Music of John Cage: An Analytic Guide.* New York: W. W. Norton, 1982.

————, Walter Brown, and William Jones. *Joachim Raff, Neglected Genius.* New York: W. W. Norton, 1939.

3. In both bibliography and footnotes, titles in foreign languages must include all diacritical marks and follow the rules of capitalization of that particular language. Learn how to enter diacritical marks in your word-processing program, and copy titles and foreign names exactly. For capitalization of titles in foreign languages, learn the rules for each language, or copy the title exactly as it appears in a reliable reference work. The basic rules for the languages you are most likely to cite are as follows. In German titles, capitalize the first word of the title and all nouns; in French, Italian, and Latin titles, capitalize only the first word and proper nouns. When in doubt, find the title in a reliable reference work and copy it exactly the way you find it.

4. In both bibliography and footnotes, if the book has a subtitle that you decide to include in your citation, it is customary to add a colon between title and subtitle. Thus, although the title and subtitle are usually printed on the title page of the book in different styles and sizes of type, without any punctuation, in bibliography and footnote entries both the title and subtitle are listed in regular type with the added colon. Thus:

Rosen, Charles. *The Classical Style: Haydn, Mozart and Beethoven.* . . .

5. In both bibliography and footnotes, additional information—such as the number of volumes, edition number, translator, or title of the collection from which the individual volume is taken—is placed after the title and before the publication information. In both bibliography and footnotes, if you are using a later edition of a book, list the publication information for the first edition first, and then add the publication information for the edition you used. Both Turabian (8:45) and Chicago (17.79, 17.83-84) specify that notations such as "second edition" and "three volumes" should use numerals and normal letters, not superscripts, for the ordinal numbers (2nd, 3rd, 4th, etc.). If your program, trying to be helpful, automatically makes those letters superscripts, figure out how to cancel this habit.

**Bibliography**
Smith, John, and William Jones. *Joachim Raff, Neglected Genius.* The Great
    Composers Series. 2nd ed. 2 vols. Translated by Edward Miller. New York:
    Norton, 1924; reprint, New York: Dover, 1989.

**Footnote**
    [1]John Smith and William Jones, *Joachim Raff, Neglected Genius,* The Great
Composer Series, 2nd ed., 2 vols., translated by Edward Miller (New York: Norton,
1924; reprint, New York: Dover, 1989).

6. In both bibliography and footnotes, if the place of publication is not a well-known city such as New York, Boston, London, Paris, or Vienna, or if there is the possibility of confusion with another city of the same name, one must add the state, province, or country for further identification.

Cambridge: Cambridge University Press, 2004.

Cambridge, MA: Harvard University Press, 2004.

Washington, DC: Smithsonian Institution Press, 2003.

Upper Saddle River, NJ: Prentice Hall, 2005.

Boston: Houghton Mifflin, 2004

Note that "Cambridge" alone means the original one in the United Kingdom; for the U.S. city, use "Cambridge, MA." Washington is certainly a well-known city, but to avoid confusion with the state it is proper to add "DC." The last two examples illustrate the basic rule—Upper Saddle River is not a well-known city; Boston is. Note also the general use of the two-letter postal codes for states (Chicago 15.29), without periods, although some guides prefer the older abbreviations for states (Calif., Mass., etc.).

When the publisher's name includes the name of the state, as in the case of many university presses, it is not necessary to add the abbreviation for the state after the name of the city, even if the city is not well known. The reader can be trusted to infer that the Indiana University Press is probably located in Indiana.

Bloomington: Indiana University Press, 1987.

Chapel Hill: University of North Carolina Press, 2002.

7. In both bibliography and footnotes, the publisher's name can be listed either as it appears on the title page or in shortened form, provided that the publisher is clearly identified. Thus, instead of "W. W. Norton & Co.," one can write "W. W. Norton" or "Norton," on the grounds that the company is well known (Turabian 8.58-59; Chicago 17.103-6). This approach is consistent with the trend toward simplifying citations. If you cite the full name of a publisher, cite it exactly as it appears on the title page, including details of spelling and punctuation, but leave out *Inc., Ltd.,* and the equivalent foreign terms. *The Chicago Manual of Style* also allows either the ampersand (&) or "and," no matter what appears on the title page.

W. W. Norton & Co. (with an ampersand or "and")

Simon & Schuster (with an ampersand or "and")

Harcourt Brace Jovanovich (no commas, no "and," no ampersand)

Consistency, as always, is important. Cite all publishers either by full name or by a shortened name, and use either "and" or an ampersand in all instances.

8. Listing the date of publication is generally easy enough; in modern books, the date is listed on the reverse of the title page, somewhere in the copyright information. If you use a modern edition of an older book, list the date of the first publication as well as the date of the version you actually used. If no date of publication is given, even in the copyright information, you may use the abbreviation "n.d." ("no date") in place of the date in the entry, or

simply list place and publisher, with a comma separating them rather than the usual colon. Listing the dates of some types of publications, such as translations and reprints of older books, can get complicated; the *Chicago Manual* (17.115-122) discusses some of the special situations that may arise.

9. All the information and examples above regarding footnotes apply to the first time the work is cited. If a work is cited a second or third time, a shorter form is used, including just enough information to make clear which previously cited work the author is referring to. For example, if only one work by an author has been cited previously, that work can be cited again by simply using the author's last name. This practice replaces a group of Latin abbreviations and the complicated rules for their use found in older style guides—*op. cit., loc. cit., art. cit.,* etc.

[1]Smith, p. 422.

If more than one work by Smith has been cited previously, the writer must specify which work he means, using a shortened form of the title. For example, if several books by John Smith have been cited previously, *John Cage Remembered* can be cited in the following way in a later footnote. If two or more authors named Smith has been cited previously, add the initial of the first name to specify the author you are citing.

[1]Smith, *Cage Remembered,* p. 422.

The main requirement is clarity—there should be no possible doubt about which work the writer is citing.

10. Finally, there is one Latin abbreviation still in use that can be quite handy—*ibid.*, an abbreviation for "ibidem," meaning "in the same place." If you want to cite the same work and same page as in the previous footnote, just write "Ibid." This term is set in roman type, not italics, and is always followed by a period, since it is an abbreviation (Turabian 8.85-86; Chicago 16.47-48). If you want to cite a different page in the same work, write "Ibid., p. 46." Or "Ibid., 46." This handy abbreviation works only to refer to the source cited in the previous note; you cannot use "ibid." to refer to works cited in any other notes or on earlier pages.

### Dissertations

Dissertations that have been published as books are cited just like other books, listing place of publication, publisher, and date as the publication information. For dissertations that have not been published, the format is different; the title is placed in quotation marks, like the title of an article, and the degree, granting institution, and date of conferral take the place of the publication information.

**Unpublished dissertation—bibliography**
Smith, Joan. "Hindemith's Early Songs." Ph.D. dissertation, University of Chicago,
1989.

**Unpublished dissertation—footnote**
[1]Joan Smith, "Hindemith's Early Songs," Ph.D. dissertation, University of
Chicago, 1989.

**Published dissertation—bibliography**
Jones, Jane. *The Ballate of Francesco Landini.* Ann Arbor: University of Michigan
Press, 1990.

**Published dissertation—footnote**
[1]Jane Jones, *The Ballate of Francesco Landini* (Ann Arbor: University of
Michigan Press, 1990).

## Articles in Dictionaries and Encyclopedias

**Bibliography—basic form for unsigned articles**   Editor of lexicon, last
name first. *Title.* Place: publisher, date; s.v. "Title of article." "S.v." is an
abbreviation for the Latin words "sub verbo," or "sub voce," meaning
"under the word"; the plural form is "s.vv." This abbreviation directs the
reader to the specific entry or entries the writer wishes to cite.

Slonimsky, Nicolas, ed. *Baker's Biographical Dictionary of Musicians,* 8th ed. New
York: Schirmer Books, 1992; s.v. "Mahler, Gustav."

**Footnote—basic form for unsigned articles**   Editor of lexicon, *Title*
(place: publisher, date); s.v. "Title of article."

[1]Nicolas Slonimsky, ed., *Baker's Biographical Dictionary of Musicians,* 8th ed.
(New York: Schirmer Books, 1992); s.v. "Mahler, Gustav."

## Notes

1. Sometimes a reference work has existed for a long time and several editors have worked on it. In those cases, the work may be alphabetized
under its long-standing name, with the present editor listed afterwards.
The one-volume dictionaries listed previously are frequently cited in this
way.

**Bibliography**
*Baker's Biographical Dictionary of Musicians,* 8th ed. Edited by Nicolas Slonimsky.
New York: Schirmer Books, 1992; s.v. "Mahler, Gustav."

**Footnote**

¹*Baker's Biographical Dictionary of Musicians*, 8th ed., edited by Nicolas Slonimsky (New York: Schirmer Books, 1992); s.v. "Mahler, Gustav."

2. In the case of larger encyclopedias such as *The New Grove Dictionary of Music and Musicians* and *Die Musik in Geschichte und Gegenwart*, which contain long articles by recognized authorities, an alternative format is to cite the article by the author and title of that article, followed by the title of the lexicon and the publishing information. When compiling a bibliography, one often finds that books and articles by the same author who wrote the article in a lexicon are already listed in the bibliography. It makes sense to include the lexicon article in the same place under the author's name. In addition, since some of the articles in these lexicons are book-length monographs, the authors deserve specific mention in the citation.

**Bibliography—basic form for signed articles**    Author's name, last name first. "Title of article." *Title of lexicon*, edition. Editor's name, volume and page. Place: publisher, date.

> Powers, Harold. "Mode." *New Grove Dictionary of Music and Musicians*, 2nd ed. Edited by Stanley Sadie and John Tyrrell, 7:334–367. London: Macmillan, 2001.

**Footnote—basic form for signed articles**    Author's name, "Title of article," *Title of lexicon*, edition, editor's name, volume and page (Place: publisher, date).

> ¹Harold Powers, "Mode," *New Grove Dictionary of Music and Musicians*, 2nd ed., edited by Stanley Sadie and John Tyrrell, 7:334–367 (London: Macmillan, 2001).

### Notes on Articles in Lexicons

1. The standard guides have little to say on the issue of citing lexicons such as the *New Grove* or MGG; their rules are clearly designed for citing well-known works such as *Encyclopedia Britannica*. They recommend omitting the publication information when citing standard sources; the citation then lists only title, edition, and specific entry. Perhaps it would make sense to use this system for the specialized lexicons that we cite frequently in music research.

2. There are different ways to cite volume and page number when listing an article in a lexicon. The listing of volume and page may appear at the end of the entry, after the publication information. Note that in the examples, the abbreviations for "volume" and "page" are omitted; the number of the volume is followed by a colon and page numbers. That system works well, as long as it is clear what the numbers mean.

**Bibliography**

Planchart, Alejandro. "Dufay. " *The New Grove Dictionary of Music and Musicians.* 2nd ed. Edited by Stanley Sadie and John Tyrrell, 8:235–279. London: Macmillan, 2001.

OR . . . . Edited by Stanley Sadie and John Tyrrell. London: Macmillan, 2001. 8:235–279.

**Footnote**

   [1]Alejandro Planchart, "Dufay," *The New Grove Dictionary of Music and Musicians,* 2nd ed., Edited by Stanley Sadie and John Tyrrell, 8:235–279 (London: Macmillan, 2001).

   OR . . . , edited by Stanley Sadie and John Tyrrell (London: Macmillan, 2001), 8:235–279.

## Articles in Periodicals

**Bibliography—basic form**   Author, last name first. "Title of Article: Subtitle." *Title of Journal* volume number (year): page numbers.

Wallace, Robert. "Poetic and Musical Structures in the Songs of the Troubadours." *Journal of the American Musicological Society* 34 (1974):14–32.

**Footnote—basic form**   Author, first name first, "Title of Article: Subtitle," *Title of Journal* volume number (year): page numbers.

**Citing the entire article**

   [1]Robert Wallace, "Poetic and Musical Structures in the Songs of the Troubadours," *Journal of the American Musicological Society* 34 (1974):14–32.

**Citing a particular passage**

   [1]Robert Wallace, "Poetic and Musical Structures in the Songs of the Troubadours," *Journal of the American Musicological Society* 34 (1974):14–32; see pp. 30–32.

**Note**   In both bibliography and footnotes, use arabic numerals for volume and page numbers, even if the periodical uses roman numerals. Note also that the date appears in parentheses after the volume number, with no punctuation in between them (Turabian 8.101). Remember also that, in the case of scholarly periodicals, there is no need to list any of the other information that might appear on the title page, such as issue number or season of the year, since the issues for a particular year are paginated continuously and eventually bound as a single volume. The only information one needs to locate the article is volume number, year, and pages.

### Articles in Collections of Essays

**Basic form, both bibliography and footnote**   The name of the author and the publication information are dealt with exactly as in the case of books. The title of the article is enclosed in quotation marks. The additional information—"In," the title of the collection in italics, the editor's name, and the page numbers of the cited article, along with any other additional information—is listed after the title of the article and before the publication information (Chicago 17.69).

**Bibliography**
Wilson, George W. "Monteverdi's Venetian Operas." In *The Monteverdi Companion,* edited by Denis Arnold, 332–359. Chicago: University of Chicago Press, 1987.

**Footnote, citing a specific page**
    [1]George W. Wilson, "Monteverdi's Venetian Operas," in *The Monteverdi Companion,* edited by Denis Arnold (Chicago: Chicago University Press, 1987), p. 356.

### Scores

Scores and recordings are often listed in a separate section apart from the listings of books and articles. Scores are cited in both bibliographies and footnotes in much the same way as books; in bibliographies they are alphabetized by the composer's last name. In both bibliographies and footnotes, the composer's name is first, followed by the title of the work. If the work cited is part of a larger work, that title comes next, followed by the name of the editor (if there is one listed), and the usual publication information— place, publisher, and date. Footnote references make the same format changes as in the case of books (Turabian 8.142–43; Chicago 17.263).

**Bibliography**
Mahler, Gustav. *Das Lied von der Erde*. Kassel: Bärenreiter, 1976.

**Footnote**
    [1]Gustav Mahler, *Das Lied von der Erde* (Kassel: Bärenreiter, 1976).

**Note**   Citing scores is not always as straightforward as this example would indicate. Scores often list editors, they may be contained in large collected sets that have their own titles and editors, works may have nicknames ("Eroica," "Farewell") that should be listed, and so forth. Generally, just as in the case of books, any additional information is placed after the title and before the publication information. Further issues about citing musical works will be discussed later in this chapter.

**Bibliography**
Bach, J. S. Cantata no. 78, *Jesu der du meine Seele*, edited by Alfred Dürr. Series I, Band 2 of *Neue Ausgabe sämtlicher Werke*, edited by Johann Sebastian Bach Institut of Göttingen and the Bach-Archiv of Leipzig. Kassel: Bärenreiter, 1954–.

**Footnote**
    [1]J. S. Bach, Cantata no. 78, *Jesu der du meine Seele*, edited by Alfred Dürr, Series I, Band 2 of *Neue Ausgabe sämtlicher Werke*, edited by Johann Sebastian Bach Institut of Göttingen and the Bach-Archiv of Leipzig (Kassel: Bärenreiter, 1954–).

## Sound Recordings

**Basic form—bibliography**   Composer, last name first. Title of the work or title of the recording if it is different from the title of the work, in italics. Manufacturer, number, date. If you wish to list principal performers, that information is listed after the title of the work and before manufacturer, number, and date (Turabian 8.144; Chicago 17.268).

> Mahler, Gustav. *Das Lied von der Erde*. Kathleen Ferrier, mezzo-soprano; Vienna Philharmonic Orchestra, cond. Bruno Walter. Deutsche Grammophon, 410 715-2, 1982.

**Basic form—footnote**   The same kinds of format changes are made as in the case of books—the composer's name is listed first name first, commas appear between items of information, publication information (here, manufacturer, number, and date) is enclosed in parentheses, and there is a period at the end.

    [1]Gustav Mahler, *Das Lied von der Erde*, Kathleen Ferrier, mezzo-soprano, Vienna Philharmonic Orchestra, cond. Bruno Walter (Deutsche Grammophon, 410 715-2, 1982).

### Citing Interviews, Correspondence, etc.

The standard resources may not be of much use for some types of specialized research, such as the study of recent music or events. Research in these areas generally involves unusual research methods, such as listening to taped interviews collected in archives or contacting knowledgeable people directly through interviews, correspondence, or e-mail. There are standard ways to cite various kinds of interviews; both *The Chicago Manual of Style* (17.204–9) and the Wingell/Herzog *Introduction to Research in Music* discuss these special format issues. Most undergraduate writing projects are not likely to involve this kind of research; should you find yourself involved in such a project, consult those sources to see how to cite interviews. Regarding the question of interviewing experts, I read recently that prominent scholars sometimes find themselves besieged by e-mail messages from undergraduate students seeking help on their assignments, sometimes apparently at the urging of their instructors. Of course it is easier to fire off an e-mail inquiry than to do your own research, but imposing on someone's time in this way hardly seems justified. The researcher can probably find books and articles in which these experts have already explained their ideas. Interviews and personal inquiries are appropriate only when you are doing highly specialized research and only after you have exhausted all the normal channels for gathering information.

### Citing Electronic Resources

In Chapter 3 we spoke about electronic resources for research. Since the researcher can now consult online journals, databases, bibliographic resources, and other sources of information, we need a standard format for citing Web sites and other electronic resources. There has been considerable change in this area since the third edition of this guide was published. At that point, the standard guides had not kept pace with the rapid growth of research sites on the Internet, and the best source for up-to-date advice was the FAQ ("Frequently Asked Questions") section of *The Chicago Manual of Style* Web site. Since then, the fifteenth edition of the *Chicago Manual* has appeared, and it includes a straightforward, helpful section on citing electronic sources (17.4-15). At the time of the third edition, the academic world seemed somewhat at a loss about citing these new Web sites; the publication of Chicago 15 has restored sense and order to this question.

Note that, as we mentioned in the Preface, the sixth edition of Turabian is coordinated with Chicago 14, an earlier edition of the *Chicago Manual;* the seventh edition, which appeared in April 2007, is coordinated with Chicago 15. By the time you read these pages, the seventh edition of Turabian will be available. I recommend following either Turabian or Chicago 15 as the authoritative guide in these matters. In addition to the general section cited above, Chicago 15 includes examples of electronic sources in each of the sections on citing various kinds of publications—books, journal articles, lexicons, etc.

**General principles**    The basic approach of Chicago 15 brings reason and logic to the discussion of this relatively new issue in the academic world. Cite electronic resources just as you cite books and articles—cite the author, if a specific author is listed, or the organization that produced the Web site; then the title of the site; next, the date of publication; and finally, the URL (Uniform Resource Locator) or address of the site. First we need to discuss some technical issues about citing URLs.

**Citing URLs**    Since, as you are aware, computers are literal and URLs are often complicated, it is important to cite URLs carefully, including all the dots, slashes, tildes, and other characters that separate elements, including the "trailing slash" that ends some URLs. The easiest way to cite a URL may be to copy and paste it from the source into your draft. Because some URLs are case sensitive, it is a mistake to change any lowercase letters to capitals or make any other small editorial changes. Even if the URL begins after a period, the first letter of the URL should not be capitalized. At the time of the last edition of this guide, in the interest of making a clear distinction between the URL and surrounding text, we were told to enclose all URLs in angle brackets (<>). Chicago 15 now regards that practice as unnecessary and incorrect, since angle brackets often have a special technical meaning in the context of computer language. In addition, it is now correct to add a period at the end of a URL if the context requires one—for example, at the end of a sentence, footnote, or bibliographic entry. It is clear that as we become more used to dealing with these once strange and exotic strings of abbreviations and symbols, we are less worried about making clear that they are distinct from ordinary text.

One technical issue in citing URLs is dealing with line breaks when it is necessary to run an URL over to a second line. The *Chicago Manual* recommends putting the break *after* a slash, but *before* a period, comma, tilde, hyphen, underline, or other symbol. The reason is clear—moving the period to the start of the second line makes clear that the URL continues on that line rather than ending on the previous line. Likewise, never add a hyphen at the line break; the reader will interpret that hyphen as part of the URL. In addition, if a hyphen is part of the URL, put that hyphen at the start of the next line, not at the end of a line. These recommendations make perfect sense if you understand how URLs work and if you are interested in citing Web sites accurately.

**Access dates**   Citing access dates is another issue in which the thinking has changed in just a few years. Guides used to think it was essential to cite the date that the writer accessed each Web site, since the Internet is in constant flux—sites appear and disappear or change constantly. Chicago 15 takes a commonsense approach—if it makes a difference or is important for some reason, cite the date of access; otherwise, it is not necessary. Papers on music frequently cite the *New Grove Dictionary* as a basic resource; as you know, *Grove Music Online* is constantly being updated, so the access date can make a difference. On the other hand, the date of each updated article is listed prominently online in the heading of the article. I think it makes more sense to list the date of the revised article in the citation, just like the date of publication of any other resource, and then omit the date of access.

**Resources available in both print and electronic versions**   A related issue is whether or not it is important to cite both the print and electronic versions of resources that are published both ways. When the content in both versions is the same—for example, journal articles that are available on the JSTOR site—it does not matter whether you sat in the library and read the article from a bound volume of the journal or read it on your laptop in Starbucks or your dorm room. On the other hand, since the JSTOR archive does not necessarily contain complete runs of all journals, it might be helpful to add "also available in the JSTOR archive online" at the end of a citation of a journal article. Perhaps it is still worth mentioning which version you used for your research; you might ask your instructor for advice on this question.

When the versions are different—for example, articles in the *New Grove* that have been revised or updated in the online version—obviously it is necessary to cite the version you used. Also, it clearly makes sense to check the online version to see if the article you plan to consult is available in a revised version. On the *Grove Music Online* Web site, the editors list their recommended ways to cite both the print and online versions of *New Grove*, which differ somewhat from the standard guides; you might check with your instructor to see whether it is permissible to follow the editors' recommendations.

Following is an example of a citation of an electronic resource, in this case an article in an online scholarly journal. The URL is necessary, since it is the only way to gain access to the article.

> Schulenberg, David. "Some Problems of Text, Attribution, and Performance in Early Italian Baroque Keyboard Music." *Journal of Seventeenth-Century Music* 4, no. 1 (1998), http://www. sscm-jscm.org/jscm/v4/no1/schulenberg.html.

This is an actual article; look it up on your computer if you have not yet browsed through an online journal. Note that it is easy to figure out what the various components of the URL mean—the Society for Seventeenth-Century Music (and its journal), a non-profit organization, published this article in its journal, Volume 4, number 1. Note also the period at the end, which is not part of the URL but ends the entry. This is a bibliography entry; a footnote would make the usual changes—the order of the author's name, and commas instead of the periods in the bibliography entry.

> [1]David Schulenberg, "Some Problems of Text, Attribution, and Performance in Early Italian Baroque Keyboard Music," *Journal of Seventeenth-Century Music* 4, no. 1 (1998); http://www. sscm-jscm.org/jscm/v4/no1/schulenberg.html.

For further examples of citing electronic resources, see the examples in Chicago 15, Chapter 17, under ways to cite various kinds of publications. In conclusion, the business of citing electronic resources is fairly new and still evolving. The editors of Chicago 15 anticipate that a simpler set of permanent identifiers for electronic sources will emerge in the future. In the meantime, follow the advice of Chicago 15 and Turabian 7 and the usual principles regarding format issues: Base your decisions on logic and common sense, and be consistent.

# THE AUTHOR-DATE SYSTEM OF CITATION

The author-date system of citation, which uses *reference lists* (or "lists of works cited") rather than bibliographies and brief *parenthetical notes* rather than footnotes or endnotes, was once used only in the natural and social sciences. It is now sometimes used in other disciplines as well. For music majors, particularly music education majors, who may be directed to use this system, the following brief guide to the system should be helpful.

The system is explained in detail in both Turabian (10.1-34) and the *Chicago Manual* (16:90-120); Turabian also adds a long chapter comparing the correct format for various kinds of publications as they would appear in footnotes, bibliography entries, parenthetical notes, and reference list entries. The fundamental difference between the two systems is that the author-date system, instead of a footnote, places within the text a brief parenthetical citation, usually consisting of the author's last name and the date of the publication. The reference list resembles a bibliography, alphabetized by last names of authors; the date is cited immediately after the author's name and directs the reader to the correct full citation in the reference list. In the author-date system, the reference list is the important element, since it is the only place in which the full citation appears. Note that there must be an item in the reference list for every parenthetical citation, and the author's name and the date of the publication must match exactly in both places. Without a corresponding item in the reference list, a parenthetical citation is of little help to the reader. We turn now to the proper format for reference lists and parenthetical citations.

### Reference Lists (Lists of Works Cited)

Reference lists are formatted very much like bibliographies, with one important exception; since the date is the crucial element in matching items in the reference list to the parenthetical citations in the text, the date appears, as noted earlier, immediately after the author's name as a separate element, rather than as the final element of the publication information at the end of the citation.

Turabian's sixth edition assumes that the author-date system is still restricted to papers in the natural sciences, and therefore discusses the conventions of capitalization of titles that those disciplines use; here we will assume that papers in the humanities use standard capitalization for titles.

Smith, John. 2003. *John Cage Remembered.* New York: W. W. Norton.

If two publications by a single author are cited, both of which were published in the same year, lowercase letters are added to the date (in both parenthetical citations and the reference list) to distinguish them, and they are alphabetized, as in a bibliography, by the first word of the title, excluding articles.

> Smith, John. 2003a. *John Cage Remembered.* New York: Norton.
>
> ———. 2003b. *The Music of John Cage: An Aesthetic Analysis.* Cambridge, MA: Harvard University Press.

Multiple authors, as well as additional information about editors, translators, titles of collections, and so forth, are handled exactly as in bibliographies; again, the only difference is the placement of the date of publication.

> Smith, John, Walter Brown, and Thomas Jones. 1997. *Joachim Raff: Neglected Genius.* Volume 7 of The Great Composers Series, edited by Ralph Cooper and Dmitri Fletcher. Boston: Houghton Mifflin.

Dissertations, periodicals, scores, recordings, Web sites, interviews, etc., are cited in reference lists just as they are in bibliographies, following the rules outlined earlier, always with the important change that the date appears as a separate item after the author's name, not elsewhere. For further information about details, consult Turabian and Chicago 15.

### Parenthetical Citations in the Text

Rather than footnotes, the author-date system inserts the author's name and the date of the cited publication in parentheses within the text. Only a space, not a comma, is used to separate the name from the date.

> (Smith 2003)

To cite a particular page or pages, add a comma after the date and then the page number or numbers.

> (Smith 2003, 34–42)

To cite several works by the same author, along with specific pages, place a semicolon between the listings of the various works.

> (Smith 2003, 34–42; 2005a, 124–35)

If two authors with the same last name are cited, the initials of their first names are added to distinguish them.

> (J. Smith 2003)
>
> (R. Smith 1997)

Multiple authors are dealt with as you would expect; if there are more than three, it is customary to cite the first name followed by "et al."—a Latin abbreviation for "et alii," meaning "and others."

(Smith, Brown, and Jones 2003)

(Smith et al. 2003)

**Placement of parenthetical citations**   Parenthetical citations can appear in any logical place in a sentence; they often are placed immediately before a punctuation mark. If the author's name appears in the sentence, the citation can omit the name and list just the date.

> Some scholars take an entirely different position (Smith 2003; Jones 1998).
>
> One scholar states that "Cage is more important as a thinker challenging the aesthetic assumptions of his time than as a musician" (Smith 2003).
>
> One scholar (Smith 2003) takes the position that "Cage is more important as a thinker challenging the aesthetic assumptions of his time than as a musician."
>
> Smith (2003) takes an entirely different position.

Note the punctuation of the second example. The final period, rather than coming at the end of the quotation, in its usual position before the quotation marks, comes after the parenthetical citation.

Parenthetical citations make no distinctions between various kinds of publications. "Smith 2003" could refer to a book, an article, a Web site, an interview, or any other form of publication; the reader must consult the reference list to find out exactly what the publication is. Note also that parenthetical citations identify an author and indirectly refer to the work cited, but they cannot fulfill the other functions of a footnote, such as explaining a term or adding further information. It may sometimes be necessary to use both parenthetical citations and standard footnotes in the same paper, using the parenthetical citations to identify works quoted or referred to and standard footnotes for other purposes.

There is no doubt that the author-date system is an efficient and appealing system; parenthetical citations are much simpler than footnotes, and the author-date system eliminates the need to repeat the same information in footnotes and bibliography entries. Students should understand how both systems work. You may not be able to choose the system to use in your papers; it goes without saying that you must follow the format and style guides recommended by your institution and your professor. Whichever system you use, you must use it carefully and consistently. As straightforward as the system of parenthetical citations seems, to my surprise I have seen it used incorrectly.

## FORMAT ISSUES RELATED TO WRITING ABOUT MUSIC

The latest editions of both the *Chicago Manual* and the Turabian guide include brief sections on format issues related to music; see Chicago 15, 8.201–5 and Turabian 8.142–46. We cannot expect the standard guides, however, to address all the technical issues that arise as we write about music, and the editors point out that many of their recommendations are not hard and fast rules. In addition, there are some standard conventions in scholarly writing about music that run counter to the recommendations of the standard style guides. Each specific musical topic, of course, involves its own particular editorial issues; here we will mention some general issues that arise in writing about music.

### Stylistic Periods

It is standard editorial practice in writing about music to capitalize the terms we use for the historical periods—thus, the Baroque era, the Classical period, the Romantic period. We do this to distinguish these technical terms from the same words used in their general senses—for example, "those baroque decorations," "classical music" (as opposed to popular music), or "the lyrical romanticism of a Mozart aria." This practice runs counter to the *Chicago Manual* (8.78–79), which recommends the use of lowercase initials for all such terms, unless they represent specific historical periods such as the Renaissance or the Age of Enlightenment or they are based on proper names, such as the Victorian era. To music historians, terms such as "Baroque," "Classical," and "Romantic" do represent specific historical eras, and the uppercase initials are useful to avoid ambiguity. On the other hand, terms that represent styles rather than specific periods of history, such as neoclassicism, impressionism, and expressionism, are not capitalized, and note that there is no hyphen in neoclassicism.

### Referring to Centuries

Many musicologists today prefer to divide the history of music by centuries rather than stylistic periods. According to the *Chicago Manual* (8.77), numerical designations of historical periods should be lowercased—the eighteenth century, the nineteen hundreds, the quattrocento. The numbers in references to centuries should always be spelled out—"the eighteenth century," not "the 18th century." Note also that there is no hyphen between the ordinal number and the word "century" when the combination is used as a noun; a hyphen is required, however, when the combination term is used as an adjective.

Brahms died near the close of the nineteenth century.

The late nineteenth-century orchestra provided a rich palette of evocative colors for composers of symphonic poems.

### Referring to Musical Works

Musical works with specific titles, such as *Fanfare for the Common Man, Orfeo, Die schöne Müllerin,* or *The Sound of Music,* are easy to cite; like book titles, they are set in italics, and the writer follows the capitalization rules of the language of the title. Format issues are more problematic in the case of generic titles (Symphony no. 42, Concerto in F Minor, Nocturne in B-flat Minor), particularly when the title also includes a subtitle, an opus number, and a catalog number; there are several options for the correct ordering of all those elements. Following are some issues that arise when referring to musical works.

**Italics or quotation marks**    In general, italics are used for specific titles of musical works; individual numbers or movements of larger works are generally put in quotation marks, as are titles or first lines of songs and hymns (Chicago 8.202).

"I Know That My Redeemer Liveth" from *Messiah*

"Come scoglio" from *Così fan tutte*

"People Will Say We're in Love" from *Oklahoma*

Bartók's *Concerto for Orchestra*

"The Star-Spangled Banner"

"Amazing Grace"

"Wachet auf" (the chorale)

*Wachet auf* (the cantata based on the chorale)

"Hey Jude"

Note that the second example contradicts the general rule that foreign words should be italicized; foreign words within quotation marks are already clearly separated from the words of the text, and hence need not be italicized.

**Generic titles**    Generic titles are set in roman type, not italic; the terms for genres (sonata, concerto, symphony, etc.) are capitalized when they are part of a title but lowercase when they are not part of a title.

Bartók's Fourth String Quartet

the last string quartet that Bartók composed

Sometimes it is difficult to decide whether a title is specific or generic. Note that in an earlier example, I italicized Bartók's *Concerto for Orchestra,* treating it as a specific title; one could argue this case is no different from the titles of Mozart's concertos for piano or Vivaldi's concertos for bassoon, which would be treated as generic titles, hence roman. Bach's *Mass in B Minor* is another interesting case—I would argue that it is a specific title for a well-known work, but one can also consider it a generic title. In such a case, consult a reliable reference work to see how it formats the title, and then, whatever your final decision is, always refer to the work that way.

Sometimes there are several possible ways to list a title; the proper procedure is to cite the title exactly the way it appears in a scholarly edition or in the worklists of lexicons such as the *New Grove.* For example, here are several ways to cite the same well-known work.

Piano Concerto in C Minor, K. 491

Concerto No. 20 for Pianoforte and Orchestra in C Minor, K. 491

Concerto in C Minor for Piano and Orchestra, K. 491

One can imagine other ways of listing this same information; imagine the range of possibilities when you cite a Vivaldi *concerto grosso,* with its list of instruments and the different numbering systems found in the three Vivaldi thematic catalogs. In such instances, follow the usual two rules—use a reliable reference work as your authority, and be consistent.

**Subtitles**    Many works with generic titles have added subtitles that appear in citations of the work; such subtitles, whether they originated with the composer, critics, historians, or the public, have become an accepted part of the title. They are put within parentheses, with either quotation marks or italics, at the end of the work's official title. According to the *Chicago Manual* (8.203), such subtitles are set in italics if the work is long and quotation marks if the work is short. Alternatively, all such nicknames may be set in roman type within quotation marks.

Haydn, Symphony No. 102 in E-flat Major ("Drum Roll") *or* ... (*Drum Roll*)

Schubert, Quintet in A Major for Piano and Strings ("The Trout")

Symphony no. 6 in F Major ("Pastoral") or (*Pastoral*)

the *Pastoral Symphony*

The companies who market recordings of classical music sometimes add subtitles to remind potential buyers that they might know these works through their use as background music in films. Thus, one sees titles such as Mozart's "Elvira Madigan" Piano Concerto, or *Also sprach Zarathrusta* (The *2001* Tone Poem) by Richard Strauss. These nicknames are marketing ploys, not real subtitles; I would avoid them in a research paper.

**Opus numbers**    If numbers are included in the citation of a musical composition, the terms "op." (for "opus") and "no." (for "number") are set in roman type and usually not capitalized (Chicago 15, 8.204). When a number is used restrictively—that is, to specify a particular work within a set or genre—it is not set off by commas; a number that follows another restrictive element in the title is set off by commas, since in that case it is no longer restrictive and merely provides additional information. When numbers are spelled out in a title, they are capitalized.

Hungarian Rhapsody no. 12

Brahms's Twelfth Hungarian Rhapsody

The Sonata in E Major, op. 45, was composed in 1822 (in this case, "op. 45" is non-restrictive).

The Sonata op. 45 was composed in 1822 (here "op. 45" is restrictive).

Sonata op. 31, no. 3, was composed . . .

Sonata op. 31, K. 415, was composed . . .

### Naming Notes and Keys

The proper way of naming notes and keys in prose is different from the systems in use in other contexts, such as analysis projects. In prose, the letter for a musical note or key should be capitalized. Uppercase letters signal the reader that they are being used as letters, not words; thus, we write "T-shirt" and "an A-frame house." We really should write "E-mail" with a capital for the same reason, but the lowercase E in "e-mail" has become the standard usage. Capitalizing notes distinguishes them from ordinary words, so that we don't write sentences such as "Chopin composed his Prelude in a flat . . ."

If it is important in your paper to specify the exact octave in which a note appears, it may be necessary to use a system of uppercase letters, lowercase letters, and superscript numbers or strokes to designate notes in different octaves. In that case, explain the system you are using early on, in a preface or one of the first footnotes, preferably with a musical example to make things clear, and then follow the system consistently. Otherwise, in normal prose, all notes should be uppercase.

Note that this practice is different from the shorthand system often used in analysis projects, in which uppercase "C" stands for "C major" and lowercase "c" means "C minor." In prose, always use the capital letter, adding the words "major" or "minor" if necessary. When the words "major" and "minor" appear in titles of musical works, they are capitalized.

**Correct**

Sonata in C Minor

The development section begins in the key of C minor.

Prelude and Fugue in E Major

Toccata and Fugue in D Minor

**Incorrect**

Sonata in c

Toccata and Fugue in d

The chromatic inflections of notes ("sharp" and "flat") and the term "natural" should be spelled out as words, both in your text and in footnotes and bibliographies. Do not use the sharp sign (#) for "sharp" or lowercase B (or a flat sign) for "flat," as in C# or Eb; after the uppercase letter naming the note, add a hyphen and then spell out "flat," "sharp," or "natural." These three words are not capitalized in titles; the combination of letter, hyphen, and qualifier is treated as a single term.

**Correct**

Rachmaninoff's Prelude in C-sharp Minor

**Incorrect**

Prelude in C# Minor

Prelude in c#

Prelude in C Sharp Minor

**Correct**

The whole-note G-sharp in the countertenor, altered to form the double leading-tone cadence, clashes with the shorter G-natural in the upper voice.
According to some scholars, Bach associated keys such as A-flat and C minor with resignation and contemplation.

**Incorrect**

. . . Bach associated keys such as Ab and c with resignation and contemplation.

### Foreign Terms

As a general rule, familiar words borrowed from foreign languages should be set in roman type, and unfamiliar foreign words should be set in italics. The problem, as you might imagine, is determining which words are familiar. Style guides used to base the distinction on the English dictionary; if a foreign word appeared in a reliable English dictionary, it was to be treated as a normal English word. Now the guides take a more nuanced approach. Foreign words "familiar to most readers" are not italicized, but may be italicized if necessary to avoid confusion (Chicago 7.54). One should also take into account the subject matter of one's paper and which foreign words are familiar in this particular field.

In the field of music, there are many terms that were once foreign words but have since become familiar English words: allegro, cello, concerto, crescendo, prelude, sarabande, sonata, sonata-rondo, soprano, staccato, and so forth. In a paper on music, these words no longer need italics. There is, however, another level of terminology in which the terms are clearly still foreign words—sonata da chiesa, viola da gamba, oboe d'amore, violino piccolo, and so forth. Current practice, particularly in the case of a foreign word that is used repeatedly in a paper, recommends italicizing the word at its first appearance, where it is defined, and setting it in roman type thereafter; if it occurs only rarely, it is better to italicize all appearances (Chicago 7.55).

In the cantata *Wachet auf, ruft uns die Stimme,* Bach calls for a *violino piccolo,* a slightly smaller violin tuned a minor third higher than the standard violin. . . . In the duet "Wann kommst du, Mein Heil?" the violino piccolo plays the obbligato line.

Another issue is how to make the plural forms of these foreign terms. "Concerto," a familiar word, is treated like an English word; the plural is "concertos." Thus, "Mozart did not write out cadenzas for most of his piano concertos." But if *"concerto grosso"* is a foreign word, then it should appear in italics, and its plural form should be *"concerti grossi."* That seems fussy and pedantic, but what viable alternative is there? "Concerto grossos"? "Concertos grosso," like "inspectors general"? Perhaps one can get away with *"oboes d'amore"* and *"violas da gamba,"* treating the compound term as two separate elements, a familiar English noun and a foreign modifier. With terms such as *concerto grosso* and *violino piccolo,* however, the only plural forms I can think of are *concerti grossi* and *violini piccoli,* pedantic or not. A better solution is to rewrite any sentence that requires these plural forms. As we said earlier, there is always another way to say anything you might want to say; back up and phrase the idea in such a way that the plural form is not necessary.

### Musical Examples

There is a standard format for the title or caption of a musical example. Students sometimes think that it is redundant to provide any information with an example, since they have already introduced it in the text, but there are reasons why captions are necessary. First, examples cannot always be placed exactly at the spot where they are mentioned in the text; therefore, they need to be identified clearly. Even if they are located near the relevant discussion in the text, musical examples are a form of quotation and therefore must be accompanied by the same kinds of information that accompany any quotation. Each musical example should be clearly identified—there should be no doubt in the reader's mind about precisely which page of which piece he or she is looking at. Every example should have a caption that includes the example number and the identification of the work quoted, including the composer's name, the title of the work, the movement (when appropriate), and the measure numbers. When you list measure numbers, remember that the abbreviation for measure is "m." followed by a space and the appropriate number. The plural form is "mm." followed by a space and the numbers. Do not use "ms." to mean "measures"; "ms." is the standard abbreviation for "manuscript." Finally, the title of each example should end with a footnote number, directing the reader to a note that cites the publication from which the example was taken and lists the publication information for the score.

## CONCLUSION

Although this chapter has devoted considerable space to questions of format, we have barely scratched the surface; look through *The Chicago Manual of Style* for a more thorough treatment. There are two central points to bear in mind: First, there is a proper way to format and present a paper; and second, you can find answers to all your format questions in the standard guides. If you are careless about the format for footnotes and bibliography entries, you cannot expect your paper to be treated as a serious piece of work. Your work will not be taken seriously—or may not be read at all—unless you submit it in a standard format and acceptable style. Knowledge of the proper format for research papers is one of the tools of your present "trade" and one of the ways in which you demonstrate your professional competence and ability to meet the exacting standards of the demanding world in which you have chosen to compete.

# CHAPTER 6

# Other Kinds of Writing Projects

Research papers are not the only written assignments you will encounter as you pursue a degree in music. There are other projects that involve the same challenges and skills, the same attention to research and organization of material, and the same careful preparation as writing a research paper. In addition, each of these tasks has its own special requirements; each deserves a brief discussion.

## THE SEMINAR PRESENTATION

Presenting a report in a seminar is in some ways the most difficult of academic assignments. Most people feel intimidated by the prospect of addressing a group, and your peers can be the most frightening group of all. Some lucky people are blessed with an inborn knack for speaking in a natural, lively, and persuasive way. Most of us, on the other hand, feel shy and nervous when addressing a group, and nervousness shows itself in various ways, none of them helpful. Some people giggle, some try to be cute or humorous, some bluster, some hide behind a stiff and formal exterior. The most effective strategy is to be prepared, be enthusiastic, and be yourself. Once you survive the experience of your first public presentation, it becomes easier to organize a good presentation and present it effectively.

Since this guide is about writing, not public speaking, our task here is not to train persuasive speakers. Spoken style is, of course, different from written style, and preparing for an oral presentation is different in some ways from the process of writing a convincing paper, but there are important similarities. Let us look at each step of the process.

### Research

The process of locating material for a seminar presentation is exactly the same as the research process for a paper. The fact that an oral presentation has to work within strict time limits does not mean that one can spend less time in research than one would for a paper. In fact, you might want to be especially thorough in your research for a seminar presentation, since some time is usually scheduled for questions and discussion. You need to have a deep and wide-ranging command of the topic so that you can answer any questions your classmates might raise. As you can imagine, nothing is more embarrassing than to fumble around, unable to answer a question on the topic that you are supposed to know about, and a weak performance in the discussion phase can negate the effect of your presentation, no matter how impressive the rest of it was. No research ever goes to waste, even if some material you discover does not fit into the presentation itself. Review the discussion of the research process in Chapter 3, and start with the basic resources listed there—your library catalog, your computer's search engine, electronic databases, *Grove Music Online,* histories, biographies, and journal articles. For a seminar presentation, you will also want to locate good recordings of the music in question, since you probably will want to include audio examples.

### Organizing the Presentation

Once you have completed your research, the process of turning a mass of information into a logical, coherent presentation is similar to the early stages of writing a paper. The first thing you need is a logical and detailed outline; review the section on outlining in Chapter 4. A clear outline is perhaps even more critical in a seminar presentation than in a paper. In the process of writing a paper, if you decide that additional material is necessary, even at the last minute, you can always add a page or two or even a new section—word limits are generally flexible. In a seminar presentation, on the other hand, you have to stay within rigid time limits; whatever time you devote to an interesting digression leaves you with less time for your main point. You need to construct a clear outline and be ruthless in deleting any ideas, no matter how interesting, which do not advance your main point. As you construct and revise your outline, there are several issues peculiar to oral presentations that you should keep in mind.

**Time limits**  Working carefully within the time constraints is the key to planning an effective seminar presentation. If the professor has allotted a definite time period, perhaps a half hour, to each presentation, you will probably have to stop when your allotted time is up, whether or not you have covered the material you planned to discuss. In my experience, some students do not take time limits seriously and thus make unrealistic plans to cover more than it is possible to discuss in the allotted time. What happens, of course, is that they are cut off when the time elapses, and the presentation, lopped off in the middle, is not a great success. The first time you prepare for an oral presentation, it may be difficult to estimate how much time each point will take and to put together a realistic plan. If you are not sure about your timing, ask one or two fellow-students whose judgment you trust to act as the audience for a rehearsal. Not only will you get a better sense of pace and timing; they can also tell you whether your presentation is clear, logically organized, and easy to follow, and whether some sections need more work.

**Recorded examples**   You may want to use recorded musical examples as illustrations. Because of the time limits, you need to be very selective about recorded examples; choose brief excerpts that clearly support what you are saying. A seminar presentation is not the appropriate time for an extensive survey of a composer's greatest hits. I remember vividly a presentation in a graduate seminar years ago; the student, unable to choose between excerpts, told us at the beginning of the presentation that he had forty-five minutes of recorded excerpts that he planned to play—during his one-hour presentation. Naturally, he was not able to finish his presentation. After he covered part of his planned outline, the presentation trailed off weakly with a summary of what he would have covered had there been enough time. He sulked for the rest of the semester, angry with me for enforcing the time limits, while his colleagues managed to fit their presentations into the time allotted.

Recorded excerpts must be chosen very carefully and timed exactly. Although compact discs allow you to locate exact starting and stopping points, it may be more convenient to rerecord your excerpts on a new disc. Everything must be carefully planned if you want to take full advantage of your limited time; you don't want to waste precious time and try the patience of your colleagues by fumbling around trying to find the excerpt you want. The time and effort you devote to preparing your musical examples will ensure that your presentation moves along briskly and creates a professional and convincing impression.

**Writing every word versus speaking from an outline**   As you edit and fine-tune your outline, you will need to decide whether you plan to speak from a detailed outline or write out every word and then read your text. If the instructor insists on your reading a fully written-out text, then of course you must. If the choice is up to you, consider the advantages and disadvantages of both strategies. Writing out the full text has the obvious advantage of ensuring that you will not have to fumble for the next word or idea. The disadvantage is that reading a paper is not the same thing as speaking to a group, and listening to someone read a paper can be deadly. Although some people can turn reading a paper into a lively experience for the hearer,

I generally encourage students to work from a detailed outline. The advantage is that your words are more direct and spontaneous. Since no one but you will ever see either your outline or your text, you can devote more time to refining your outline and preparing your recorded examples and spend a little less time editing a written text. If you decide to speak from an outline, it should be very detailed, so that you know exactly where you are going and how you plan to get there. In particular, you must know in advance exactly how you plan to begin and how you want to end. It may be advisable to write out your introduction and conclusion, so that you get under way smoothly and wrap up the presentation with a strong conclusion rather than trailing off weakly with something like "Well—that's about all I have to say." In your notes, you must also have all direct quotes written out or detailed directions to find them, including book titles and page numbers. The same is true for examples or illustrations. It is deadly to sit through a long pause while the presenter pages through a book to find a passage or an illustration he or she wants to share with the group.

**Preparing a handout**   As you fine-tune your outline, deciding exactly what you want to cover and how you plan to proceed, consider assembling a handout of three or four pages to distribute to the class. There are several advantages to handouts. First, some kinds of information—bibliographic notes, a list of the composer's works, or an outline of the main events of a person's life—are much easier for your audience to read off a page than pick up by ear. Besides, it is useful for the listeners to have a short bibliography for their files, should they wish to review the presentation or return to the topic at some time in the future.

You might also consider including in your handout a carefully chosen musical example or two. If all members of the class have the same measures of music in front of them, you can discuss specific details of musical style that would be difficult to make clear by your words alone. As you put the handout together, you can mark the pages of music to draw attention to the details you plan to discuss.

Some students go to extremes in preparing handouts, as if the grade for the presentation were determined by the size, weight, and cost of the handout. I have seen handouts of twenty or thirty pages, filled with elaborate illustrations photocopied from books and page after page of photocopied score. Producing an impressive handout is not the same as preparing an effective presentation; in fact, if all your time goes into gathering materials, the presentation itself will be ill-prepared and ineffective. It is costly and probably illegal to make multiple copies of large sections of scores or movements. Be as selective with musical examples as you are with recorded examples; you can probably illustrate any point you wish to make by including a few short musical examples or by creating your own diagrams or graphics to illustrate large-scale organization or structure. At the other extreme, some students distribute handouts that are not very helpful—perhaps a hastily assembled bibliography in need of editing and proofreading. Anything you distribute with your name on it should be put together and edited with the same care you would use on a research paper.

There are other ways besides handouts to provide scores for the class; one alternative is to bring multiple copies of the appropriate scores. If you choose this method, think carefully about the logistics and keep the time constraints in mind. If the scores are different editions with different page numbers, or if some students will be reading piano-vocal scores and others orchestral scores, the members of the class may spend all their time trying to figure out where they are supposed to be in the scores. If your plan calls for the group to look at several short examples from different collections, the presentation can turn into a complicated and distracting exercise in circulating and collecting scores, and no one will hear what you have to say. Once an important point is made clear through close reading of one selected score example, it may be better to listen to other recorded examples rather than try to provide a score for each recorded example. After all, music majors should be able to listen analytically and make stylistic judgments by ear, particularly after their attention has been drawn to the point you are trying to illustrate. Difficult choices have to be made, just as they do in a paper; every example, whether it is a page from a score, a diagram, or a recorded example, must clearly support the point you are trying to make.

Once you have your outline, your plans for the handout, and your recorded examples clearly in mind, if you still have doubts about whether your plan is realistic, you may want to consult your instructor for a preliminary reaction, particularly if your presentation is scheduled first; the person in this position is at an obvious disadvantage. Your instructor can tell you whether your plans seem realistic and whether it is likely that you can accomplish what you intend to accomplish in the time allotted.

**Multimedia presentations**   Students who have the ability and equipment to produce multimedia presentations should consider using multimedia tools to enhance their presentations. At the simplest level, one might show a few slides of helpful illustrations. Other students might want to experiment with PowerPoint presentations incorporating audio and video clips. Working out an impressive presentation, however, should not occupy all your time and effort; the multimedia resources should be used only to enhance solid research and careful organization of the material.

### Tone and Approach

Finally, as you prepare your outline, handout, and examples, and as the time for your presentation gets closer, think about the impression you want to create. Imagine yourself standing in front of the group, and think about your own experience sitting in class over the years; you know exactly what sort of approach appeals to you as well as those that annoy you or put you to sleep. Audiences generally come to a lecture or presentation with an interest in the topic and a willingness to listen. As long as speakers appear to know what they are talking about, are well prepared, and are enthusiastic about communicating their insights, people will listen. Their willingness to listen will last through the whole presentation unless the speaker interferes with that interest by fumbling around, appearing nervous or unprepared, or not knowing what is coming next. To hold the attention of a class, one need not be a superb public speaker. Think about your favorite professors over the years. I would bet that the good ones stand out in your mind because they knew and loved the material they taught and communicated it clearly and effectively, not necessarily because they were great orators. As you know from your own experience, students cannot tolerate having their time wasted by anyone, faculty or student, who is not prepared or does not seem to care whether anyone is listening or what comes next.

The impression you want to create is that you know what you are doing, you are interested in your topic, you have spent considerable time in research, and you will move crisply through your outline. Walk up to the front of the room the way you walk out on stage for a performance, looking as assured as you can, not as if you were heading to the dentist for root canal work or to the IRS office to have your tax return audited. You should assume that the audience is interested in your topic and make clear by your look and behavior that you will not waste their time. Think of yourself as a competent professional; you stand before your colleagues not as a preacher exhorting them to some action, or as an entertainer trying to amuse them. You are there as a researcher reporting on the insights and knowledge you have gained, sharing your vision of some specific musical works or historical developments with them. If you have done the necessary research and planned your presentation carefully and you present yourself in this way, the experience will be a satisfying one, both for you and for your audience.

## CONCERT REPORTS

Another type of assignment that involves writing about music is the concert report. Although professors who assign reports generally make clear exactly what they expect the student to do, there are a few useful generalizations we can make about this kind of assignment.

### Purpose

While each instructor may have particular goals in assigning concert reports, most view these reports as extensions of the classroom discussions.

Concert reports are an example of what psychologists call second-order learning—applying newly acquired conceptual information and understanding to new experiences. It is one thing to absorb what an instructor says in class and be able to repeat it in an examination; it is another thing altogether to be able to use the insights discussed in class to understand and appreciate new musical experiences.

The focus of a concert report should therefore be on the music and musical style. Too many concert reports, either by students in Music Appreciation classes or by music majors, waste a great deal of time discussing issues that have nothing to do with music—descriptions of the hall, the audience, what the performers were wearing, or the writer's evaluation of the quality of the performance. A concert report is different from music criticism, which is a form of journalism. Although questions of performance practice may be relevant to your discussion of musical style, discussion of the quality of the performance can too easily degenerate into negative criticism of the playing or comments about problems of ensemble coordination, intonation, and the like. I have even read concert reports that opened with complaints about how hard it was to find the concert venue or a place to park. My response is "Get over it, and tell me about the music."

What instructors want to see in concert reports is discussion of the music that was performed, especially if the student can connect it with pieces and issues discussed in class. Classes studying early music, for example, are frequently asked to attend concerts of music composed before 1750 and discuss what they hear in terms of the stylistic developments discussed in class. Comparisons to specific works discussed in class are always welcome. Discussion of performance practice issues is also welcome; instructors expect that the students will apply the information they have learned in class to future musical experiences. If the report is an assignment in a Music Appreciation class, students should discuss the music they heard in terms of their newly acquired knowledge about the elements of music—rhythm, texture, color, harmony, and so forth.

### Research

It sometimes surprises students to find out that they might have to do some research before attending a concert and writing a report on it. Listeners who attend a concert already armed with an understanding of the history, background, and style or structure of a particular work will be in a much better position to discuss the work from a stylistic viewpoint and to judge whether the performance was stylistically valid. Lack of preparation or lack of understanding of what a work is about sometimes leads students to resort to repeating the commentary printed in the program notes or discussing irrelevant questions such as the appearance, size, or behavior of the audience. We should add that copying the printed program notes instead of writing about your own ideas and reactions is an example of plagiarism, and probably copyright infringement as well. If discovered, this behavior could result in a failing grade for the course and a hearing before the committee on student conduct.

### Writing the Report

Students often wonder how to begin writing a concert report. The opening paragraphs should provide the basic information about the concert—who, what, where, when. Who were the performers—a professional orchestra, a student ensemble, a chamber group, a soloist? Did the group include unusual instruments or the standard ones for that type of ensemble? Which works were performed? After providing that basic information, decide which works you want to discuss in detail—perhaps the pieces that relate most closely to the class or the ones you found most interesting. It may be possible to focus most of your attention on one work, the one closest to the material of recent class discussions, and summarize the rest of the concert in a sentence or two. In discussing the music, use the analytic categories and the technical vocabulary that you use in class. Obviously, one expects more technical detail about issues such as structure, harmony, and orchestration from music majors than from nonmajors, but both groups should be able to use what they are learning in class in their discussions of the concerts they attend. Music majors might approach their discussion from the point of view of comparing their expectations before the concert to what they actually heard. Were there surprising or unique elements in any of the pieces, or did they stay fairly close to what the informed listener would expect? Did the live performance help to underline some things about the music that one would not be able to observe in the same way from a recording? Preparation, sensitive listening, and imagination will lead you to choose the best direction for your discussion.

The main topic to keep in the forefront of your mind as you draft your concert report is always musical style. If you focus on stylistic issues, you are demonstrating to your instructor that you have thought about class discussions and that you can handle stylistic questions competently and intelligently. An informed, focused, and thoughtful report that grapples with musical issues will be a success.

Finally, a word of caution. Students, particularly those who are not music majors, do not always realize that putting on a recital or concert is a complicated enterprise and that problems can arise at the last minute. Performers get sick, a difficult piece just doesn't come together in time, the performers decide at the last minute that changing the order of the pieces on the program would make a more unified or more logically organized performance, and so forth. Even professional recitals and concerts make changes at the last minute; pieces are substituted, the order is changed, or the artists perform an encore or two after the official program is over. Since the printed program has to be produced in advance, it may not represent exactly what was actually played at the performance. You can see where this is going; students sometimes pick up a program at the door, assume it will be followed exactly, and then go home to write up their concert reports without staying to hear the concert. It is not even safe to leave at intermission; changes can happen in the second half. I have read glowing accounts of performances that never happened because the pieces were cancelled or changed at the last minute. Even if your instructor or teaching assistant does not attend the concert, other students who stayed for the concert will report on the changes in the program, and what you thought was a slick way to save time can leave you in serious trouble. Go to the concert or recital, listen carefully, take some notes, and report on what you actually heard and how it relates to material discussed in class.

## PROGRAM NOTES

At some point during your life as a student or later in the professional world, you will probably be asked to write program notes for a recital or a concert. Program notes present a special challenge to the writer because of their special purpose and because of the severe space limitations that are usually imposed.

### Purpose

Program notes are different from research papers. Papers are written to demonstrate competence as a researcher and scholar and therefore must include the standard scholarly apparatus of footnotes and bibliography. The purpose of program notes, on the other hand, is not primarily scholarship, although whatever you write must be based on solid research and analysis. The purpose of program notes is to increase the audience members' understanding of the music to be performed and therefore their enjoyment of the concert. If listeners have the opportunity in advance to learn something about the background of the piece, its special purpose, or the ways in which it is unique, they have something specific to listen for and are less likely to sit passively, letting the music wash over them. Intelligent listeners appreciate informative, well-written program notes.

### Who Is the Audience?

It is often difficult to gauge the background and knowledge an audience brings to a concert; it is therefore difficult to estimate the level of technical knowledge you can assume in your writing. You should avoid overly technical analysis that will make no sense to the majority of the audience. Conversely, the program notes should not insult the audience's intelligence by assuming that they know nothing at all about music. Obviously, people who devote their valuable time and money to attending concerts already have an interest in music. Most members of concert audiences collect classical recordings and have a fair general knowledge of the history of music. Write for an imaginary nonmusician who is interested in music and is fairly well read. If the program consists of standard works, your imaginary reader probably already knows something about them and probably has heard other live or recorded performances of these pieces. This listener still appreciates being reminded, or told for the first time, about the special circumstances surrounding the composition of a particular work, the composer's intent, and what makes the work unique.

The question of writing for a particular audience can be particularly troublesome when you are writing notes for a recital presented as part of your work toward a degree. The audience will probably include relatives and friends who are there because they are proud of you, not because they have any special interest in the pieces you will sing or play; teachers, who will judge the recital on technical grounds; and your student colleagues, who will bring their special knowledge and background to the experience. In that situation, I would not write for either your relatives or your teachers, but for your colleagues, somewhere in the middle between the two extremes. In such situations, try to write at a more technical level than would be appropriate for a general concert audience, while avoiding the other extreme of assuming that everyone knows the music as intimately as you and your teacher do.

### Research

Approach the research for program notes in the same way you approach research for a paper, using the same resources and methodology, beginning with the standard resources. It may seem strange to pursue the same sort of research to write a few short paragraphs of program notes as you would for a twenty-page paper, but whatever you write in program notes, no matter how brief, must be based on a thorough understanding of the music, as well as awareness of the background of the work, where it fits in the composer's output, and the composer's intent. In writing program notes, one rarely uses all the information uncovered in one's research, but it is a serious mistake to simply toss off a few casual comments. If you are going to perform the work you are writing about, you have probably analyzed it already, but you may need information on the background of the work, the composer's intent, and so forth. When you do not already know the work thoroughly, that must be the first step in your research—no one should ever write about a musical work without studying the score and hearing a recording, if possible.

The audience may not realize that the few paragraphs they read are based on hours of careful research, but each sentence you write must be based on thorough knowledge. The world does not need any more vague, fanciful, or flowery program notes; quite enough of that sort of prose has been written already. The process of researching musical topics is explained in Chapter 3.

### Working within Limits

The main constraint on program notes is always limited space. If you are told that there is room in the program for 500 words, you must stay within that limit. If you go over the word limit, you cause endless problems for the people who are printing the program. If there is time, they might ask you to shorten your prose, or they might do it themselves; they might even leave out the notes altogether. If your limit is 500 words, then everything you say must fit on somewhat less than two pages of double-spaced type-script with normal margins. Every word you write must be carefully chosen. Space limitations are not always that severe, but the writer must always stay within whatever limit is imposed.

In some ways it is more difficult to discuss a piece of music in a paragraph or two than to write a twenty-page paper about it. In a paper, one has the leisure to develop ideas at some length, cite long quotations, and include extended analytical discussions. There is no room in program notes for footnotes; quotations must be brief and be chosen with great care. It can be very helpful to quote a composer's words about what he had in mind for a particular work, but all quotations must be short and effective. One usually cannot include musical examples, and extended analyses are impossible because of the space limitations. The writer hopes to draw the listener's attention to something interesting or unique about a particular work; frequently, that is all one can accomplish. Program notes are not research papers, but neither are they collections of vague sentiments about music in general or about a particular composer. Through a kind of sleight of hand, the writer tries to convey an understanding of a particular work in a few well-chosen words.

As you can see, it is a challenging task to write effective program notes. Sometimes, in an attempt to meet a deadline, one is tempted to simply copy or paraphrase material from published collections of program notes or from the notes that come with a recording. Needless to say, such copying constitutes plagiarism, an illegal act in both the academic world and the publishing world, and a serious mistake, just as it would be in a paper. Some published notes and record jackets are written in a flowery style that would be difficult to pass off as your own work, and some have little worthwhile to say about the music. It is clearly better to do your own research, study the music, and try to communicate your insight in a clear and informative manner in the short space allotted to you.

### Special Problems

Some kinds of concerts present special challenges for the writer of program notes. The following brief comments offer general guidelines for writing program notes in these special situations.

**Early music**    The music of the medieval, Renaissance, and Baroque periods was usually written to be performed in a context far different from today's concert hall. Early music, at least that portion that was written down, was generally performed either in church or in court. Composers and performers worked for the church or the aristocracy and succeeded as long as they continued to provide the kind of music that would satisfy their powerful patrons.

It is often helpful for the audience to be reminded of the special circumstances for which a work was written. Think, for example, of the pieces discussed in Chapter 2. Listeners would be better prepared to appreciate a performance of Dufay's "Nuper rosarum flores" if they understood that Dufay was trying to model his musical structures on the architectural proportions of the new dome. Even if a listener cannot hear the mathematical relationships between the two slow-moving lines, it is helpful to know what the composer was trying to do. At a concert performance of a Bach cantata, the audience should understand that the cantatas were not written as concert pieces, but as part of the long Sunday morning service of the German Lutheran church, a way to illuminate the message of that particular day's Gospel reading.

There are other historical questions that may deserve comment. In the Middle Ages and the Renaissance, and often in the Baroque and Classic periods, composer and performer were the same person, not two different specialists. Music was often written for instruments and vocal groups different from the ones that usually perform the music now. In addition, most early music was written in shorthand form; performers learn to reconstruct the musical details rather than follow complete directions set down by the composer. The audience should understand these historical differences in the fundamental relationship between composer and performer, and should be aware of the decisions for which the performers are responsible, as well as the circumstances for which the music was originally written. If modern instruments are substituted for the instruments that the composer intended, that fact should be noted. One need not construct an elaborate defense of the practice, but neither should the writer pretend that the composer wrote these works for modern instruments. If pianists want to perform Bach on twelve-foot Steinways, they have a perfect right to do so, provided they understand something of Baroque style, but the listener should be aware that Bach wrote for a different instrument altogether, and that using modern instruments may alter the sound the composer had in mind. If large choruses choose to perform sixteenth-century madrigals, listeners should be aware that these pieces were written for chamber vocal groups with one voice on each part and performed in much more intimate venues than the modern concert hall. Whatever the writer can convey about the original purpose and sound of the music will help the audience appreciate the performance better and will equip them to make an intelligent judgment about the success of the performers' reconstructive work.

**Transcriptions, arrangements, and editions**    An allied issue is the question of the relationship between what the performers play and what the composer actually wrote. To appreciate the performance, the listener should be told something of the history of a work. If a clavier concerto by Bach, for example, is a transcription of a violin concerto by Vivaldi, the notes should certainly mention that fact. If the score used in a performance is a modern transcription or arrangement of an earlier work, that fact should also be noted. Another example from the music of Bach comes to mind. Cellists enjoy performing the so-called gamba sonatas of Bach; these works, however, were transcribed by Bach for solo gamba and harpsichord with an obbligato right-hand part from earlier trio sonatas written for two treble instruments and continuo, in which the harpsichord part consists of a figured bass line. Again, this information is interesting to the intelligent listener. In the same way, modern editions or restorations of the original versions of works from the Romantic period, or from any period, should be noted. Reminding an audience that, for example, they are about to hear the chamber orchestra version of Copland's *Appalachian Spring* should focus their listening and make them think about the differences between that version and the familiar version for full orchestra. The audience certainly wants to know whether what they hear is the original work, a version "corrected" by an editor, or a modern reconstruction of the original version.

**Recent music**    World premieres and recently composed music can pose problems for the writer of program notes. The usual research resources are of limited use; lexicons and books on twentieth-century music may contain useful information about the composer and his or her place in contemporary music, but not about recently composed works. If you are writing the notes for your own performance, you can work from your knowledge of the score; if not, it may be difficult to gain access to a score. In that case, you may have to contact the composer or another knowledgeable person—a performer or concert presenter who knows the work—by mail or in person. Some composers are very helpful in explaining the genesis and the structure of their works; others dislike discussing their creations, prefer to let their music speak for them, and if pressed for comments, embark on disquisitions about Eastern philosophy, higher mathematics, or antiwar sentiments. Still, the diligent investigator can usually find out something of what the composer had in mind and where the work fits in the evolution of musical styles. Any information of this sort is helpful to the listener, who then is saved from the danger of judging the work against the wrong set of expectations. The composer's ideas may or may not be audible in the performance, but at least the listener knows what to listen for and can judge the work on the grounds of whether it communicates what the composer had in mind.

**Familiar repertory**   The writer faces the opposite problem when writing program notes about works everyone knows, such as the Beethoven symphonies or some of the better-known late Romantic works. One feels tongue-tied and a bit foolish when trying to write about these works; what can there be left to say about the "Eroica," for example, or the Chopin preludes? The way to approach this situation is exactly the way one approaches any writing about music—research. One can always discuss issues such as the background of the work, the composer's intent, the structure of the work, or the qualities that make it unique. Since vast amounts of commentary have been written about the better-known composers and their works, it is certainly easy to find material. Published letters of composers may contain information about what the composer thought of the work, the circumstances of the first performance, and the reaction of the audience and the critics. It is easy to find the writings of well-known composers; a carefully chosen quotation may give the reader a new slant on a familiar work.

### Texts and Translations

One final issue that should be discussed is the question of providing texts and translations of vocal music. In general, the listener should always be provided with the text, whether the singers will be singing in English or in a foreign language. If the performance will be in a foreign language, listeners should have at hand both the foreign text and an English translation, so that they can follow the text as it is performed and can consult the translation in case they do not read the foreign language with facility.

The principle is clear enough, but some situations present special problems. If a text is extremely long or if there are a large number of texts, as in a *Lieder* recital, reprinting texts and translations may take a large amount of space. In that case, a separate insert containing the texts and translations can be added to the program. Some texts are familiar to most listeners; if a choral group is performing a Renaissance setting of the Ordinary of the Mass, for example, most members of the audience will know the familiar liturgical texts and what they mean in English. Even in that case, however, programs frequently contain both text and translation. If you have a choice, always choose the most literal translation, rather than the most beautiful English version; when the translation stays close to the original word order, the members of the audience are in a better position to judge the aptness of the musical setting to the individual words of text. If the translator's name is known, it should always be included with the translation. Remember also that it is illegal to reprint a published translation without dealing with copyright issues and permissions. Finally, when you have gone to the trouble of providing texts and translations, make sure there is enough light in the hall during the performance for the audience to read them. It makes little sense to provide texts and then turn the house lights down until the hall is too dark for reading.

### Conclusion

Writing program notes can be a daunting challenge because of the severe space limitations and the special problems posed by some kinds of repertory. Informative and carefully written program notes, however, are welcomed by interested audience members and can add greatly to the listening experience and therefore the success of the concert.

## ESSAY EXAMINATIONS

There is another type of writing about music that is very much part of your life as a student—answering essay questions about music in examinations. As you can imagine, reading a large number of essay questions can be a daunting task; few people can produce effective prose under the pressure surrounding an examination. Answers usually vary enormously in quality, from unorganized facts scrawled in incomplete and awkward sentences to the occasional well-organized and convincing essay. Knowing how to approach essay questions can materially affect your examination grades and therefore your academic success. This section will discuss the purpose of essay questions, how to prepare for them, the steps to follow in writing a successful essay as part of an examination, and some common errors.

### Purpose

Professors do not include essay questions in their examinations just to be cruel or because they have a compulsion to read stacks of student prose. Essay questions are important because they are the only way students can demonstrate their grasp of important material, and because they call for insight, understanding, and the ability to synthesize large amounts of information and focus on what is most significant. After all, neither art nor life is multiple-choice. For a professor to ask only objective or short-answer questions is to do an injustice to the material covered, since the history of music is much more than a series of unrelated factoids. Essay questions are the only way to test the student's grasp of the big picture, as well as important trends and connections.

### Preparing for Essay Examinations

One of the advantages of essay questions, from the instructor's point of view, is that preparing for them can give shape and coherence to the process of reviewing the material. Studying for the examination thus becomes an important and useful part of the learning experience, not simply an exercise in memorizing facts.

There are several steps involved in preparing for essay questions. First, find out in advance whether there will be essay questions on the examination, and if so, how many there are likely to be. When you find out that there will be essay questions, make a list of those areas that you think are particularly important—the material that was given special emphasis by the instructor. If you pick out four or five areas that you think are obvious choices for essay questions, you can be fairly sure that some of those questions will appear in some form on the examination. You have survived examinations before, and you know how they work. Professors naturally give special emphasis to those areas they think are particularly important, and they know it would be pointless to ask essay questions about side issues or unimportant details. Assume that your professor is a reasonable and logical person even when making up examination questions. If you go over your notes with an eye to what the professor emphasized, you can predict what the questions will be and plan your answers. You can even design outlines for the answers to the questions you think are most likely to appear so that your answers will be logical, coherent, and organized. If you go about preparing in the right way, there is no reason why you should be surprised or taken unawares by the questions your professor chooses. It seems so simple; when there is a perfectly legal way to find out about the examination questions in advance, one wonders why more students are not better prepared for essay questions.

### How to Proceed

Once you are actually writing the examination, when you get to an essay question the main trick is to pause and think before you start writing. That is not easy to do; students usually approach examinations in a state of high anxiety, their minds crammed with recently reviewed facts, pencils poised to write as much as possible as quickly as possible before all the information flies out of their heads. Working quickly and impulsively is usually not a bad strategy, particularly when dealing with objective questions, but it is not the way to answer essay questions.

The first thing to do is to read the question a second time to be sure you understand it. Ask the instructor if you are not sure what the question means. Look for key words. Does the question ask you to *outline* the important stages in the evolution of a particular style, to *discuss* a particular work or a particular artistic movement, or to *compare and contrast* two works, styles, or composers? There are only a few kinds of essay questions, and professors try very hard to frame their questions as clearly as possible. Pause and think about the question. Does the question set limits? What is included? What is not? Are there terms that need to be defined as the first step?

The next step is to outline your answer and tinker with the outline for a while. Maybe your answer would make better sense if you changed the order of ideas, or perhaps there is something in your outline that you feel prepared to discuss but does not really fit with the question. Accept the fact that you may not get a chance to demonstrate every little bit of your recently acquired knowledge. It is better to answer the question briefly and stay on the point than to write three pages of brilliant prose about some other topic.

After you are satisfied that your outline adequately covers the area specified by the question and that you have not left out anything important or included something irrelevant, then start writing your answer. If there is time, write a rough draft and edit it before you copy your final version. Stay on the point, and force yourself to follow your outline. Avoid the tendency to spew out unrelated facts, and do your best to produce a piece of writing that flows logically and coherently. Finally, assuming there is still time, edit and proofread your answer, make sure it is legible, and delete anything that is ungrammatical, incoherent, or not relevant to the question. Remember that your aim is to demonstrate understanding, insight, and the ability to organize information, not to produce a long string of unrelated facts. Remember also that your professor will have to read a large stack of examinations. After a few hours of grading papers, imagine what a pleasure it is to encounter a clearly organized, carefully written essay. Even if two essays contained the same information, the one that is a coherent and careful piece of writing will be more successful than a rambling, disorganized scrawl. The trick is to organize the information, not just regurgitate it.

### Common Errors

The common mistakes that students make when writing essay examinations are easily avoidable. The main mistake is not reading the question and the instructions carefully. Some students pounce on a key word that triggers a flood of facts, without first asking which facts are relevant. If the question, for example, asks you to compare and contrast impressionism and neoclassicism in the twentieth century, some students see the word "impressionism" and launch into a description of Debussy's life and career, without stopping to realize that that is not what the question is about. Focus on exactly what the question asks for. If the question is "Trace the evolution of the motet from Notre Dame polyphony through the French Ars Nova," do not write about the English school, no matter how thoroughly you have reviewed Dunstable's motets. If the question is "Discuss *The Rake's Progress* as an example of Stravinsky's neoclassical style," do not ramble on about the Octet for Winds, even if you have performed it and know it much better than *The Rake*. Even if you are convinced that the octet is a better example of neoclassicism than the opera, you still have to write about *The Rake's Progress*. Although it seems obvious that the key to success is to answer the question posed by the instructor rather than writing on a topic you like better, time and again students wander off into areas specifically excluded by the professor's carefully written questions.

Another mistake in writing essay questions is to spew out an unorganized jumble of facts more or less related to the question, rather than a thoughtful, coherent essay. Many students seem to think that their task is to write everything they can think of, a sort of stew filled with chunks of unrelated information, leaving it to the instructor to pick out whatever he or she wants. All the important facts are in there somewhere, if the instructor is willing to dredge for them and does not care about the order in which things appear. When asked to compare and contrast two different schools or styles, for example, some students write two separate, detailed descriptions of the two styles, never directly addressing the question of the ways in which they are similar or different. That approach is surprisingly common; it may be a result of the overemphasis on isolated facts in some music history books, as well as in our educational system in general. Some blame this tendency on the television age, with its emphasis on sound bites and short bursts of information, or on the nervousness with which students approach examinations. Never underestimate the importance of logical organization and coherence. If you read the question carefully, stay on the point, and try to write decent prose, you will succeed—it's that simple—provided, of course, that you have something to say.

Another common error is careless use of technical terms. In their haste, students sometimes mix up important technical terms and thus make it hard for the reader to know what they are trying to say. An examination is not the place to throw around technical terms loosely; a mistake like that can ruin what otherwise might be a fine answer. Chapter 8 has a section on proper use of technical terms; review that section with the examination situation in mind.

The last common error is failing to proofread and edit your essay. Your professor has no way of knowing how well you have answered the question if your answer is not legible. See that your comments can be read, correct as many misspellings and grammatical errors as you can in the remaining time, copy the essay over if it needs it, and make the essay look as competent and professional as you can, granting the pressures of the examination situation.

To summarize, remember that the object of essay questions is not to produce a knee-jerk, reflex response or isolated bits of information, but to demonstrate your mastery of the topic and your ability to select the most significant events and trends relevant to the question and organize your ideas in a thoughtful and convincing fashion. Essay questions are a test of understanding and insight, not a test of whether you have memorized an impressive list of bits of information. Logic, coherence, and clear writing will be much more successful than several pages of hastily scrawled facts.

## CONCLUSION

Besides the projects discussed above, there are other kinds of writing projects that challenge music students. The lecture-recital, for instance, is an especially daunting challenge, combining a kind of seminar presentation with a public performance. Lecture-recitals are not discussed in this chapter because they are seldom required of undergraduate majors. However, you can imagine what the lecture part of the event would require—extensive research, careful writing and editing, and consideration of materials such as slides or handouts to help present your ideas effectively.

As you reflect on the different kinds of projects discussed in this chapter, note that, as different as the challenges of these various activities are, there are important common elements in writing a paper, giving a seminar presentation, writing a concert report, writing program notes, or writing an essay in an examination. Two basic concepts will guide you successfully through any of these challenges. The first is research. No one, whoever the writer is and whatever the context is, should ever write or speak about music without being solidly grounded in creative and thorough research. Even a fifteen-minute presentation or brief program notes should be based on solid research. The second requirement in all these situations is a professional attitude toward preparing and presenting your ideas.

# CHAPTER 7

# Writing Style

Chapters 7 and 8 discuss basic ideas about writing effective prose. Since most students passed a writing course early in their college careers, much of this material will probably serve as a review rather than new information. Many books on writing treat these matters in much more detail; this section is a brief guide, included here for your convenience. Although much of this discussion applies to any expository writing, we will also discuss issues that arise in papers on musical topics. This chapter reviews some general principles and details of effective writing style; Chapter 8 discusses common writing problems that detract from the effectiveness of student papers.

## SOME BASIC IDEAS ABOUT WRITING

After reading hundreds of student papers as well as producing various kinds of writing myself, including textbooks, articles for scholarly journals, and program notes, I have become convinced of some basic truths about writing.

1. *Effective writing is a learned skill, not an inborn talent.* It is frustrating to hear students say "I don't write very well," or "I've always been a poor speller," with a shrug, as if this lack of skill were an endearing imperfection over which they had no control. The ability to spell correctly or write well is not genetic; it is a skill we learn and refine through years of effort. Writing convincing, effective prose is hard work; there is no particular mystique about it, and it is not a kind of magical power conferred on a few lucky persons. Anyone willing to work at it can learn to write clearly and forcefully.

2. *We all can improve our writing skills.* Assuming that you have the basic skills for writing English prose, you do not need special courses, tutors, or technical training to hone these skills. Naturally, if English is your second language and you have difficulty speaking and writing it correctly, you may

need the help of special courses and tutors. Most students have some writing skills; what they need is to improve them. We all can improve our writing; even prominent scholars and writers sometimes produce prose that is less than perfect, and much of the material we read each day could be improved by further revising and editing. Good writers work harder than you might imagine to make the words say exactly what they want to say, and they constantly strive to improve their writing style. Read about Ernest Hemingway and the way he worked. He is famous for editing and cutting his drafts ruthlessly, until the final version was one-fourth the size of his original draft, or less, and the prose was finally distilled down to the lean, direct style that is the hallmark of his writing.

3. *Music students should think of their papers as a kind of performance and try to attain the same professional standard in their writing as they do in their performances.* If you want to be taken seriously as a student and you expect your ideas and insights to be taken seriously, you must learn how to communicate them effectively in a carefully written and edited paper. I am amazed that the same students who present themselves as consummate professionals in their performances sometimes tolerate low standards in their academic work. Imagine what their recitals would be like if they prepared and presented them with the same casual attitude with which they sometimes approach their written assignments. Performers dressed in shorts and T-shirts would wander on to the stage a half-hour late, stumble through a slapdash performance, and then feign shock when their teachers disapproved. Recitals like that don't happen, because musicians understand the high standards expected in performance. Extend that same concept of high professional standards to your written work.

4. *There are different types of writing, each with its own standards and rules.* What might be perfectly appropriate in poetry, fiction, or personal letters may not be suitable in a research paper. For example, there is a memorable line in a love poem by e. e. cummings (he insists on the lowercase initials): "If a look should April me ..." He turns the name of a month that calls up associations with spring, melting snow, soft rains, and new life into a verb, a wonderfully expressive poetic device, an example of the creativity and striking language that we expect of poets. That same creative approach, however, would be out of place in a research paper. Research papers are an example of expository prose, as opposed to poetry or fiction, and the overriding goal of expository prose is clarity and persuasiveness, not the startling and allusive use of language that creates poetry. Expository prose is not as demanding an art as poetry is; not everyone is a poet, but anyone can learn to write expository prose.

5. *There are specific steps you can take to improve your writing.* First, read. Read all sorts of writing—novels, mysteries, short stories, essays, history, biography. Don't confine your reading to what you have to read for class;

turn off the television and the computer and read for pleasure when you have a spare moment. Read critically, with an eye to appreciating good style. Second, write. The only way to learn how to write better is to write and rewrite. Write a draft, then revise, edit, cut, polish, get critical opinions from reliable critics, and continue rewriting. There are no shortcuts to producing a first-quality paper, any more than there are shortcuts to a fine performance.

## DIFFERENT KINDS OF PROSE

Expository prose is different from much of the writing we see each day, because it is designed to inform and explain. Other kinds of writing have different purposes. Advertising copy, for example, is often designed not so much to convey information as to surround the product with an aura of pleasant associations; the prose often speaks to our emotions rather than to our minds. Think about the way cars are advertised on television. Many ads hardly mention equipment, horsepower, or safety features. Instead, the words and pictures are designed to make us feel good about the car and convince us that we would feel better about ourselves if we only owned that car. Note that the people in automobile ads never use their shiny cars to drop off the kids at school, return a video, or run to the grocery store. They sometimes drive on city streets, but the streets are remarkably empty and there are lots of empty parking spaces. These cars never get near crowded freeways. They are usually speeding along scenic, empty roads in the Colorado Rockies or through a picturesque desert in New Mexico. The ads don't highlight facts; they promise freedom and the wind in your hair. Look at the men in most beer ads. They are not accountants or salesmen or algebra teachers, and certainly not music students; they are always deep-sea fishermen, steelworkers, or construction workers, real he-men who go for the gusto and like their pleasures big and brawny. The implication is that we would be like them if only we drank the right beer. The ads are about feelings, not facts.

Just as advertising prose is designed to create appealing associations around a product, prose can be written to mask or sanitize unpleasant ideas, through what is called *euphemism*. Politicians speak of "revenue enhancement strategies" instead of "raising taxes," trying to hide the real meaning from suspicious voters. Politicians refer to social programs run by religious organizations as "faith-based programs," avoiding the word "church," trying to forestall any outcry about the separation of church and state. The military is expert at creating euphemisms; "friendly fire" and "collateral damage" are bizarre examples of neutral, pleasant-sounding terms for ugly realities. Similarly, a person looking for a home quickly learns how to translate the special language of real estate ads. "Needs a little love" means that it will take $30,000 in repairs to keep the place standing for a few more years, and "cute" usually means the space is unbelievably tiny.

Frequently, prose is designed to make the writer look important rather than to explain ideas. A network chief recently was quoted discussing the idea of making the network's shows accessible on different media: "The issue is how do we get that content before new eyeballs on new platforms with money attached to it." We understand the idea, but why is the language so crude? Why "eyeballs" instead of "people" or "viewers"? I suspect that this language is intended to convey that the speaker, despite his astronomical salary and lavish perks, is really just a regular guy. Perhaps for the same reason, the world of business seems overly fond of sports jargon. Numbers are "ballpark figures," not "approximate estimates," and other sports terms are used constantly—"slam dunk," "full-court press," "third and long," "step up to the plate," "home run."

While businesspeople act tough by using the language of professional sports, educators like to show off their business sense by adopting the jargon of the business world. University administrators now say things like "using our Web site to build brand recognition," "selling our program in a whole new market," and even that jarring business cliché, "growing our program." Keep your ears attuned to the words that surround us. Language is employed in the pursuit of many different goals; straightforward transmission and explanation of ideas is only one of its uses.

Read the prose that comes your way with a critical eye, listen to the ads on television, and ask yourself what the writer's purpose is and how it is achieved. Once you begin to understand the manifold ways in which words can be used, the purpose of expository prose should be clearer as well, and you will better understand the tone and style appropriate for it.

## TONE

Since the purpose of expository prose is to inform and explain, its main goal is clarity. Your goal in a paper about music is to convey ideas and insight about a complex art as clearly and directly as possible. The focus should be on communicating concepts, not on making yourself sound important. Your prose should be as direct and as simple as you can make it, so that the reader will be informed and enlightened. The tone of your writing should be crisp, professional, and businesslike. That is not to say that you should avoid using technical terms. Like the jargon of all fields, technical musical terms exist because we need them. There is no other economical way to communicate a complex concept such as "fugue" or "sonata-allegro structure"; these terms convey precise information to the musically informed reader. As to the rest of your language, however, clarity and crispness of expression are the goals.

Two extremes are to be avoided. Expository prose is different from speech and informal writing, such as personal letters. A slangy or cute tone is therefore completely out of place in a formal paper. Sometimes student papers contain sentences like "I was bummed when I discovered that ..." or "The tenor is all 'I love you,' but the soprano is all 'No way.'" Such casual language is inappropriate in a research paper. Sometimes students add quotation marks around words they know are questionable, as if that somehow absolves them of responsibility for them. Putting quotation marks around "bummed," for example, would not exonerate the writer from the charge of poor word choice. In fact, it makes things worse—now there is the additional problem of using quotation marks when there is no valid reason for them.

It is more common to see student writers go to the other extreme and adopt a stilted, artificial style. Perhaps they were taught to use overly formal language in their papers or they feel that such a style creates an impression of scholarship. One frequently sees awkward impersonal constructions such as "It has long been assumed that ..." and "The present writer finds it well-nigh impossible to agree with this position," instead of "I disagree." Sometimes the writing becomes overly flowery and dramatic, as in the following example.

> When Josquin entered the service of the Duke as a young choirboy, little did the world suspect that in the future he would have such a profound impact, not only on the history of music, but on all of Western culture.

You see the problem—that sentence calls for a dramatic drum-roll. The proper tone for expository writing is somewhere between these two extremes. The first priority should always be clarity. Individual concepts must be explained as clearly as possible, and your ideas must be set forth in a unified and coherent way. Your writing should be clear, crisp, economical, and businesslike, neither casual and slangy nor stilted and artificial.

## THE STANCE OF THE WRITER

Related to the question of tone is the issue of the writer's stance, or how involved the person of the writer should be in the prose. Again, there are two extremes to avoid. The first extreme is for the writer to be too intrusive. Some students write with a tone of breathless discovery, as if no one had ever heard this music or considered these ideas before. This approach tells the reader more about the naïveté of the inexperienced researcher than about the topic.

The other extreme is the elusive or invisible writer. As we explained earlier, research means more than merely reporting the ideas of others. As a researcher, you are expected to design a thesis and argue it by studying the evidence, reviewing the secondary literature, analyzing the music, and forming your own conclusions, based on your critical judgment. After the writer cites expert A and expert B, the reader waits for the other shoe to drop—what does the writer think? To stay aloof from your prose, reluctant to get involved and take a stand, is to shirk one of the fundamental responsibilities of the writer.

## REFERRING TO YOURSELF

The question of the writer's stance brings up the question of referring to yourself in your prose. Many of us were trained to avoid the first person pronoun in our writing and find it difficult to write the word "I" in a paper. Most instructors now agree that "I" is perfectly acceptable, provided that it is reserved for those moments when the writer is sharing his or her own thoughts. Clearly, "I" is out of place when discussing someone else's ideas, but there are few alternatives to "I" when it comes to the writer's own conclusions. "The present writer" is an awkward and distracting phrase; "I" seems much more natural in a sentence like "A says this and B says that; I agree with B." One can, of course, avoid pronouns altogether by writing something like "A says this, B says that; considering all the evidence, B's position seems more compelling."

"I" is not the appropriate pronoun to use in a general statement that any informed reader would take for granted. Consider the following sentences.

> As I look at the number of cantatas Bach composed in his first few years at Leipzig, I am astounded.
>
> As we look at the number of cantatas . . . , we are astounded.
>
> As one looks at the number of cantatas . . . , one is astounded.

The first version, using "I," doesn't feel right; it sounds simultaneously arrogant and naïve. The writer did not suddenly discover that Bach wrote a lot of cantatas in his first years at Leipzig; the chronology of Bach's cantatas is common knowledge and has been in print for years. Emphasizing your astonishment simply points out that you are new to the research game. Both "we" and "one" are adequate for sentences like this, but people object to both. "We" can sound pretentious, like the "royal we," as in "We are not amused." Some are uncomfortable with "one," feeling that it is a stiff or old-fashioned construction; I think it still works in general statements of this sort. If choosing a pronoun makes you uncomfortable, find another way to write the sentence—you can always find another way to say anything. In this case, you can avoid using any pronouns by turning the sentence around.

> The number of cantatas composed by Bach . . . is astounding.

In summary, use "I" when the idea is really yours, when you are sharing your own views or stating your conclusions, based on your research and analysis. Use other pronouns, or avoid pronouns altogether, when you are making more general statements, and "the present writer" belongs in the dustbin with other phrases no longer in use.

There are two excellent ways to get a sense of the proper tone and level of sophistication in your writing. The first is to browse through journal articles with an eye for the tone of the writing; scholars present their ideas as clearly and forcefully as they can. Another helpful way to judge the tone of your own writing is to put the draft aside for a few days and then reread it. After a pause of a few days, inappropriate language is generally quite clear. When you return to an old paper a week, a month, or a year later, the passages of slangy or pretentious language are obvious and embarrassing. Whenever you sit down to draft a paper, assume the frame of mind of a competent scholar, trying to explain as clearly as possible important ideas about the art of music.

## WRITING EFFECTIVE SENTENCES

The act of writing, whether the work is expository prose, fiction, or poetry, consists of choosing and assembling the words that will convey one's ideas as effectively as possible. In a way, the writer's responsibility boils down to choosing the next word, just as the composer's task ultimately consists of deciding what the next note or chord should be. Our discussion of writing style therefore begins at the level of choosing appropriate words and then moves on to good and bad combinations of words and questions of sentence structure.

### Word Choice

The basic work of writing is the selection of appropriate words to convey the idea you have in mind. Care and precision in choosing the right words is what makes the difference between a convincing paper and one that is weak or dull. There are a few general principles that will help you make appropriate choices.

First, bear in mind that the English language, because of its long and involved history, is richer in vocabulary and synonyms than many other languages. Over the centuries, English has adopted words from Anglo-Saxon, old Scandinavian languages, Norman French, Greek, Latin, modern French and German, Spanish, Italian, Arabic, and a host of other languages. You therefore have at your disposal an incredible wealth of synonyms for any word or idea, each with its own particular flavor and force. Browsing through a dictionary or a thesaurus gives one a sense of the vast vocabulary of English; most of us use only a tiny fraction of the words available to us. The huge vocabulary of modern English means that the writer has no reason to settle for awkward or inappropriate words or words that do not quite fit the idea. Here are some specific recommendations about word choice.

**Slang**    Use words in their original senses; avoid any slang usage that is different from a word's standard sense. As you know, slang changes rapidly; as soon as the general population adopts a colorful slang usage, the group that originated the slang phrase stops using it and invents new ways to keep their language private. In a formal paper, avoid using normal words in their slang senses, and, of course, avoid words that exist only in slang. "Twelve-tone music is so over!" may be fine in a conversation—the question here is usage, not the truth of the assertion—and "over" is a legitimate English word, but this slang usage of the word would not pass muster in a paper. Even the slang words that are standard in some contexts in the musical world, such as "fiddle" for "violin" and "chops" for "technical competence," should not be used in formal papers.

**Anglo-Saxon and Latin roots**    Words derived from Anglo-Saxon roots are usually shorter, more concrete, and more forceful than words derived from Latin roots. "Church music" is more forceful than "ecclesiastical music"; "went mad" is stronger than "suffered a complete personality disintegration." I remember a counselor, worried about a troubled teenager, saying, "His emotional stability factors are in severe imbalance." I can think of crisper, livelier ways to put that—perhaps "That kid needs help" or "Watch out for that one." You cannot avoid Latin roots altogether, any more than you can avoid technical terms, but always stop to consider whether you can find a simpler, livelier way to say what you want to say.

**Foreign words**    Foreign words may sometimes be unavoidable in your prose. Since many foreign words have no exact equivalent in English, using a foreign term may be the best way—or the only way—to say exactly what you want to say. It is a mistake, however, to use foreign words just for effect. A flood of foreign words gives your prose a stuffy and pedantic flavor and creates the impression that your goal is to show off your erudition, not to argue your thesis. Consider the following sentence.

> The *Weltschmerz* that permeates the early songs is in keeping with the *Zeitgeist* of *fin-de-siècle* Vienna.

That sentence sounds pedantic; it tells us more about the author's pretensions than about Vienna or the songs in question. Although you can convey the same idea using English words, you might choose to retain one of the foreign terms, since their meanings are different in subtle ways from the English translations, and some foreign words nearly defy translation. In revising this sentence, you might decide to keep *Weltschmerz* or *fin-de-siècle*, because of their particular nuance or connotation. An occasional foreign word is fine; a string of them creates a pretentious effect.

**Use words literally**    Respect the literal force of words and use them the way the world at large uses them. "Unique," for example, means "the only one in the world." Therefore, to describe a piece of music as "somewhat unique" or "totally unique" is meaningless; it is impossible to be somewhat unique, just as it is impossible to be somewhat dead. "Hopefully" used to mean "in a spirit of hope," not "I hope that," although every day one hears it used in the latter sense. A sentence such as "Hopefully, the performance will reach a higher level once the orchestra has a few more rehearsals" is common usage today, but careful writers avoid it. "Literally" means "actually," or "without exaggeration," but people use it carelessly as an intensifier, as in "The audience members were literally glued to their seats," which is nonsense unless someone actually painted glue on the seats. Lately, "decimate" is widely used as a synonym for "devastate," in sentences like "The town was decimated by the flood." "Decimate," from the Latin *decima* ("tenth"), means to destroy ten percent of something; it describes, for example, the practice used by occupying armies to punish resistance by lining up the inhabitants of a town and killing every tenth person. Since I first drafted this section in 1989, the battles over "hopefully" and "decimate" apparently have been lost; careless usage has once again won. I still think a careful writer should use words correctly, whether the world at large does or not. We could go on with other examples, but the point is clear—respect the literal meaning of the words you use.

**Creating new words**    Use existing words; there is no reason to create new words by piling prefixes or suffixes onto existing words. In everyday English, there is a tendency to tack "-ize" or "-wise" onto every other word. The resulting neologisms, such as "prioritize," "finalize," and "background-wise," are awkward and unnecessary. The writer should be able to find a respectable English word or phrase that will convey the idea in a more natural and graceful manner. Sometimes music students create hybrids such as "analyzation," "texture-wise," and "a minuet-type movement." "Analyzation" is not even a real word; I suspect it is an attempt to create a Latinistic form of the term "analysis," which is actually a borrowed Greek word. If you want to sound educated and profound, Greek trumps Latin every time, so "analysis" is perfect as it is. "Texture-wise" and "minuet-type" are ungainly, and there are better alternatives. Take the trouble to find the appropriate word from the rich vocabulary of standard English, and do not resort to artificial creations.

In musicological studies based on new critical methodologies, one sees strange new words constructed by adding suffixes to familiar roots—words such as "narrativity," "narratology," "commodification," "contextualiza-tion," and even "recontextualization." These words, however, are not care-less substitutes for ordinary English words; they were created because the new critical approaches needed a new technical vocabulary. That process is different from jamming roots and suffixes together and creating your own new words for no reason.

**Nouns are nouns and verbs are verbs**  Respecting what words mean includes using words as their proper parts of speech. There is a tendency in some modern English to make nouns out of verbs, verbs out of nouns, adjectives out of nouns or verbs, and so forth. "All systems are definitely in a go configuration" may be normal language at NASA headquarters, but it is unacceptable in a paper; "go" is a verb, not an adjective. "He's their go-to guy" appears regularly in sports pages, but "go-to" is a very odd kind of adjective, not something you would use in a paper. Similarly, "That was a fun rehearsal" may be fine in conversation, but you can't say, "*The Barber of Seville* is a fun opera" in a paper, since "fun" is a noun, not an adjective. In standard English, "access" is a noun, not a verb; "I was unable to access the primary sources" is standard language in computer science classes, but not in a humanities paper. This last example, turning a noun into a verb, represents the recent tendency to turn all words into verbs. One reads, for example, that music "transitions" from one section to another and groups meet to "interface," "dialogue," and "conference" with each other. In the new schools of critical theory, scholars "gender" texts and write that Eurocentric literature courses "privilege" the works of white male writers. I assume that the justification for this practice is that these artificial verbs are needed as new technical terms. All the words in quotation marks in those sentences are nouns dragooned into service as verbs, a practice some call "verbing." The perfect comment on verbing appeared in a now-defunct comic strip called *Calvin and Hobbes,* when one character announced, "Verbing weirds language." Use nouns as nouns and verbs as verbs.

### Word Combinations

It is not enough to choose the right individual word; sometimes a perfectly appropriate word is inappropriate in context because it already appears in the previous phrase or is used nearby in another sense. This issue is complicated further when one writes about music; one must reserve the words used as technical terms for that use alone, and not try to use them as ordinary English words. You confuse your reader if you use words such as *key, major, minor, development,* and other technical terms both as general English words and as special musical terms. Sentences like the following cause confusion.

> The key element in sonata-allegro structure is key areas.
>
> One of the new developments in the Romantic symphony is the emphasis on the development sections.

These sentences can easily be rewritten, reserving the musical terms for use as technical terms and substituting synonyms where they are used in a nonmusical sense.

> The determining factor in sonata-allegro structure is key areas.
>
> One important change in the Romantic symphony is the new emphasis on development sections.

**Noun strings**    There is a tendency in modern English to create phrases out of strings of loosely related nouns. We have already mentioned phrases like "revenue enhancement strategies" and "curriculum evaluation criteria," which are awkward noun strings and inflated, pretentious phrases. The Department of Agriculture, concerned about the presence in schools of vending machines filled with chips and snack cakes, referred to these foods as "low-nutrition density options" instead of the standard two-syllable term, "junk food." In papers on music, one sees phrases like "the composer control issue," "remote key area harmonies," and "the patron/composer relationship." A slash or hyphen between two juxtaposed nouns does not solve the problem; those phrases are still strings of vaguely related nouns, not correct English phrases. To make standard English of a noun string, rearrange the words, using prepositional phrases, apostrophes, or other grammatical means to express the relationship between the different nouns. The above examples can be rewritten as "the issue of the composer's control," "chords in remote keys," "the relationship between patron and composer," or other alternatives.

**Redundant couplets**    In modern English one frequently sees combinations of adjectives and nouns that are redundant because both words mean the same thing. Common examples are "general consensus," "subject matter," and "end result." In each case, one of the words is unnecessary padding. Consensus is by definition general—there can be no such thing as a private consensus; the same logic applies to the other examples. Avoid these padded constructions. Papers on music sometimes use a peculiar couplet—"in-depth analysis," a pretentious and ugly wording. First, *in-depth* is a stale catch phrase; it is also an artificial adjective constructed by jamming together a preposition and its object. Second, the phrase is redundant; all analysis is necessarily "in-depth," since analysis means breaking a phenomenon down into its parts and studying each in detail. Also avoid redundant prefixes in creations such as "interrelationship." "Inter-," a prefix borrowed from Latin, means "between"; since relationships exist only between or among two or more entities, the prefix is unnecessary.

**Stock couplets**    Stock couplets are combinations of adjectives and nouns that always seem to appear together. "Abject poverty," "utter despair," "reckless abandon," and "extenuating circumstances" are common examples. By now, "extenuating" seems to have lost its meaning of "helping to explain or excuse," having become a meaningless appendage routinely attached to the word "circumstances." One student's concert report contained the following sentence.

Unfortunately the first piece listed on the program was not performed because of extenuating circumstances.

I assume that the student meant "unforeseen" or "unavoidable" circumstances—otherwise, the sentence is meaningless. Try to avoid stock couplets because they have lost their original force. When describing music, find alternatives for stock phrases like "lyrical second theme" and "dramatic opening gesture."

**The "not un-" construction** Avoid the pretentious "not un-" construction, as in "It was not uncommon during the Renaissance for composers to begin their careers as choirboys in the chapels of the great courts." That construction is weak and affected, and overuse of it rapidly becomes, in the famous words of Strunk and White, "not unannoying."

**Dependence on modifiers** In general, rely on strong nouns and verbs rather than modifiers to convey your ideas. One sure way to tighten up your writing is to eliminate all qualifying adverbs such as *somewhat, virtually, literally, perhaps,* and *very*. If the nouns and verbs have been chosen with care, qualifiers rarely add anything to the sentence; in fact, they weaken the force of your writing. If you choose strong, colorful verbs, you won't have to rely on modifiers. Consider the following sentences.

> The conductor walked quickly to the podium, raised his arms, and briskly conducted the orchestra in the loud, dramatic opening of the tone poem.

> The conductor bounded to the podium, raised his arms, and unleashed the full fury of the orchestra.

The second sentence, whatever else you might think of it, is certainly tighter and livelier than the first, because it relies on strong verbs—"bounded" and "unleashed"—to paint the desired picture. We mentioned earlier that English is a language rich in synonyms; if you stop and think for a minute, you can find many colorful synonyms for a word like "walk." Let me suggest a few alternatives; try to create more yourself. The conductor "marched" to the podium, or "leapt," "pranced," "strode," "lurched," "plodded," "raced," "danced," "shuffled," "charged," or "swiveled through the violins." One sure way to improve your writing is to delete the modifiers and rely instead on strong verbs.

Lately, spoken English seems to rely not only on single modifiers, but also on loosely connected modifying phrases, introduced by words such as "in terms of," "as to," or "from the standpoint of," to bear the weight of the sentence. One hears and reads sentences like the following.

> The new principal horn will be a great addition to the orchestra in terms of her mastery of technique and her beautiful tone.

> The new conductor is doing wonderful work from the standpoint of precision and the ensemble sound.

Those sentences are weak; in both cases, the real point comes only at the end after a loose connective that serves as useless filler. If you see weak sentences like this in your own writing, stop for a moment, think about what you are really trying to say, and then make the important ideas the subject or verb of the sentence, not a loosely attached afterthought. Here are some revised versions; there are, of course, many other ways to make stronger sentences out of these two examples.

> Her rock-solid technique and beautiful tone make the new principal horn a great addition to the orchestra.
>
> The new principal horn, with her technical mastery and beautiful tone, will be a great addition to the orchestra.
>
> The new conductor has greatly improved the orchestra's precision and ensemble sound.
>
> The orchestra's new precision and ensemble sound are a tribute to the new conductor's ability.

One reason we rely so much on modifiers to convey our ideas is that many of the words we use constantly have lost their force. "A brilliant performance" sounds like high praise, but if you describe as "brilliant" any performance in which the players manage to end more or less together, then you have to find something stronger, such as "exceptionally brilliant," "truly brilliant," or "quite frankly brilliant," to describe a truly superior performance. If everyone who has ever set foot on a stage, appeared in a film, or made a recording is called a "star," then exceptional performers have to be classified as "superstars." Once terms like "superstar" have been cheapened by being applied to everyone in the business, we will need still another category—perhaps "megastar" or "demigod." If you choose strong, colorful nouns and verbs, you will not need to tack a modifier onto every word. Eliminating useless modifiers will mean that you need fewer words to convey your ideas, and your writing will automatically become tighter, more forceful, and more effective.

### Sentence Structure

Writing effective expository prose is not simply a matter of choosing the right words. No matter how appropriate each word is, your prose can still turn out to be boring or difficult to understand, depending on how you deal with the matter of sentence structure.

**Passive voice**    One kind of sentence structure that frequently weakens student prose is the passive voice. Some students seem to feel that constructions based on the passive voice are especially appropriate or perhaps even required in scholarly writing. The passive voice is not always wrong; it is the correct choice when you want to emphasize the action itself, rather than the subject who is performing the action. Compare the following sentences.

American opera companies frequently perform *Peter Grimes.*

Britten's *Peter Grimes* is performed regularly by American opera companies.

If your point is that *Peter Grimes,* in contrast to many other twentieth-century operas, has become part of the standard repertoire, the second sentence, passive voice and all, is a clearer way to state your idea. The first version is not exactly the same, and seems to emphasize the idea that *American* opera companies perform the work, as opposed to English or German companies. Passive voice is not always wrong, but it should be reserved for these special cases. Generally, the active voice is more forceful. Some uses of passive voice, such as the following impersonal constructions, are especially weak.

It has often been stated . . .

In this study, several examples of the Baroque concerto grosso have been analyzed.

John Cage has frequently been viewed as . . .

In each of these sentences, the language is vague, awkward, and indefinite. It's the kind of language used by politicians caught in an act of malfeasance—"Mistakes were made," suggesting that nobody was responsible for these actions. On seeing these constructions, the reader naturally wonders about the missing agents. So who exactly has often stated this, analyzed these concertos, or viewed Cage in this way? The active voice, with a clear subject, verb, and object, is nearly always better than the passive voice. Avoid those impersonal "it" constructions altogether.

**Word order**   Since English grammar depends on word order rather than on inflected endings to indicate the case of nouns, changing the word order changes the meaning you convey, in both gross and subtle ways. Consider the different force and emphasis of the following sentences.

1. After the large-scale works of his early period, Stravinsky turned to a new idiom, the neoclassical style, which represents his chief contribution to twentieth-century music.

2. After the large-scale works of his early period, which represent his chief contribution to twentieth-century music, Stravinsky turned to a new idiom, the neoclassical style.

3. Stravinsky turned to a new idiom, the neoclassical style, which represents his chief contribution to twentieth-century music, after the large-scale works of his early period.

4. After the large-scale works of his early period, Stravinsky turned to a new idiom, his chief contribution to twentieth-century style—neoclassicism.

The first sentence is perfectly clear, and the word order is acceptable. The second version, by putting the subordinate clause after "period" rather than "idiom," changes the idea entirely; now the sentence states that the large-scale early works, rather than the neoclassical works, represent Stravinsky's chief contribution to twentieth-century music. The third version is correct but weak, since, after making its point, the sentence trails off with a relatively unimportant adverbial phrase. The fourth version is the strongest, since it puts the important term, "neoclassicism," in the strong final position. When you edit your work, try changing the order of elements in your sentences until the words not only say what you want to say, but also say it with the exact shade of emphasis that you intend. The question of word order is related to another issue, correct placement of modifiers, whether they are single words, phrases, or clauses; that question will be addressed in the next chapter.

**Parallel constructions**   When you want to emphasize the relationship between parallel elements or ideas, or the contrast between them, keep the sentence structure parallel. Consider the following sentence.

> Typical examples of the symphonic poem are *Les Préludes* by Liszt and *Ein Heldenleben* by Strauss; another example is Smetana's *Ma Vlast*.

The problem here is that Smetana seems added as an afterthought or placed in a secondary, subsidiary position. The reader wonders exactly what the writer meant to say. The idea is much clearer when the series is kept in parallel construction.

> Typical examples of the symphonic poem are *Les Préludes* by Liszt, *Ein Heldenleben* by Strauss, and *Ma Vlast* by Smetana.

Parallel construction is also the clearest way to emphasize the contrast between two ideas. Compare the following sentences.

> Bach, a church musician, composed cantatas and Passions; Handel, on the other hand, did not specialize in those genres, but rather in opera and oratorio. The explanation for this difference is that Handel worked for the English court rather than the church.

> Bach, a church musician, composed cantatas and Passions; Handel, a court musician, composed operas and oratorios.

The second sentence, with its tight parallel structure, states the contrast between the two composers more clearly and strongly than the first sentences.

When you are trying to utilize parallel construction, you must be sure that all the elements match grammatically. If the first element consists of a verb and its object, then each of the later elements must be constructed the same way. You cannot put different grammatical units in parallel. The parallel elements need not be the same length; one element can be longer, provided that all the elements are grammatically the same. Consider the following sentences.

**Incorrect:** His favorite pastimes are listening to music, chess, and to go on hikes.

**Correct:** His favorite pastimes are listening to music, playing chess, and hiking.

**Correct:** His favorite pastimes are music, chess, and the outdoors.

**Correct:** His favorite pastimes are listening to music, especially Baroque music and jazz, playing chess, and hiking.

Parallel constructions can be very effective, particularly when you are trying to make an important point in your argument. It takes some time and care to arrange parallel constructions correctly, but it is well worth the effort if the effect is strong and persuasive.

**Variety of sentence structure** Just as well-chosen words will not produce effective prose if sentence structure is not handled correctly, individually correct sentences do not result in effective paragraphs unless there is variety in the sentence structure. A series of short, subject-verb-object sentences creates a choppy and childish effect; a string of long, involved sentences makes it unduly difficult for the reader to follow your thought. Since any structure becomes tiresome when it turns into an invariable pattern, one key to effective writing is to vary the sentence structure. Consider the following paragraphs.

William Byrd was born in Lincolnshire in 1543. He studied with Thomas Tallis. He was appointed organist of Lincoln Cathedral in 1568. He was elected a member of the Chapel Royal in 1570.

William Byrd was born, probably in Lincolnshire, although the documentary proof of this fact is less than definitive, in 1543. It is commonly assumed, in the absence of incontrovertible proof, that he studied music with Thomas Tallis, another organist, Gentleman of the Chapel Royal under several English monarchs, and co-holder with Byrd of a royal patent for the publication of music, although that of course did not occur until much later, after Byrd had begun his career as an organist and been himself elected to the post of Gentleman of the Chapel Royal, while still retaining his organ position, at least for some years.

The style of the first paragraph is choppy and childish. The second is just the opposite. By the time readers finish that second rambling sentence, with all its afterthoughts, qualifiers, and digressions, they no longer know or care who the original subject was. When your syntax gets that tangled, stop, back up, and think about exactly what you want to say. Much of that material should be eliminated, and the syntax should be greatly simplified.

Complex sentences divide statements into main ideas and subordinate or secondary clauses. Since complex sentences single out one action as the main idea, they are generally clearer and stronger than compound sentences, which treat all the ideas as equal in importance. Compare the following sentences.

1. Byrd studied music with Thomas Tallis, then he was appointed organist of Lincoln Cathedral, and shortly thereafter he was elected a Gentleman of the Chapel Royal.
2. After he studied music with Thomas Tallis and served as organist of Lincoln Cathedral, Byrd was elected a Gentleman of the Chapel Royal in 1570.

The first sentence treats the three events as a series of equally important ideas, and the effect is choppy. The second pushes the material about Bryd's training and early career into the background in a subordinate adverbial clause and puts the main emphasis on Byrd's appointment to the Chapel Royal. What the sentence really wants to say should be the main clause; put the rest into subordinate clauses or modifying phrases.

You can see why the process of writing and editing takes time. The struggle to find exactly the right word and exactly the right grammatical structure to convey what you want to say, and with the proper emphasis, takes time and effort. Once you have a series of good sentences, you also must worry about variety of sentence structure. Whenever the structure of a sentence is confusing, back away for a moment and focus on exactly what you are trying to say. Once your ideas are clear, you should be able to find language that will convey them clearly and effectively.

## EFFECTIVE PARAGRAPHS

A paragraph is more than a series of correct sentences: It is a unified exposition or explanation of a single idea. A paragraph focuses on a single thought; the chief quality it must have is coherence. The paragraph must have a topic sentence that clearly states the single idea the paragraph will develop, and the rest of the paragraph must be closely related to that single idea. When you are editing your prose, check the paragraphs for unity; if there is anything in a paragraph that does not relate closely to the topic sentence, delete the unrelated material or find a better place for it. If a paragraph begins by discussing one idea and then moves into an extended discussion of a second idea, make that discussion of the second idea a new paragraph with its own topic sentence. Read through the following paragraph.

> Mahler's Second Symphony, also known as the "Resurrection" Symphony, is one of his best-known works. Following the example of Beethoven's Ninth Symphony, Mahler uses voices in the final climactic section of the work. After a long, agitated, and highly developed first movement, there follows an Andante in the easy, folksong-like

rhythm of an Austrian *Ländler.* The third movement is a symphonic adaptation of one of the *Wunderhorn* songs, and the brief fourth movement is a new setting, for contralto solo, of still another poem from this collection. The finale, after a vivid orchestral section depicting the day of Resurrection, leads to a monumental setting for soloists and chorus of a Resurrection ode by the eighteenth-century German poet Klopstock. This finale is reminiscent of Part II of the Eighth Symphony, a monumental movement for soloists and chorus, which nearly constitutes a complete secular oratorio. As other examples of secular oratorios, one might cite the "Faust" Symphony by Liszt, usually classified as a program symphony; his oratorio *St. Elizabeth,* which perhaps is difficult to fit into the "secular" classification; and even Wagner's *Parsifal.*

The errors in this paragraph should be obvious. Aside from ungainly expressions such as "folksong-like," our concern here is coherence. After a brief description of each of the movements of the Second Symphony, the author wanders off into a discussion of Part II of the Eighth Symphony. The similarity of the Second and Eighth symphonies certainly deserves brief mention, like the earlier reference to Beethoven, but the last two sentences go far beyond brief mention. By introducing the provocative notion that the secular oratorio is an important genre and then arguing that this genre includes such works as a program symphony, a religious oratorio, and an opera, the writer has let the digression go much too far. The last sentence is filled with complex ideas that have little to do with Mahler's Second Symphony and call for much more explanation and justification than the writer provides. The reader is distracted and confused by this material. Those last sentences should be shortened considerably, and perhaps the writer should consider eliminating the discussion of the finale of the Eighth Symphony. If that comparison is useful to the topic and demands some explanation, it should be discussed in a separate paragraph. One of the major tasks of the editing process is cutting and pasting—moving sentences and ideas from one paragraph to another or from one section to another, so that each paragraph is a logical unit and all the material relevant to each point is grouped in one place.

## THE EFFECTIVE ESSAY

Earlier, in Chapter 4, in the section on outlining a paper, we discussed the elements that make a good essay. That same material merits brief mention here in order to complete our discussion of the qualities of an effective essay.

A series of paragraphs related to a single topic does not of itself constitute a good essay. The paragraphs must be ordered and connected in such a way that the argument moves along logically. The order in which ideas are presented makes a difference in the effectiveness of the essay as a whole. Like each paragraph, the entire essay must have a thesis, expressed in the main topic sentence; that thesis will determine which paragraphs should be included and which should be cut, as well as suggesting the order in which the material should be discussed.

In the process of turning a series of paragraphs into an essay, the writer may need to add some material in order to create the large-scale unity the essay must have.

### Introduction

An essay cannot begin with the first paragraph of the main body of discussion. The essay needs an introduction that leads into the topic, states the main thesis of the essay, and outlines for the reader how the essay will proceed and what kinds of argumentation will be used. Introductions often begin with a general statement, move to the particular area the essay will discuss, and then state the thesis that the essay will defend. Introductions can also move in the opposite direction, from mention of a particular detail or description of a particular event or performance to discussion of a more general idea, followed by the thesis of the essay.

A good introduction avoids two extremes. It is wrong to start abruptly, so that the reader has no chance to see what you plan to do and where your topic fits in the larger view of the history of music. It is also wrong to get so carried away with your introductory ideas that the introduction becomes a long, independent essay or brings up ideas and arguments that will not be taken up later in the essay. It is difficult to generalize about the proper length for an introduction; style guides generally state that the introduction should be about one-tenth of the complete essay. Sometimes, of course, a longer introduction may be necessary in order to clarify complex concepts or terms that are essential to your argument.

### Transitions

The reader of an essay should know at all times where he or she is in the course of the argument and where the material he or she is reading fits into the overall discussion. Therefore it is sometimes necessary to add transitional material as you move from one topic to another. The reader has to know when the introduction is over and the main body of the paper is beginning; the reader also must be aware that you are moving from one argument to another in the body of the paper. Transitions need not be elaborate or long; a word or two, a phrase, or a clause may be enough to indicate a shift of ideas. Simply leaping from one argument to another is awkward and confusing. Paragraphs and ideas are not connected into a unified argument by simple proximity; they need to be joined together gracefully. The relationships between sections and the reader's position in the logical chain of argumentation must be clear at all times.

### Conclusion

An essay of any length must be summarized in a concluding section. If the essay trails off with the last paragraph of argumentation, readers are left with a feeling of incompleteness and, left on their own, must somehow gather all the detailed exposition and argumentation into a single, coherent whole. The conclusion need not be as long as the introduction and need not be world-shaking. Some sort of closing section, however, is necessary.

To understand the necessity for a concluding section, consider the analogy with musical structure. The longer a composer has sustained tension and suspense in a piece, the longer the final resolution needs to be. The short and straightforward codas appended to classical symphonic movements would never suffice to conclude the longer and more dramatic movements of the Romantic period. In the latter, since so much accumulated tension has been built up, the listener needs a proportionally longer period of resolution and calm. When you move from a few short paragraphs to an essay of ten or twenty or thirty pages, the reader needs a proportionately longer introduction and conclusion in order to tie all the ideas together into a convincing statement.

One final warning about conclusions: The conclusion should be written in the same tone and style as the rest of the essay. Since conclusions are difficult to write, students sometimes resort to a hortatory or flowery tone that is inconsistent with the tone and style of the rest of the essay. Remember that the purpose of expository prose is to inform and explain, not to preach, urge the audience to action, or dramatize. Maintain the same competent, informed, and professional tone as the rest of the essay, and bring your work to a clear and forceful close.

## SUMMARY

Each level of writing—the individual word, the sentence, the paragraph, and the essay as a whole—has its own demands and requires the writer's careful attention. At every stage of producing a paper, including planning, drafting, and editing, the writer must be attentive to the specific demands of each level. Variety of sentence structure, coherence and unity in the paragraphs, and a clear overall organization, along with a graceful introduction, transitions, and a conclusion, are just as important as the choice of individual words. An effective prose style results from the writer's understanding of the challenges present at each of these levels and success at meeting those challenges. Read articles in the standard journals with an eye to large-scale organization; note how the author introduces the subject and the thesis, and see how transitions and the conclusion link all the paragraphs into a single argument. Once again, be aware that good writing is a complex process, requiring work at several different levels and several separate stages.

# CHAPTER 8

# Common Writing Problems

This chapter will discuss problems that appear frequently in student papers—both general writing problems and the special problems involved in writing about music. Although these issues may seem elementary to some readers, they occur frequently in student papers at both the undergraduate and the graduate levels. I have included only a selection of these problems, based on my experience reading student prose. The standard guides to writing style, such as *The Chicago Manual of Style* or the *Simon & Schuster Handbook for Writers,* contain much more detailed advice on writing correctly and precisely. We will deal first with basic writing errors, and then with the special problems connected with writing about music.

## ERRORS IN BASIC GRAMMAR AND WRITING

### Incomplete Sentences

To constitute a complete sentence, a group of words must have at least a subject and a predicate. Some student papers contain incomplete sentences like the following:

1. Byrd, after studying with Thomas Tallis, a Gentleman of the Chapel Royal, being appointed a cathedral organist, and later winning a position as a court composer.
2. Impressionism can be understood as an extension of the late Romantic aesthetic expressed through new musical means. Likewise with expressionism.

These examples represent the two situations in which incomplete sentences or sentence fragments usually occur. The first consists of the subject followed by a long subordinate clause or string of participial phrases. The writer forgets that he or she has left the subject hanging, without a main verb. The second example starts with a perfectly good sentence, but then adds a shorthand afterthought as a separate unit. This sort of construction is common in spoken style, but should be used only rarely, and for good reason, in a formal paper. Such a fragment might create a fine rhetorical effect in a conclusion, for example, but in general, it is better to write complete sentences.

### Run-on Sentences

The opposite error is to jam too many subjects and verbs into the same sentence, without the proper punctuation or conjunction necessary to separate the complete sentences or clauses.

> Ockeghem wrote extremely long lines, with widely spaced cadences, Josquin constructed lines that have a much clearer phrase structure and regularly occurring cadences.

This long sentence is actually two complete sentences, and the comma by itself is not sufficient to separate them. This sort of construction often appears with an adverb such as "however" or "yet" in the second half, after the comma. Even with the adverb, that is still a run-on sentence. It is easy to correct this mistake; following are several correct ways to state the same idea.

> Whereas Ockeghem usually wrote extremely long lines with widely spaced cadences, Josquin composed lines . . .
>
> Ockeghem usually wrote extremely long lines . . .; Josquin, however, composed lines . . .
>
> Ockeghem usually wrote . . . no clear phrase structure. Josquin, on the other hand, composed lines that have . . .

Note that it is always possible to break a run-on sentence into two sentences. If you want to keep the two clauses in the same sentence, you have two choices—either connect the two main clauses with a conjunction (and, but, whereas, etc.) or a semicolon, or form a complex sentence by turning one into a subordinate clause and keeping the other as the main clause. In a complex sentence, the comma is sufficient punctuation between the two clauses.

### Agreement: Subject and Verb

One of the fundamental rules in most languages is that the subject and the verb must agree in number. Students sometimes break this basic rule, usually in long and unwieldy constructions that blur the identity of the real subject. Consider the following sentence.

> No innovative composer, not even the twentieth-century composers usually classified as members of the avant-garde, such as Cage, Stockhausen, and Wuorinen, have ever totally abandoned their musical roots.

What happens here is that the singular subject ("No composer") gets buried under the subsequent verbiage, with its plural nouns and the series of names; by the time the writer gets to the verb, he or she is thinking in the plural. If you correct the sentence by using a singular verb ("has ever totally abandoned"), the sentence is correct but sounds awkward. In such a situation, delete the whole thing and start again, after forming a clearer idea of exactly what you want to say.

If the subject is a collective noun such as "committee," "quartet," or "orchestra," choosing the proper number for the verb is not always a straightforward question. As a general rule, collective nouns take singular verbs when the group is thought of as a unit acting together.

> That orchestra has a real flair for late Romantic music.
>
> The committee recommends that Professor Smith be awarded tenure and promotion.

When the group is thought of as a collection of individuals acting separately, the collective noun takes a plural verb. The following sentences sound strange, but are actually correct, because the individuals in the group are depicted acting as separate individuals.

> Once the orchestra pack up their instruments and go home, they seem to forget everything they learned in the rehearsal.
>
> Since the committee fight constantly over every tiny question, they rarely accomplish anything.

The easiest way to smooth out these strange-sounding sentences is to add a plural noun, such as "members" or something similar, to the subject.

> Once the orchestra players pack up their instruments and go home, they seem to forget everything they learned in the rehearsal.
>
> Since the members of the committee fight constantly over every small question, they rarely accomplish anything.

### Agreement: Pronoun and Antecedent

Pronouns must agree with their antecedents in number, a straightforward rule that usually is easy enough to follow. Two special situations cause problems. The first is choosing the proper pronoun for collective nouns such as the examples in the previous section. Collective nouns considered as a single group take singular pronouns; when thought of as a collection of individuals, they take plural pronouns. In the first two sentences below, the groups designated by the collective nouns are thought of as acting as units; since the antecedents are singular, the pronouns referring to them are singular as well. The antecedents in sentences 3 and 4 are also collective nouns, but the groups are treated as individuals acting separately; the verbs and possessive pronouns referring to them are therefore plural. Once again, addition of a plural noun such as "members" helps.

1. The orchestra has worked very hard to refine its sound.
2. The Executive Committee insists on its right to review all decisions affecting the requirements for the various majors.
3. The quartet (players) spend too much time tuning between movements, breaking the flow of the music.
4. The committee (members) cannot agree on how to discharge their responsibilities.

Another special case of agreement between a pronoun and its antecedent arises in the case of general statements like the following.

Every student must bring his anthology to each class meeting.

Any student wishing to enter the concerto competition must submit his application by October 15.

The use of a masculine pronoun when the writer obviously has students of both genders in mind now strikes us as wrong. Using "his" to refer to any human being, masculine or feminine, used to be acceptable, but then orchestras consisting only of old white men, with perhaps a woman or two playing the harp or flute, seemed natural to us, too. In today's world of equality, we need gender-neutral language, ways to write without appearing to treat words such as "composer," "conductor," "performer," "department chair," and "dean" as masculine nouns. In the same way, we need to find a way to write general statements that is not gender-biased. Some people have proposed using a gender-neutral plural pronoun, even with the singular antecedent, thus:

Any student wishing to enter the concerto competition must submit their application by October 15.

That solution seems extreme; there are better ways to avoid biased language than abandoning logic and the rules of syntax. This sentence can easily be rewritten in a way that avoids both gender bias and incorrect grammar. In fact, this particular sentence can easily be rewritten without any pronoun, avoiding the issue altogether.

Any student wishing to enter the concerto competition must submit an application by October 15.

When that strategy is not available and the sentence doesn't work without a pronoun, there are several ways to avoid the masculine pronoun.

1. Make the sentence plural.

Students wishing to enter the concerto competition must submit their applications by October 15.

2. Put the sentence in the second person.

   If you wish to enter the concerto competition, you must submit an application by October 15.

3. Put the sentence in the passive voice, if possible; in this particular example, the passive voice seems awkward.

   Applications from those wishing to enter the concerto competition must be submitted by October 15.

4. Or just rewrite the sentence so that no pronouns are necessary.

   The deadline for applications for the concerto competition is October 15.

Once again, remember the general advice we keep returning to: There is always another way to say what you are trying to say. Rather than settling for awkward or ungainly wording, back up, think about exactly what you are trying to say, and try to find a way to say it that is both correct and graceful.

### Proper Cases of Pronouns

English, unlike some other languages, does not use cases for its nouns; it does, however, retain case-specific forms for some pronouns. These pronouns have three cases—nominative, possessive, and objective; the writer chooses the correct form based on the grammatical function of the pronoun in its context. The case-specific forms that we still use are listed in the following table.

| Nominative | Possessive | Objective |
| --- | --- | --- |
| I | my | me |
| he | his | him |
| she | her | her |
| they | their | them |
| who | whose | whom |
| whoever | whosever | whomever |

Some writers seem to choose from among these forms randomly, operating on instinct or sound rather than on the grammatical function of the pronoun in the sentence. One frequently hears incorrect cases in compound phrases like the following.

My parents frequently took my brother and I to concerts and plays.

The conductor offered George and I an opportunity to join the trombone section for the next concert.

In the first sentence, "I" is one of the direct objects of the verb "took"; in the second, "I" is one of the indirect objects of the verb "offered." In both cases, therefore, the nominative case is wrong; the proper form is the objective case—"me." People who would never say "They took I to concerts" or "He offered I an opportunity" somehow feel that "I" sounds more educated in compound phrases like these, no matter which case is required by the context. To choose the correct form in sentences like this, separate the compound object into its components.

### Relative Pronouns

The grammar books define relative pronouns as pronouns that introduce adjectival clauses and some kinds of noun clauses; among the important relative pronouns are "who," "which," "that," "what," and "whoever." "Who," "which," and "that" are used to introduce adjectival clauses that provide more information about an antecedent. "Who" is the correct relative pronoun when the antecedent is a person. "Which" and "that" usually refer to things or sometimes to groups of people considered as a collective unit. "That" is usually used in restrictive clauses, those that make a general subject more specific. "Which" is usually used in nonrestrictive clauses—that is, in clauses that add information about the antecedent rather than making a general antecedent more specific. Restrictive clauses are not set off by commas; nonrestrictive clauses are. Therefore, "that" is usually correct in clauses without commas, and "which" is correct in clauses with commas. The following sentences illustrate the proper punctuation and choice of relative pronouns for the two types of clauses.

> *Otello*, which was one of Verdi's last operas, is written in a style considerably different from that of his earlier operas. (The clause is nonrestrictive; it simply adds more information.)

> The opera that made Verdi a success was *Nabucco*. (The clause is restrictive; it limits and specifies "opera," a general noun.)

The distinction between restrictive and nonrestrictive phrases and clauses is discussed in more detail later in this chapter in the section on the correct use of the comma. For now, it is enough to connect "which" with nonrestrictive clauses and "that" with restrictive clauses.

In the table, note that "who" and "whoever" have case-specific forms. The choice of the correct form is based on the grammatical function of the pronoun in the context of the sentence. The following sentences are correct.

> Ockeghem, who taught several of the younger composers of his time, . . .

> The patron in whose service he worked . . .

> The master whom he chose to imitate . . .

> The Grammy is usually awarded to whoever sold the most recordings that year.

> I will work with whomever the committee selects to fill the conducting position next year.

In the first sentence, "who" is the subject of "taught" and therefore nominative case. In the second, "whose" is possessive, modifying "service." In the third sentence, "whom" is the object of the verb "chose," and therefore objective case. In the fourth sentence, it might appear that "whoever" is the object of the preposition "to," and therefore should be in the objective case, but actually, the object of "to" is the entire noun clause that follows. Within that clause, "whoever" is the subject of the verb "sold," and therefore is in the nominative case. In the fifth sentence, the entire noun clause is again the object of the preposition "with"; "whomever" is the object of "selects," the verb of that clause, and therefore is in the objective case.

Sometimes the grammatical context is complicated by additional clauses. Consider the following sentences.

> Whom do you think they will choose for the principal flute position?
>
> The Dean is the one who we believe should have the final word on personnel issues.

In the first sentence, "Whom" is correct because it is the direct object of the verb "will choose." In the second, "who" is the subject of "should have," and therefore nominative case. The way to make these choices is to divide the sentence into its constituent clauses and then strip each clause down to its basic elements—subject, verb, and object—and choose the correct form to fit the grammatical structure.

"Whom" is not used in casual conversation; in writing, one should still choose the proper case based on the grammatical context. Note the following sentences; most people would use the second version in conversation, but the first version is the correct one for written style.

> She is a sensitive accompanist on whom you can always rely.
>
> NOT
>
> She is a sensitive accompanist who you can always rely on.

If you can't imagine yourself writing that first sentence, remember that there is always another way to say whatever you want to say. Here are two alternatives.

> She is a sensitive accompanist; you can always rely on her.
>
> She is a sensitive and reliable accompanist.

### Misplaced Modifiers

Modifiers, whether they are single words, phrases, or clauses, can add important elements and color to your writing, but one must use care in locating them so that they are clearly connected with the appropriate words and ideas. Putting modifiers in the wrong place can make nonsense or unintended comedy out of your sentences and, unfortunately, is a frequent error in student prose.

**Single words**   I recently read this quote: "We are trying to turn this mess we find ourselves in around." The operative phrase is "turn around," but the modifier, "around," is placed too far from "turn," the word it modifies. "Turn this mess around" would work, because the modifier is still fairly close to the word it modifies, but in this example it is too far away, and the effect is awkward and confusing.

"Only" is a useful and important adverb; for the sake of logic and clarity, it should be placed as close as possible to the word or idea that it modifies. In the following sentences, note how changing the location of "only" changes the meaning and emphasis of the sentence.

> Only I attended the rehearsal yesterday. (No one else did.)
>
> I only attended the rehearsal yesterday. (I didn't take part in it, record it, or do anything else except watch.)
>
> I attended only the rehearsal yesterday. (Not the performance.)
>
> I attended the rehearsal only yesterday. (That recently.)

A common error in the use of "only" is to place it too early in the sentence, usually before the verb, when it belongs with a later word or phrase. "I only have eyes for you," the refrain of an old standard pop tune, illustrates this error; the sentence should read, "I have eyes only for you." Consider the following sentences.

> **Incorrect:** He only achieved success as a performer late in his life.
>
> **Correct:** He achieved success as a performer only late in his life.

**Misplaced phrases**   A modifying phrase put in the wrong place can easily create an illogical or comic effect. Consider the following sentences.

> Fortunately, my roommate found my wallet walking through the parking lot.
>
> Lying in plain view right next to my car, my roommate found my wallet.

Both these sentences paint bizarre pictures. The first sentence pictures a walking wallet; the second has the roommate, not the wallet, lying on the ground next to the car. "Walking" and "lying" are participles, which function both as verbs and as adjectives modifying nouns. They must be located near the nouns they modify. These sentences can easily be corrected by moving the modifying phrases to their proper places.

> Fortunately, my roommate, walking through the parking lot, found my wallet.
>
> My roommate found my wallet lying in plain view right next to my car.

One can also fix these sentences by changing the construction; one way is to turn the participial phrase into a clause with its own subject.

> Fortunately, my roommate found my wallet as he was walking through the parking lot.
>
> My roommate found my wallet, which was lying in plain sight right next to my car.

**Dangling participles**   A particular kind of misplaced participial phrase is the so-called "dangling participle" or "dangler." The problem with these participles is not that they are located too far from the nouns they modify, but that there is no appropriate noun anywhere in the vicinity to serve as an antecedent. The result is an abrupt shift of grammatical gears in mid-sentence.

> Pacing nervously in the wings, the orchestra began the overture.
>
> Turning to the second movement, a quiet introduction featuring a beautiful solo for the English horn leads to the main theme.

You see the problem. Who is pacing nervously in the wings? Surely not the orchestra—it's hard enough to play together sitting in one place. The sentence paints an illogical and comic picture. The same problem exists in the second sentence; the introduction is not turning to the second movement. The way to repair these sentences is either to supply an appropriate subject in the main clause for the participle to modify or to rewrite the phrase as a clause with its own subject.

> Pacing nervously in the wings, the tenor heard the orchestra begin the overture.
>
> As the tenor paced nervously in the wings, the orchestra began the overture.
>
> Turning to the second movement, we hear (or "one hears") a quiet introduction . . .
>
> As we turn to the second movement, a quiet introduction . . .

A dangling participle may appear after the main clause as well as before; in either place, it still needs a logical noun to modify. The following sentence appeared in a student's concert report.

> The "Stabat mater" is obviously a favorite text for composers to set, having heard Pergolesi's setting just last week.

Again there is no appropriate noun for the phrase to modify; the "Stabat mater" did not hear Pergolesi last week. To correct this sentence, either supply an appropriate subject in the main clause or turn the modifying phrase into a clause.

> Having heard Pergolesi's setting just last week, I gather that the "Stabat mater" is a favorite text for composers to set.
>
> Since I heard Pergolesi's setting just last week, the "Stabat mater" is obviously a favorite text for composers to set.

Like run-ons and sentence fragments, danglers usually result from sloppy thinking or flagging concentration.

**Modifying clauses**   Clauses that serve as modifiers, either adjectival or adverbial clauses, must also be located correctly in the sentence, so that their modifying function is clear. Following is an example of a misplaced adverbial clause.

> When he was still very young, Mozart's father presented him at the Habsburg court.

The problem here is the pronoun in the subordinate clause, which should refer to the nearest antecedent, "Mozart's father." The way the sentence stands, Mozart's *father* was still very young when this happened; the statement as it stands makes no sense. This sentence can be repaired by moving the clause, or better, by rearranging the nouns and pronouns so that the sentence makes sense. In this case, one might also distinguish between father and son by using their first names.

> Mozart's father presented his son at the Habsburg court when Wolfgang was still very young.
>
> When Mozart was still very young, his father presented him at the Habsburg court.
>
> When Wolfgang was still very young, Leopold presented him at the Habsburg court.

The way to clean up all types of misplaced modifiers is to back away from the sentence, think about what you are actually trying to say, and design a clearer way to say it. The answer to jumbled sentences like the incorrect examples above is not to add additional phrases or clauses in an attempt to clarify things, but to delete the jumble and start again, always with the basic idea in mind: Who is doing what to whom? Who is the subject, what is the action, and who or what is the object?

### The Split Infinitive

Related to the problems of word order discussed above is an old grammatical rule that forbids splitting an infinitive, as in the following sentence.

> His goal in the symphonic poems was to as vividly as possible describe the main ideas or feelings depicted in the story.

The rule states that the infinitive, "to describe," should not be interrupted by another word or phrase. The sentence should read as follows.

> His goal in the symphonic poems was to describe as vividly as possible . . .
>
> OR
>
> . . . as vividly as possible to describe . . .

Some recent books on writing style allow the occasional use of split infinitives, provided that only one word comes between the two parts of the infinitive, or if it seems the most graceful way to convey your thought. In formal papers, however, it is probably better to keep infinitives together in all situations. Deciding whether the modifying word or phrase should be placed before or after the infinitive ("as vividly as possible to describe" versus "to describe as vividly as possible") is a question of choice. In the case above, I think "to describe as vividly as possible" is more natural and smoother than the other choice, but both are correct.

### Mixed Metaphors

Beyond the fairly cut-and-dried questions of correct grammar, one must also consider questions of style in one's writing. Two perfectly correct sentences can vary widely in their force, elegance, and persuasive power, depending on variations in the style of the writing. In Chapter 7, we discussed stylistic issues such as word choice and sentence structure; here we want to single out one stylistic error that creates the same kind of illogical or comic effect as misplaced modifiers and danglers—the mixed metaphor.

Metaphors are related to similes. A simile is a comparison between two realities, expressed using "like" or "as"; metaphors are comparisons expressed without the words "like" or "as."

**Simile:** She sings like an angel. He tore through the finale like a man possessed.

**Metaphor:** When the conductor humiliated me publicly, that was the last straw.

Both similes and metaphors can add color and elegance to your writing. "That was the last straw" is an economical and forceful way to state the idea; it certainly is stronger than "that was the deciding factor in my decision to quit." Problems arise when we use familiar metaphors like "the last straw" or "light at the end of the tunnel" and forget that they are metaphors based on colorful pictures. We get into trouble by trying to extend metaphors too far or by mixing incompatible metaphors. Mixed metaphors create the same confusing and comical effects as misplaced or dangling modifiers. Think about the following sentences.

It was the sort of last-minute red herring on which an entire election can hinge.

The whole house of cards is built on sand.

Once he bit the bullet, rolled up his sleeves, and began practicing seriously, he could see the light at the end of the tunnel.

These sentences create startling, jarring pictures; the reader is brought up short, startled by the odd combinations of pictures, and the argument is momentarily derailed. The first two examples—the red herring and the house of cards—are taken from actual political rhetoric; I found both on the editorial pages of one of the country's great newspapers. It is difficult to suppress a smile when you read these gaffes; the writer's righteous indignation becomes funny rather than serious. If writers actually thought about what their metaphors were saying, they would not create these absurd mixtures.

When you venture into metaphor, be sure the comparison you choose is helpful rather than distracting, stay with a single comparison, be sure it does not get out of control, and abandon the metaphor the instant it no longer serves your purpose.

## SPELLING ISSUES

### Using a Dictionary

English, as we pointed out previously, is a wondrous language, rich in vocabulary and synonyms, but it does have the disadvantage of illogical and inconsistent spelling. Study the following list of words, circle the ones that are misspelled, and write the correct spellings in the space at the right.

| | |
|---|---|
| accommodate | liaison |
| anomaly | millennium |
| calendar | occasion |
| consensus | parallel |
| desperate | predilection |
| embarrassment | resistance |
| exhilarate | sacrilegious |
| fallacy | supersede |
| indispensable | tranquillity |
| judgment | weird |

How many mistakes did you find? Actually, all these spellings are correct; check a reliable dictionary. The point was not to trick you, but to illustrate that English spelling is difficult. Even professional writers and editors keep a reliable dictionary handy and consult it frequently; you may have noticed as you studied the above list that the longer you look at a word, the stranger it looks. Even common words begin to look wrong if you stare at them long enough.

There are two ways to improve your spelling skills. The first is to accept the fact that spelling matters; unless you take correct spelling seriously, it will always seem random and impossible. Secondly, you have to own and use a good dictionary. No one expects every undergraduate student to own one of the oversize dictionaries, such as *Webster's Third New International Dictionary,* but you need to own and use a good college dictionary, one of the standard hardbound dictionaries, such as *Merriam-Webster's Collegiate, American Heritage College, Random House Webster's College,* or *Webster's New World.* Note that dictionary titles sound similar and frequently contain the same names, such as Merriam and Webster. *Merriam-Webster's Collegiate* is presently in its eleventh edition, and is a reliable standard work, frequently revised. In any dictionary, when two spellings are listed for a word, assume that the first one is the standard and use it in your writing.

One group of words that students frequently misspell is adjectives and nouns derived from Latin participles. In American English, the final vowel in words such as "predominant" and "occurrence" is pronounced as a *schwa* (an "uh" sound). Therefore, one cannot spell these words correctly simply by sounding them out. Since the choice of vowel depends ultimately on the conjugation of the Latin root, the only way to be sure of the spelling, short of learning Latin, is to look it up, and continue to look it up, until you are sure of it.

### Forming Possessives

The rule for forming possessives is this: Add an apostrophe and an "s" to form the possessive of a singular noun; add an apostrophe to form the possessive of plural nouns. An exception is plural words that end in letters other than "s," such as "women" and "children"; the plural of these words is formed by adding an apostrophe and "s" (Chicago 15, 17-22). Note also that one should add an apostrophe and an "s" to proper nouns that end in "s" or another sibilant, except for any multisyllabic name with an unaccented ending pronounced "-eez," such as "Euripides" or "Sophocles." Thus, in current practice, the following possessives are correct.

| | | |
|---|---|---|
| Dickens's | Berlioz's | Demosthenes' |
| Marx's | Ives's | Albeniz's |
| Burns's | Brahms's | Josquin des Prez's |

These possessives, although they are correct, look strange and sound awkward when you read them aloud. One can always avoid the problem by rewriting the phrase.

the symphonies of Ives **instead of** Ives's symphonies

the motets of Josquin des Prez **instead of** Josquin des Prez's motets

the influence of Berlioz on later program music **instead of** Berlioz's influence on later program music

### Plurals of Borrowed Latin and Greek Words

Some students find it difficult to remember the singular and plural forms of borrowed Greek and Latin words; society at large has the same trouble. Writers frequently forget that "data" and "media," for instance, are the plural forms of "datum" and "medium," not singular nouns.

**Incorrect:** The media has blown this problem all out of proportion.

**Correct:** The media have blown this problem all out of proportion.

**Incorrect:** The data proves that lab rats prefer Mozart to Schoenberg.

**Correct:** The data prove that lab rats prefer Mozart to Schoenberg.

In order to use borrowed Latin and Greek words correctly, one must either memorize the correct form or consult a trustworthy dictionary. Following is a list of frequently misused borrowed Greek and Latin words, with their correct singular and plural forms.

| Singular | Plural |
|---|---|
| addendum | addenda |
| alumnus (masculine) | alumni (masculine or mixed genders) |
| alumna (feminine) | alumnae (feminine) |
| crisis | crises |
| criterion | criteria |
| curriculum | curricula |
| datum | data |
| erratum | errata |
| medium | media |
| phenomenon | phenomena |
| thesis | theses |

### Foreign Words

Related to the issue of spelling is the question of correct treatment of foreign words. As a general rule, all foreign words are set in italics. A foreign word that you plan to use frequently is often set in italics at its first appearance, where it is defined, and set roman after that. When foreign words are proper nouns or appear within quotation marks, as in a title, they need not be set in italics, since the capital letter or quotation marks already set them off from the text.

Foreign words and names must be copied exactly as they appear in reference works, with all the appropriate accents, umlauts, tildes, and other diacritical marks. To omit any of these marks is to misspell the word or the name. It is no longer necessary to add these marks by hand; learn the proper commands and keystrokes to get your word-processing program to print these marks. Unless you have studied the foreign language in question, it is difficult to remember the exact nature and location of each accent mark, especially when dealing with Slavic names, such as Dvořák, or with long foreign titles, such as the French title of Debussy's *Prelude to the Afternoon of a Faun*. Consult a reliable reference work such as the *New Grove* or the

*Harvard Dictionary* and carefully follow the exact spellings found in those resources.

Recently there have been changes in the standard ways of transliterating names from foreign alphabets. There is a new method of transliterating Chinese characters; we now write "Beijing" instead of "Peking." There have also been changes in the standard way of transliterating Russian names from the Cyrillic alphabet. One now sees spellings such as "Rakhmaninov," rather than the older Germanic spellings. It is always safe to follow the spellings found in standard reference works, provided that one follows the spelling consistently. When a project focuses on a single composer or a few works, the writer quickly becomes accustomed to the correct spelling and accents of the names that appear frequently. One must rely on standard reference works and then be rigidly consistent in using one standard spelling.

### Medieval and Renaissance Names

Some students have difficulty with the names of medieval and Renaissance personages, referring incorrectly to "da Vinci" or "de Vitry" as if those were family names. One standard way of naming people in those periods was by given name and place of origin—"Guillaume de Machaut," "Guido of Arezzo," "Leonardo da Vinci," "Giovanni Pierluigi da Palestrina." At other times, people were known by their given name and an epithet, a description of something characteristic of them—"William the Conqueror" (known as "William the Bastard" before his famous victory in 1066), "Prince Henry the Navigator," "Richard Lion-heart," "Notker the Stammerer," and "Charles the Bald." Compounding the confusion, medieval and Renaissance names often appear in several different languages, so that one can find many different versions of the same name. Petrus de Cruce, as he is known in Latin, is sometimes referred to as "Pierre de la Croix," and the Italian Trecento theorist is referred to as "Marchettus Padovensis," his Latin name, or "Marchetto da Padova" in Italian; in English his name is "Marchetto of Padua." However you choose to refer to one of these personages, do not mix languages—"Marchettus of Padova," mixing three languages, is wrong—and use the same form consistently.

Unfortunately, we have not been consistent in referring to these historical figures; we commonly speak of "Machaut" and "Palestrina" as if those were the composers' last names, rather than the towns where they were born. Libraries alphabetize Machaut correctly under "G" for "Guillaume," whereas Palestrina is usually found under "P." Incidentally, the only reason that we have been able to use "Machaut" and "Palestrina" to refer to these individuals is that no one else of historical importance came from those towns. We could not use the same system for other places and use "Paris," "Rome," "Venice," or "London" as the names of specific persons.

When you are working on a project that involves names such as these, consult a reliable reference work and be consistent in referring to them exactly as the sources do.

## SOME TROUBLESOME WORD PAIRS

This section singles out for discussion a few similar pairs of words that are frequently confused in student papers.

### *Its* and *It's*

It should not be difficult to distinguish these two tiny words and use them correctly. "Its," without an apostrophe, is the possessive form of the pronoun "it"; "it's," with the apostrophe, is a contraction of "it is." The common error is to use "it's" to indicate possession, probably because we associate the apostrophe with possession.

**Incorrect:** The committee will announce it's decision on Monday.

**Correct:** The committee will announce its decision on Monday.

Just remember that "its" is the possessive pronoun. "It's," the contraction, would seldom be appropriate in a formal paper, since contractions are generally out of place in that context.

### *Your* and *You're*

A similar situation exists with these two words. "Your," without the apostrophe, is the possessive form of the second person pronoun; "you're," with the apostrophe, is a contraction for "you are." The common error is to use "you're" to indicate possession, again probably because of the association of the apostrophe with possession. "You're," the contraction, is not likely to be appropriate in a formal paper.

**Incorrect:** You're solo in last night's concert was beautiful.

**Correct:** Your solo in last night's concert . . .

### *Whose* and *Who's*

A similar situation exists between "whose," the possessive form of the relative pronoun "who," and "who's," a contraction of "who is." The common mistake, as in the two previous cases, is to write the contraction instead of the correct possessive. Once again, awareness that contractions are generally out of place in a formal paper will help you to avoid these errors.

**Incorrect:** Leonard Bernstein, who's works span a wide variety of genres and styles . . .

**Correct:** Leonard Bernstein, whose works span a wide variety . . .

### Affect and Effect

These two words cause great confusion for writers. Put as simply as possible, "affect" is generally a verb meaning "to produce an effect or change." It also can be used as a noun meaning an emotion. "Effect" is generally a noun meaning "the result, consequence, or outcome of something." It can also be used as a verb meaning "to achieve or bring about." In the following sentences, the two words are used correctly.

Her performance affected me greatly.

The effect of her solo was startling.

Music is a powerful way to portray affects such as love and yearning.

If the committee manages to effect a change in the entrance requirements, the effect on the school will be enormous.

### Due to and Because of

Student writers sometimes confuse "due to" and "because of." "Due" is an adjective, not a conjunction; therefore, "due to" can be correctly used only after some form of the verb "to be," as a predicate adjective. "Due to" is not correct at the beginning of a sentence.

**Incorrect:** Due to the troubled political climate in Italy, Verdi constantly had trouble with the Austrian censors.

**Correct:** Because of the troubled political climate in Italy, Verdi constantly had trouble with the Austrian censors.

**Correct:** Verdi's constant trouble with the Austrian censors was due to the troubled political climate in Italy.

### Fewer and Less

"Fewer" and "less" are both antonyms of "more." "Fewer" means a smaller number of individual, countable things; "less" means a smaller amount of a single thing. The common error is to use "less" to apply to countable things instead of "fewer."

**Incorrect:** The band would sound better with less clarinets.

**Correct:** The band would sound better if there were fewer clarinets.

**Correct:** That soprano would sound better with less vibrato.

### Like and Such as

In everyday speech, we use "like" to introduce specific examples of something general—"composers like Bach and Handel," "double-reed instruments like the oboe." Taken literally, these phrases refer not to Bach and Handel, but to other composers, composers *similar to* Bach and Handel, and to other double-reed instruments, not the oboe itself. If you mean to refer to Bach and Handel as examples, write "composers such as Bach and Handel"; if you want to include the oboe, write "double-reed instruments such as the oboe." The distinction may seem fussy, but think of the literal meaning.

### *Predominant* and *Predominate*

"Predominant," like "dominant," is an adjective; "predominate," like "dominate," is a verb. The common error is to use "predominate" as an adjective. The words are used correctly in the following sentences.

The predominant composer of the high Renaissance was Josquin des Prez.

The predominant aesthetic credo of the Romantic period . . .

The aesthetic view that predominates over the entire period . . .

### *Principal* and *Principle*

"Principal" is generally an adjective meaning "main" or "most important," although it can also be used as a noun meaning "the head of a school" or "an amount of money." "Principle" is a noun meaning "a fundamental law or doctrine." In the following sentences the two words are used correctly.

The new principal horn of the Philharmonic is Ignaz Feuermann.

The new principal of the high school has greatly improved the music program.

A good essay must be based on the principles of unity and coherence.

He is a man of principle.

The discussion of troublesome pairs of words could go on much longer. We have discussed only a few; the style guides have much longer lists. All these issues go back to a principle discussed earlier: The writer should treat words with respect and choose them carefully, conscious of their literal meaning and import.

## PUNCTUATION

Correct punctuation is another troublesome area for many student writers. Consult Chapter 6 of *The Chicago Manual of Style* or Part VI of the *Simon & Schuster Handbook* for authoritative discussions of the proper use of punctuation. Students who have trouble with punctuation should also know about some lighter, more entertaining guides to punctuation, such as *Lapsing into a Comma*, by Bill Walsh; *The Comma Sutra*, by Laurie Rozakis; and *Eats, Shoots &*

*Leaves,* by Lynne Truss, which they might find very helpful. Here we will mention a few situations that seem to cause problems for students.

### The Period

The period is used after every complete sentence. It is also used after abbreviations such as "m." for "measure," "mm." for "measures," and "ms." for "manuscript." All footnotes end with a period. In bibliography entries, a period appears between the author's name and the title, between the title and the publication information, and at the end of the entry. See Chapter 6 for discussion of the proper format for footnotes and bibliographies.

In a typed paper, it is accepted practice to put a space after every period, particularly after periods that follow abbreviations. Thus it is incorrect to write "m.5" and "mm.15–22"; the correct way is "m. 5" and "mm. 15–22," with the space. There should also be a space after the period following an initial in a name—thus, "J. S. Bach," not "J.S.Bach" or "J.S. Bach." Academic degrees, on the other hand, do not include spaces between the initials— thus, "B.A.," "M.A.," "M.M.," "D.M.A.," and "Ph.D."

**Note**  Many of us were trained to double-space after a period or any other punctuation mark at the end of a sentence. That practice has fallen into disuse; the usual explanation is that that extra space is not necessary, now that most fonts have proportional spacing. There still are situations when I think the extra space is an improvement, for instance at the end of a sentence that ends with a quotation followed by a period, quotation marks, and a footnote number. At this point it seems to be a matter of choice or the writer's preference. Whatever you choose to do, you must do it consistently throughout the paper.

### The Comma

Some student writers seem mystified by the comma and its proper use; some situations seem particularly troublesome.

**Series**  In a series containing more than two items, commas should separate each item, including the last one.

> The leading composers of the Mannheim school were Johann Stamitz, Ignaz Holzbauer, Christian Cannabich, and Carl Stamitz.

Some style guides now allow the omission of the last comma, before "and," provided that a comma is not required for clarity. That style of punctuating a series is common in journalistic style, but not in scholarly papers; *The Chicago Manual of Style* (6.19) requires the inclusion of that final comma, which is referred to as a "serial" comma. If one chooses to omit it, there is always the danger that the last two items will be read as a two-part single item, like Gilbert and Sullivan or macaroni and cheese.

**Appositives**    If a phrase simply tells us something more about a noun, rather than making a general noun more specific, it should be set off by commas.

Monteverdi's *Orfeo*, an opera in the Florentine style, was first performed in 1607.

If an appositive phrase is restrictive—that is, if it makes a general noun specific—then commas are not used.

Verdi's opera *La Traviata* is based on a novel by Dumas.

If commas were used to set off the title in that last sentence, the writer would be saying that *La Traviata* was the only opera Verdi composed—Verdi's one opera.

**Restrictive and nonrestrictive clauses**    Commas are used to set off nonrestrictive clauses, just as they are used to set off nonrestrictive appositives; commas are not used to set off restrictive clauses.

Arnold Schoenberg, who fled from Nazi Germany in the thirties, . . .

The composers who fled from Nazi Germany in the thirties . . .

In the first sentence, the relative clause is nonrestrictive; it adds information rather than making a general subject more specific, since we already know who the subject is. Therefore, commas must be used. In the second sentence, the relative clause is restrictive, making the general noun "composers" more specific; the clause answers the question "Which composers?" Therefore, commas are not used.

**Compound and complex sentences**    A comma is used between the clauses of a compound sentence, provided that they are joined by a conjunction. If the clauses are short and there is no possibility of confusion, the comma may be omitted.

Berg used the twelve-tone system freely to create a style we usually describe as expressionist, but Webern extended the twelve-tone idea into new areas.

Bach played and his wife sang.

A comma is used between the clauses of complex sentences.

Although much of the music of the postwar period can be traced to the influence of Webern, the neoromanticism of recent years can be interpreted as a return to the freer and more expressive style of Berg.

**Introductory phrases**    A comma is generally used after all introductory phrases. If the introductory phrase is short and there is no possibility of misinterpretation, the comma may be omitted. Both the following sentences are punctuated correctly.

Judging from the correspondence, we can conclude that Brahms was very worried about the first performance of his First Symphony.

In 1723 Bach accepted the post of Cantor at the *Thomaskirche* in Leipzig.

In the case of a short introductory phrase, if there is any possibility of confusion or what the *Chicago Manual* calls "mistaken junction," the comma should be included to ensure clarity.

**Confusing:** Soon after the concert was interrupted by loud catcalls and angry denunciations.

**Clear:** Soon after, the concert was interrupted by loud catcalls and angry denunciations.

Without the comma, the eye sees "after the concert" as a prepositional phrase, confusing the reader.

Commas are also used in some other situations:

In titles, dates, and numbers:
Friday, September 4, 1596; 425,000.

To set off parenthetical elements, interjections, and words of direct address:
Bach, it is believed, was born on March 21.
The evidence, dear reader, supports my conclusion.

To separate complementary or antithetical elements:
Bach's harsh, though at the same time brilliant, criticism was not lost on the town council.

To separate elements forming a confusing conjunction:
To Gilbert, Sullivan was an enigma.

In elliptical constructions to indicate omission:
Beethoven wrote nine symphonies; Brahms, four.

### The Semicolon

The semicolon marks a more important break in the flow of a sentence than breaks marked by a comma. In particular, the semicolon is used to separate the two parts of a compound sentence when they are not connected by a conjunction.

Stravinsky performed as a pianist and conductor all his life; Schoenberg was a university teacher.

**Note**   Words like "however," "still," "yet," and "hence" are adverbs, not conjunctions. Therefore, if the second clause starts with one of these words, a comma is not sufficient punctuation between the clauses; a semicolon is necessary. As an alternative, one can rewrite the sentence as two separate sentences.

**Incorrect:** Stravinsky performed as a pianist and conductor all his life, however Schoenberg was a university professor.

**Correct:** Stravinsky performed as a pianist and conductor all his life; Schoenberg, however, was a university professor.

**Correct:** Stravinsky performed as a pianist and conductor all his life. Schoenberg, however, was a university professor.

Semicolons are used to separate items in a series when they are long and complex and when they contain internal commas.

Among Verdi's most popular works are *Rigoletto,* produced in Venice in 1851; *La Traviata,* produced in Venice in 1853; and *Aïda,* produced in Cairo in 1871.

### The Colon

The colon is used to mark a greater break in the flow of a sentence than breaks marked by the semicolon. In expository prose, the colon has two main uses. The first is to introduce a formal statement or quotation; the second is to introduce a list. Note that if the material after the colon is a complete sentence, the first word after the colon is capitalized.

The rule may be stated thus: Material that appeared in the dominant or in another related key in the exposition returns in the tonic in the recapitulation.

He answered as follows: No prince may force me to compose at his whim.

Rosen's book deals with the composers whom he views as the chief exponents of the Classical style: Haydn, Mozart, and Beethoven.

### Quotation Marks

In Chapter 5 we discussed the proper format for brief and long quotations and the conventions one should follow when citing the words of someone else. You may want to review that section. Here we need to add a few rules about quotation marks in combination with other kinds of punctuation. Note that American practice diverges from British practice in this matter; we will explain American practice.

1. Periods and commas required by the context of the sentence are placed inside the quotation marks, whether or not the period or the comma is part of the quoted material. Logical or not, the following sentences are correctly punctuated.

At the conclusion of "Sempre libera," we know much more about Violetta's character and her ambivalence about love.

A striking example of Ives's technique of quotation is "Decoration Day."

This rule seems to cause more objections and discussions than any other. What bothers students is that the comma in the first sentence is not part of the quoted title, any more than the period is part of the title of "Decoration Day." Nevertheless, in the United States those punctuation marks are placed inside the quotation marks. Period.

2. Semicolons, colons, question marks, and exclamation points required by the context of the sentence are placed outside quotation marks. Thus:

A good example of his collage technique is "Decoration Day"; a clear example of his impressionist style is "The Housatonic at Stockbridge."

Again this may seem to defy logic. The only difference between these two clauses is the fact that they use different punctuation marks; the semicolon after the first clause goes outside the quotation marks, but the period at the end goes inside. That's the way we do it here in the United States. Compare an article published in America with one published in Britain, and you will see the difference in the way we handle this matter.

### The Hyphen

The hyphen is used to divide the first part of a word at the end of a line from the second part at the beginning of the next line. Students frequently err in the way they divide words. Short or one-syllable words should not be divided at all; longer words may be divided, provided that you follow the rules for dividing words correctly. Consult a dictionary to check the proper division of the word, which is often different than you might guess, or keep the word together and start it on the next line.

Hyphens are also used in compound constructions such as "two-voice," "one-syllable," "time-consuming," and "long-neglected" provided that they function as adjectives and appear before the nouns they modify. Generally, compounds are not hyphenated when they appear as predicate adjectives after the sentence's verb.

A well-read person would not make a glaring mistake like that.

I like talking with him because he is well read.

It is impossible to keep straight in your mind all the compounds that are hyphenated versus the ones written as one word or written as two words. Accepted practice seems to be moving in the direction of using fewer hyphens; "lowercase," "neoclassical," and "nonconformist," for example, are standard now. One should consult an up-to-date dictionary if there is any doubt whether or not a compound should be hyphenated. Even if standard usage does not require a hyphen, it may be necessary to use a hyphen in some situations to avoid confusion.

The so-called suspended hyphen can be used in compound constructions, but it can be confusing and should be used with great care. It is correct to write "three- and four-voice polyphony," or "four-, five-, and "six-voice madrigals," meaning "three-voice and four-voice polyphony," and "madrigals for four, five, and six voices," but be careful that your meaning is clear and your punctuation is correct.

On most keyboards, a hyphen is also used to indicate ranges of numbers, as in "pp. 45-48" or "1984-87." Publishers use a small dash, called an "en dash," larger than a hyphen and smaller than a regular dash, for that purpose. If your program allows that, fine; otherwise, use a hyphen.

### The Dash

Long dashes, called em dashes, can be used in expository prose to interrupt a sentence's structure to add information, such as a definition, an explanation, or a reaction or comment. Although this construction should be used with restraint, it can be effective.

> The composers of the late madrigal—Marenzio, Monteverdi, and Gesualdo—based their musical style on rhetorical effects.

There are several other ways to convey that idea without using the dashes. Note also that on most keyboards now, you can form a continuous em dash rather than the two hyphens formerly used as a substitute; note also that no space appears before or after the dash.

### Parentheses

Parentheses are used to enclose additional information that breaks up the flow of the sentence. The most common error in the use of parentheses is to overuse them. If the material in parentheses is important, it deserves to be included in the regular text, without parentheses. If it is not important, don't include it in the text at all—leave it out or put it in a footnote. Parentheses are a way to fit in last-minute additions and afterthoughts; constant use of parentheses means that the writer has not thought out clearly what he or she wants to say.

There are many other rules and details about punctuation. There is no need to discuss exclamation points here, since they are of little use in expository prose. Experience with student papers shows that the most critical need is for students to learn the correct use of the comma. For further details of correct punctuation, consult Chapter 6 of *The Chicago Manual of Style,* Chapter 3 of the Turabian guide, or Part VI of the *Simon & Schuster Handbook for Writers.*

## SPECIAL PROBLEMS INVOLVED IN WRITING ABOUT MUSIC

### Technical Terms

Every field of study has its own vocabulary of technical terms. We need these terms so that we can describe musical events with some accuracy and precision, and so that readers can understand exactly what we are trying to say. If we did not have terms such as "sonata-allegro form," "Wagner style," or "impressionism," we would have to write long descriptions of what we mean. In order to use this powerful means of communication effectively, we should be aware of some guidelines for the use of technical terms.

**Using technical terms correctly**    First, treat technical terms with respect, and use them carefully. Each term, like any other word, has its own particular force and connotation, and the writer should use that term only when that precise force and connotation is appropriate. There are several terms, for instance, for polyphonic texture: imitation, canon, fugue, fugato, stretto, etc. These terms are not interchangeable. Each has its own special shade of meaning, and, if the writer carelessly uses them as if they were synonyms, the reader will not get a true impression of what the writer is trying to say. Technical terms should be used with care and respect.

Second, choose standard technical terms; do not try to make up new ones. Sometimes students coin ungainly new terms to describe musical phenomena, such as "a fugue-type texture," or "a sonata-like structure." In the first instance, the student probably means "an imitative texture," or "a polyphonic texture." The standard terms are much clearer and much more elegant than awkward, newly invented pseudo-terms.

Third, be careful about anachronistic use of technical terms. An *anachronism* is something inappropriate for the time under discussion; it would be an anachronism if, in a production of *Romeo and Juliet,* Romeo pulled out a cell phone and called Mercutio in the middle of the balcony scene. Anachronistic terminology frequently appears in students' discussions of early music; some students use the term "fugal" to describe imitative writing in Renaissance Masses and motets. "Fugal" mean something different from the compositional practice in question; "fugue" as a technical term refers to eighteenth-century musical practice, and is inappropriate in discussions of Renaissance music. Other obvious examples of anachronistic use of technical terms would be writing about secondary dominants in Machaut motets, modulation from key to key in Gesualdo madrigals, or, moving in the opposite direction, isorhythm in Stravinsky's Mass. It takes work to uncover complex ways of organizing and relating musical events in a composition; it also takes care and precision to find or choose the appropriate term to describe what you see and hear going on.

Finally, as we pointed out in Chapter 7, once you use a word as a technical term, it is no longer available for use in its general, nontechnical sense; you cannot use the term in both senses.

**Genre, form, and style**    Musicological writings regularly use some general terms to express the nature and characteristics of the music under discussion. Among these terms are *genre, form,* and *style,* three important terms that overlap to some extent but actually represent distinct points of view in regard to musical works. Because there is some overlap, one can find examples in which writers appear to use them almost as synonyms; no wonder students have some difficulty using the terms precisely and convincingly in their writing. Let us try to make clear the distinctions among these terms.

***Genre*** is a general term for the category or kind of musical work represented by the example under discussion; examples of genres are terms such as "symphony," "motet," "concerto," and "opera." Genres are generally very inclusive terms; the genre "symphony" includes works as diverse as Haydn's "Drum-roll," Beethoven's Ninth, Bruckner's Seventh, Mahler's "Resurrection" Symphony, and Stravinsky's Symphony in Three Movements, among hundreds of others. "Symphony" does not imply a specific form, unless the context makes clear that the writer is talking about a group of similar works such as the Mozart symphonies. Even then, although there may be formal or stylistic implications associated with the term, the fact that an individual work departs from the standard expectations does mean that it is not a symphony. Other inclusive genres include "opera," which includes works as diverse as *Orfeo, Giulio Cesare, Don Giovanni, Salome,* and *Nixon in China;* and "Mass," which includes works by, for example, Josquin des Prez, Bach, Mozart, Beethoven, and Stravinsky. On the other hand, some genres are confined to a narrower time period, and therefore connote more details about matters of form and style. An example of that sort of genre is "ballata," nearly always used for Italian Trecento vocal pieces in a particular form—AbbaA, like the *virelai.* Still, as a genre, the term first and foremost connotes a category of music, not a form or style.

*Form,* our term for the way musical ideas are organized to create coherent larger compositions, seems to be a more straightforward concept than "genre" or "style." "Form" implies something observable, quantifiable. We regard terms such as "sonata-allegro form," "rondo," "fugue," "theme and variations," "ABA form," "strophic form," and "ritornello form" as clear and definite, standing for a specific pattern that either is or is not present in a few pages of score. But even here, things are not always that clear. "Sonata-allegro" and "fugue," for example, are often defined as processes rather than specific forms. In addition, a term such as "sonata-allegro form" can be applied to vastly diverse musical works; although we associate the term first with Mozart and Haydn, Tchaikowsky's "Romeo and Juliet" Overture can be analyzed as a huge, overblown sonata-allegro structure, with a slow introduction five minutes long, as long as the entire first movement of a typical Classical symphony. Although we often use the term "rondo" as an abstract formal term for any structure we can diagram as ABACA or ABACABA, no matter what the period or style is, the term has always carried connotations of a dance form, a lighthearted romp, suitable for the finale of a symphony or concerto. Even the concept of form is not as simple as it might seem, but form seems to be easier to grasp than the cloudier concepts of genre and style.

*Style* refers to the specific characteristics of a piece of music that give it its specific identity. "Style" embraces the details of every facet of a musical work—its melodic contours, rhythm and meter, articulation, harmonic vocabulary, instrumentation, and so forth. The concept of style is what we use to identify and understand a musical work as we listen to it; the term embraces the details that we identify and process to create a mental picture of the music. In addition, the term "style" is connected with the general concept of "stylistic periods," such as Renaissance, Baroque, Classical, and Romantic, or seventeenth- and eighteenth-century. "Baroque," if you think about it, cannot possibly be a term for a single style, since, like any arbitrary historical construct, the period we call the Baroque era embraces works as stylistically diverse as monodies by Monteverdi and Rossi, polychoral motets by Schütz, experimental violin sonatas by Biagio Marini, Lully operas, Handel oratorios, and Bach cantatas.

Perhaps an example will help clarify the distinctions among these three terms. Let us imagine that you are looking at the first movement of a Haydn string quartet. The genre of this piece, in the broadest sense, is "chamber music," as opposed to orchestral music, solo vocal music, piano music, choral music, etc. The specific genre, of course, is "string quartet." Like the other terms for genres, "string quartet" is a very inclusive term, including works as diverse as quartets by Mozart, Beethoven, and Bartók. The correct term for the form of a Haydn first movement is probably "sonata-allegro form," but might be "sonata-rondo" or some other form; you have to read through the score to be sure. The style of the movement embraces all the musical details—the nature of the melodic ideas, meter and rhythm, the interplay between the four instruments, the harmonic language, etc. In a listening exam, the stylistic details are the evidence you use to identify the genre, form, and general style of the piece.

Keep these concepts clear in your head; knowing how these three related but distinct terms are used will not only help to clarify your thinking about musical works; using them correctly will help establish your understanding of music and ability to discuss it intelligently.

### Describing Musical Events

We pointed out in Chapter 1 that it is not easy to describe musical events. Finding a clear way of expressing what occurs in a musical work is sometimes a difficult challenge. Three particular questions deserve discussion.

**Point of view: Subjects and verbs**    One area to consider carefully is how to describe what happens in a musical work. If you want to describe a striking cadenza in a violin concerto, for example, there are several ways of stating your idea. Consider the following sentences.

> The solo violin embarks on a brilliant exploration of motives taken from the first theme.

> The composer turns the soloist loose in a brilliant cadenza based on motives taken from the first theme.

> Motives taken from the first theme are woven into a brilliant cadenza.

None of these descriptions is completely satisfactory. The first seems to ascribe the cadenza to the instrument rather than to the composer or the soloist; the second overpersonalizes the interaction between composer and interpreter; the third falls into the passive voice. Perhaps the following versions are more suitable.

> A brilliant cadenza for the soloist continues to explore motives taken from the first theme.

> The soloist then plays a brilliant cadenza based on motives taken from the first theme.

Experiment with several versions of musical description until you find one that avoids the multiple pitfalls of pretentious language, overly personal description, and weak passive-voice constructions.

**Point of view: Tenses**    It is not always easy to choose the proper tense of the verbs when describing musical events. In general, the present tense is appropriate when the reader's attention is focused on the music itself. If the emphasis is on the composer's act of creating the music or on the details of a particular performance, the past tense is appropriate. Consider the verb tenses in the following sentences.

> In the opening chorus of Cantata No. 4, the sopranos sing the chorale melody in long notes, while the other voices sing free counterpoint.

> In the opening chorus of Cantata No. 4, Bach assigned the chorale tune to the sopranos and composed free counterpoint for the other voices.

> Near the end of the coda, the brass section repeats the main theme once more, bringing this long movement to a dramatic conclusion.

> In typical Romantic fashion, Liszt chose to restate the main theme once more near the end of the coda, assigning it to the brass section.

One reads statements like "Bach assigns the chorale tune to the sopranos," but that wording is jarring—after all, Bach died a long time ago. Even when describing ongoing or repeated actions that took place in the past, the past tense makes better sense than the present.

> Schubert consistently chose the texts for his songs from the works of a few favorite poets.

> Bach based many of his cantatas on the chorale tunes that had been traditional in the Lutheran church for 200 years.

Another error is to use both present and past tenses in the same sentence or paragraph. If you start by using the present tense, choosing as your point of view the style and organization of the music rather than the composer's creative choices, stay with that point of view and that tense. Constant vacillation between present and past tense is confusing to readers.

**Finding appropriate ways to state qualitative judgments**    Another challenge in writing about music, or any art, is finding appropriate ways to state qualitative judgments. It is not enough for the writer to label everything "beautiful." The writer must search through the huge store of synonyms in the English language to find the exact word that says what he or she wants to say. The weakest possible critical term is "interesting"; that is what one mumbles when standing, baffled, in front of the latest avant-garde painting or installation. Words like "stirring," "ravishing," "majestic," "eerie," or "chilling" might be appropriate to describe late Romantic works, but would hardly be the right words to describe a Renaissance Mass or some of the more abstract and cerebral styles of twentieth-century music. On the other hand, "original," "challenging," "intriguing," "tightly organized," or "cerebral" may work to describe modernistic music, but are probably not the correct terms for late Romantic tone poems.

It takes thought and creativity to come up with exactly the right word to describe the aesthetic effect of a particular piece of music. One wants to avoid both extremes—dull words like "interesting," and affected or pretentious language. Finding the right evaluative word to use in your summary or conclusion may seem to be the most difficult part of writing a paper, but it is worth the struggle to find the one word that will say exactly what you want to say and provide a strong, effective conclusion.

## SUMMARY

This chapter has discussed some problems that mar student writing in any field, along with some of the special difficulties of writing about music. The advice is intended to be practical and helpful; if you approach your writing assignments armed with an awareness of common writing errors and ways to avoid them, your task should be easier. You should be able to write and edit your assignments with a greater sense of security, confident that your papers are more likely to be taken seriously as representative of the high quality of your work.

# Conclusion

Since the purpose of this book is to provide practical advice about writing research papers and other projects on musical topics, the emphasis in the second half of the book has been on the mechanics and technical details of writing. These details are important; carelessness about these seemingly minor matters can defeat the writer's goal of conveying his or her ideas to the reader. The unifying theme of this book, running through all the discussions of details, is that effective writing takes time, care, and precision. Each step in the process of writing a paper—research, drafting, editing, printing, and proofreading—demands that the writer understand each specific task and expend the necessary time and effort to do things in the proper way. In order to succeed as a writer, you must take sufficient pride in your work to care about technical matters such as proper format, correct spelling, and careful editing. Students will never succeed in their writing assignments until they develop a competent and professional prose style.

It is time now to step back from the details and return to the larger perspective with which the book began. Competent and careful writing can vastly improve a paper, and a careless writing style can lessen or even destroy altogether the effectiveness of a paper. Important as it is to develop an effective and persuasive writing style, however, a good writing style is not enough in itself to produce convincing prose about music. The ability to write clear, well-organized prose is only a means of communicating the writer's insight and vision about the art of music. To write well about music, the writer needs two different things: vision and insight about music and the writing skill to communicate that vision clearly and forcefully. Unless the writer has the analytical skills to understand a musical work, the aesthetic sensitivity to appreciate its beauty, the historical insight to understand its significance in the history of music, and the awareness to see how it relates to cultural issues, all the writing skill in the world will not produce prose worth reading. Even an understanding of music and its history is not enough to produce a good paper; one also needs the imagination and creativity to design a thesis or point of view that gathers all the data into a unified, forceful statement. One needs to have both something to say and the skill to say it clearly and persuasively. I have presumed throughout this book that the student writer has something to say; my mission has been to provide practical assistance in the craft of saying it clearly.

I want to close with a plea to all students: Read as many books and articles about music as you can. Read voraciously. After you read the books and articles that are required in connection with your classes, read everything else you can. Read widely but critically, with one eye on the content and the other on the writing style. When you come across a writer whose style impresses you with its clarity and eloquence, find other writings by the same author, no matter what the subject, so that you can understand what makes this writer's style effective. Find models that impress you, and try to isolate exactly what it is about the writer's skill that makes his or her writings so clear and enjoyable to read. Learn from all your reading, always looking for ways to improve the force and clarity of your own writing. Improving your writing is a lifelong task, one that is never finished, but every effort to improve it, even in a small way, will make your writing more effective and your academic work more successful.

# Sample Paper

The fourth edition of this guide closes, as the earlier editions did, with a sample paper, an example of how all the matters discussed in the book come together to create an interesting and convincing research paper. The sample paper is a real research paper written several years ago by a real student; it is reprinted here with the permission of the writer, who is now a professor of music at a small Midwestern college. Read this paper carefully, taking note not only of what the writer is saying—the topic, thesis, and argumentation— but also of how he says it. This writer exercised exemplary care and precision in dealing with every phase of the process: research, organization, writing, editing, footnotes, bibliography, and format issues.

I like everything about this paper. I think the topic is creative and thought-provoking; it is always fascinating to glimpse the inner working of the creative process and the collaboration between librettist and composer. In addition, the writer has a definite thesis, which he argues convincingly, relying on his thorough control of the literature about these important artists and solid analysis of the music. He raises questions that pique our curiosity and defends his viewpoint on these questions with authority. His bibliography is remarkably extensive for a paper of this size, and he uses his sources well.

Close study of this paper would make a useful class project; it also would be a good exercise for you to undertake on your own. After scanning the paper quickly to get a general sense of the topic, thesis, and arguments, go over the paper again, carefully, page by page, sentence by sentence, trying to grasp how the writer dealt with the various issues and processes involved in writing. The following questions should help to guide your analysis of the paper.

1. What is the *topic* of this paper? Does the title accurately reflect what the actual topic is, or did it create expectations in your mind that were not met in the paper?

2. What is the *thesis* of this paper? Remember, the thesis is the topic sentence of the entire paper; it has to be a sentence, not just a word or two. Find the one sentence in the paper that you think states the thesis most clearly. Exactly where does this sentence appear in the paper? Does it appear early enough to guide the reader's thoughts? Too early? Too late? Are there several different sentences that you might single out as the best statement of the thesis?

3. List the main *arguments* the writer uses to defend his thesis, stating them in complete sentences. Are there any arguments that are not explained or defended sufficiently? Are the arguments discussed one by one, or do ideas from one argument bleed into another? Does the writer let you know when he is moving from one argument to another? Is the logical progression of his thought easy for the reader to follow?

4. Are there ideas that require more explanation? Does the writer assume too much prior knowledge in the reader? Do you understand his ideas and arguments, or do you feel left in the dark about anything?

5. Do you think he added anything to your ideas about the topic, or did he simply rehash familiar ideas and approaches? Did you feel that his arguments were convincing?

6. How about the *tone* of his language—Did he use too many technical terms or big words for you? Did he seem focused on arguing his ideas forcefully, or on establishing his knowledge of arcane facts?

7. Does the *introduction* lead smoothly into the topic, or did you feel it was either too short or too long? Does it contain ideas that you think need more explanation?

8. Does the *conclusion,* in your opinion, wrap up the whole project gracefully and convincingly? Did it leave you with the feeling that you would like to know more about this topic?

9. Look again at his *musical examples*. Were they well chosen? Was the point of each example clear? Did they advance his arguments effectively?

10. Finally, discuss your general reaction to the paper in a paragraph or two. How would you grade it, compared to other examples of student prose you have read? Would you call this writer a good writer? Is there anything you would change? In your opinion, are there sections of the paper that need to be expanded or need to be shortened? If you were the professor grading this paper, what grade would you assign to it?

At this point I could give you my own answers to these questions, but the point of the exercise is for you to develop your own critical skills. As I noted earlier, I consider this a model paper, a fine example of what first-rate student writers can achieve. I should speak to one possible problem that you may have noticed; the writer refers to the complex philosophical notion of word and deed in Goethe's *Faust* in one short introductory sentence and then moves immediately into his discussion of Strauss and Hofmannsthal. Perhaps you singled out that sentence as an example of an important concept that needs more explanation, or perhaps you felt the need for a longer introduction. There is a good reason for this brief reference. The paper was written for a class that had spent a great deal of time discussing Goethe's *Faust* and its influence on nineteenth-century literature and music; in this context, an elaborate explanation of the concept of word and deed in *Faust* was not necessary. Granting that one special circumstance, this paper is a fine model, one that you would do well to imitate in matters of argumentation, style, and format, as well as in general approach.

Finally, bear in mind that the process of analyzing prose about music is the same, whether you are reading a book, an article from one of the journals, or a student paper. Think of this same list of questions whenever you are reading expository prose about music or any other topic; reread a journal article that impressed you and ask those same questions. The more you try to take apart good prose—extracting the topic, thesis, and arguments, checking the outline, asking yourself whether the arguments are clear and convincing, thinking about the level and tone of the language, judging the effectiveness of the introduction and conclusion, and looking at details of format—the better you will understand the writing process and the more ways you will find to improve your own writing. Read everything you can, and read analytically, questioning the organization, content, language, and format of what you read. The best way to improve your writing is to read voraciously, read critically, and try to incorporate the good qualities of what you read into your own writing.

# ECHOES OF *FAUST*:
## Word versus Deed in the
## Recognition Scene of *Elektra*

Andrew Whitfield
MUS 896
May 3, 1999

When he addressed the question of word versus deed in *Faust,*[1] Johann Wolfgang von Goethe (1749–1832) raised an aesthetic dilemma that echoed throughout the nineteenth century. This dichotomy also represented a crucial factor in the artistic collaboration of Hugo von Hofmannsthal (1874–1929) and Richard Strauss (1864–1949), a relationship which officially began in 1906, when Strauss consented to set Hofmannsthal's drama *Elektra* to music. Although Hofmannsthal's free adaptation of Sophocles offers remarkably complex psychological characterizations, its plot centers on Elektra's obsession with the *deed* of revenge. Strauss telescoped Hofmannsthal's drama as much as possible because he "knew instinctively how important it was to reduce a text to its essentials in order to produce a good opera text."[2] Yet despite these exhaustive cuts, Strauss asked for additional text from Hofmannsthal when he needed more *words* in order to attain his musical goal. This paper will examine the ways in which the dramatic ideal and the musical ideal are affected by Strauss's musical and textual insertions in one of these key moments, the scene of recognition between Elektra and Orestes.

In order to understand the nature of Hofmannsthal's drama, one must first consider the defining aesthetic factors that governed Hofmannsthal's creativity in *fin-de-siècle* Vienna. Hofmannsthal began his literary career in Vienna as a poet at the age of seventeen, "quickly

[1]See Goethe's *Faust,* I: 1224–1237, where Faust is translating the opening line of the Gospel of John. In the Norton Critical Edition translation by Walter Arndt, Faust ultimately renders "In the beginning was the Word" as "In the beginning was the Deed."

[2]Bryan Gilliam, *Richard Strauss's Elektra* (Oxford: Clarendon Press, 1991), 36.

absorbing the fashionable poetic and plastic culture of all Europe."[3] The problem with this aesthetic direction for Hofmannsthal was that it felt too narcissistic and too solipsistic; the poet, who has a great dependency on and love for fashionable *words,* was condemned to seek the meaning of life "purely within his own psyche."[4] This meant that the poet's words would gradually cease to reflect human experience. Although the society that favored his poetry seemed perfectly content to live in this artistic "prison," Hofmannsthal rejected the notion of art as separate from society. According to Bryan Gilliam, "Hofmannsthal sought to forge connections between art and experience, between the individual and civilization."[5] Ultimately, Hofmannsthal recognized the potential for art to awaken the human instinct. Through an affirmation of the instinctual, the artist would then be released from his own psyche, and "the door to the life of action and society" would be opened again.[6]

It was at this point in his career that Hofmannsthal focused his attention on drama, and *Elektra* represents Hofmannsthal's first foray into this new artistic genre.[7] Although Hofmannsthal admired the fusion of the arts in theatre, the real importance of the medium was its use of gesture (as opposed to the *words* alone of poetry) as a means of expression.

[3]Carl E. Schorske, *Fin-de-Siècle Vienna: Politics and Culture* (New York: Vintage Books, 1981), pp. 15–16.
[4]Schorske, 16.
[5]Gilliam, 21.
[6]Schorske, 19.
[7]Gilliam, 23.

"A pure gesture is pure thought. . . . In pure gestures the true personality comes to light," observed Hofmannsthal in his 1911 essay *On Pantomime.*[8] For Hofmannsthal, words did not maintain this purity of gesture; they tended to "generalize rather than reveal pure thought."[9] This interest in gesture led Hofmannsthal to favor mythic subjects "reworked with a contemporary sensibility."[10] In the preface to *Die Ägyptische Helena,* Hofmannsthal defended his preference for mythological subjects:

> If this age of ours is anything, it is mythical—I know of no
> other expression for an existence that unfolds in the face of
> such vast horizons—for this being surrounded by millennia . . .
> for this immense inner breadth, these mad inner tensions. . . . It
> is impossible to catch all this in middle-class dialogue. Let us
> write mythological operas! Believe me they are the truest of
> all forms.[11]

Thus, for Hofmannsthal, the power of a mythological subject, such as *Elektra,* lay in its potential for the truest gesture contained in the truest form; furthermore, such an absolute gesture is the product not of words, but of action ("the *deed.*") Gilliam observes that this division between "language and gesture—between word and deed" is a primary theme in Hofmannsthal's *Elektra.*[12]

---

[8]Quoted in Gilliam, 22.
[9]Gilliam, 22.
[10]Robert Marx, "Act Two," *Opera News* 63, no. 9 (March 1999): 19.
[11]Quoted in Marx, pp. 19–20.
[12]Gilliam, 22.

It was in 1906 when Richard Strauss, having initially declined to write a ballet on Hofmannsthal's *Der Triumph der Zeit,*[13] consented to set *Elektra* (1903) to music. Although this was the beginning of a long artistic relationship between the two men, this particular project did not require much collaboration, since Strauss was the "major figure behind *Elektra's* transformation from play to libretto."[14] Gilliam estimates that Strauss reduced Hofmannsthal's text by nearly one-third.[15] While these intense cuts may have removed some of Hofmannsthal's psychological complexities, they certainly reinforced the drama's focus on gesture or action. In fact, one of the critical arguments with which Hofmannsthal convinced Strauss to set *Elektra,* despite its apparent similarity to *Salome*, was the intense burst of dramatic action which consumes the last third of the drama:

> What is more, the rapid rising sequence of events . . . which leads up to victory and purification—a sequence which I can imagine much more powerful in music than in the written word—is not matched by anything of a corresponding, or even faintly similar kind in *Salome.*[16]

Here, Hofmannsthal highlighted the "rapid rising sequence of events" as a key element of the work and alluded to the power of music to convey

[13]*The Correspondence between Richard Strauss and Hugo von Hofmannsthal,* trans. Hanns Hammelmann and Ewald Osers (London: William Collins Sons & Co. Ltd., 1961), 1.
[14]Gilliam, 18.
[15]Gilliam, 36.
[16]*The Correspondence between Richard Strauss and Hugo von Hofmannsthal,* 4.

this gesture better than words alone. All that Strauss did to telescope the drama for the operatic stage seems to support the overall nature of Hofmannsthal's drama.

Although Hofmannsthal did not participate in the task of reducing his play to a manageable opera libretto, Strauss did ask Hofmannsthal to provide additional text in several cases. In a letter of 1908, Strauss wrote in regard to the opera's finale:

> Enclosed herewith your final verses which I am asking you to extend as much as possible. . . . Nothing new, just the same contents, repeated and working towards a climax.[17]

Although there is no doubt that the purpose of Strauss's request is to satisfy his overall musical plan, it seems to negate his previous efforts to reduce the text to its most necessary elements. Furthermore, by asking for more of the same words, Strauss's artistic goal seems to contradict Hofmannsthal's celebration of gesture above word.

One scene that may serve as another example of this aesthetic conflict between the two artists is the scene of recognition between Elektra and her brother, Orestes. Elektra's father, Agamemnon, was betrayed and murdered by Elektra's mother, Klytämnestra, and her paramour, Aegistheus. Elektra cannot forgive her mother and lives to avenge her father's murder. After Elektra fails to persuade her sister, Chrysothemis, to help her, Elektra is left alone. A stranger enters, and

---

[17]*The Correspondence between Richard Strauss and Hugo von Hofmannsthal*, 18.

soon Elektra discovers it is her brother, Orestes, whom she believed to be dead. It is at this moment in the drama that Elektra realizes her destiny; in Orestes she has found someone to carry out the *deed* of revenge.

In a letter of June 22, 1908, Strauss remarked:

> . . . I need a great moment of repose after Elektra's first shout: 'Orest!' I shall fit in a delicately vibrant orchestral interlude while Elektra gazes upon Orestes, now safely restored to her. I can make her repeat the stammered words: 'Orest, Orest, Orest!' several times. . . . Couldn't you insert here a few beautiful verses until I switch over to the sombre mood . . . ?[18]

Though Hofmannsthal reworked his verses to fit into the tender mood while Elektra gazes upon Orestes, the real concession here comes in the addition of a long orchestral interlude followed by a lyrical, closed aria for Elektra. In the following example from the libretto, note the indication of Strauss's musical insertion and the places where Strauss repeated Elektra's cry of "Orest!" In Hofmannsthal's original text, she calls out the name only once, at the beginning of the passage.

Elektra[19]
Orest!
[Strauss's "delicately vibrant orchestral interlude"]
Orest! Orest! Orest! Es rührt sich niemand! O lass deine
Augen mich sehen, Traumbild, mir geschenktes Traumbild,
schöner als alle Träume! Hehres, unbegreifliches, erhabenes
Gesicht, o bleib' bei mir! Lös' nicht in Luft dich auf, vergeh'
mir nicht, vergeh' mir nicht, es sei denn, dass ich jetzt gleich

---

[18]*The Correspondence between Richard Strauss and Hugo von Hofmannsthal,* 16.

[19]Hugo von Hofmannsthal, *Elektra,* libretto included with sound recording, trans. Boosey & Hawkes, Inc. (London OSA1269, 1966–1967), 20.

sterben muss und du dich anzeigst und mich holen kommst:
dann sterbe ich seliger, als ich gelebt! Orest! Orest! Orest!

Elektra
Orestes!
[Strauss's "delicately vibrant orchestral interlude"]
Orestes! Orestes! Orestes! No one is stirring! Oh let your eyes
gaze at me, dream-phantom, a vision which has been granted
me, fairer than any dream! Sublime, ineffable, noble counte-
nance, oh stay with me, do not melt into air, do not vanish
from my sight. Even if now I have to die, and you have re-
vealed yourself to me and come to fetch me, then I will die
happier than I have lived! Orestes! Orestes! Orestes!

It would be an error to imply that this musical extension in the
form of an aria has no precedent or context at all within the opera. It is,
in fact, based on the music we hear in Elektra's opening monologue,
when she tenderly laments the loss of her father. These following
measures in A-flat major, taken from that monologue, show Elektra's
"longing for her father's love."[20]

**Example 1**, from Elektra's monologue, six bars before rehearsal 46[21]

[20]Paul Bekker, "*Elektra*: A Study by Paul Bekker," trans. Susan Gillespie, in
*Richard Strauss and His World,* ed. Bryan Gilliam (Princeton, NJ: Princeton University
Press, 1992), 384.

[21]Richard Strauss, *Elektra,* piano/vocal score (London: Boosey & Hawkes, 1943), 25.

It is this motive of longing that is re-awakened when Elektra recognizes Orestes, and it forms the basis of her fifty-four-measure aria. The aria, which recalls the A-flat tonality of the longing in her monologue, ends with the following bars that echo Elektra's previous lamentations:

**Example 2,** from Elektra's aria, rehearsal 154[a] [22]

In some senses, it is almost is if time stops for a moment while Elektra absorbs into her being the reality that her innermost desires for revenge may be fulfilled. While this might seem a likely moment of repose in another drama, it undermines the "rapid rising sequence of events" that Hofmannsthal found integral to the nature of his drama. Some contemporary critics were quick to praise Strauss's musical

[22]Strauss, *Elektra*, 187.

choice here. Recently, Lawrence Gilman wrote of the recognition scene:

> . . . Here we have once more the deeper and finer Strauss, the supremely moving tone-poet who portrayed the homecoming and death of Don Quixote, who gave us the tranquil close of "Ein Heldenleben." This scene is the musical apogee of the work. It has a richness of emotion, a depth of sorrowful tenderness, which set it among the noblest things in music.[23]

Paul Bekker, however, believed the result of the extension was a very noticeable attempt by Strauss to leave the audience with something musical to remember.

> The fact that passages of this kind make the strongest impression on the public cannot mislead more serious observers as to their lack of originality. I have no hesitation in judging the much-lauded A-flat-major passage—for many listeners the single refreshing moment of the evening—to be one of the weaker parts of the work. I do not even believe in the artistic-aesthetic necessity of this last-minute insertion. . . . May Strauss not have felt—consciously or unconsciously—a secret wish to offer something to those listeners who were inclined to indulge their ears?[24]

Even Lawrence Gilman admitted that aside from the musical success of the recognition scene, there are many passages "which are far from memorable—passages in which . . . the music declines from power and vitality into lamentable emptiness and commonness."[25]

---

[23]Lawrence Gilman, "Strauss and the Greeks," in *Nature in Music and Other Studies in Tone-Poetry of Today* (Freeport, NY: Books for Libraries Press, Inc., 1966), 129–130.

[24]Bekker, 399–400.

[25]Gilman, 130.

The real argument against what some praised as Strauss's musical greatness is that the end result suspends the dramatic action for too long. Perhaps this was Strauss's narcissistic attempt to leave the audience with a memorable "musical" moment. This flash of a self-serving aesthetic would definitely conflict with the thrust of Hofmannsthal's original text. Paul Bekker remarked:

> I almost wish that Hofmannsthal had not agreed to this alteration. The score of *Elektra* would be deprived of one of its most sure-fire effects, but its unity would not have been interrupted by this lyrical flourish.[26]

The fact that in later collaboration Strauss always deferred to Hofmannsthal's choice of subject is a great tribute to the librettist; in a way it almost re-established a "pre-eminence of the libretto which was all but completely gone since Metastasio."[27] However, in the case of *Elektra,* it seems as if Strauss either could not or would not operate on the same aesthetic principles as his esteemed librettist. In this case of the recognition scene, one sees the *words* of Strauss's music superseding the *deed* of Hofmannsthal's drama.

[26]Bekker, 400.

[27]Patrick J. Smith, *The Tenth Muse: A Historical Study of the Opera Libretto* (New York: Schirmer Books, 1970), 364.

# Bibliography

Bekker, Paul. "*Elektra*: A Study by Paul Bekker," trans. Susan Gillespie. In *Richard Strauss and His World,* ed. Bryan Gilliam, 372–405. Princeton, NJ: Princeton University Press, 1992.

*The Correspondence between Richard Strauss and Hugo von Hofmannsthal,* trans. Hanns Hammelmann and Ewald Osers. London: William Collins Sons & Co. Ltd., 1961.

Gilliam, Bryan. *Richard Strauss's Elektra.* Oxford: Clarendon Press, 1991.

Gilman, Lawrence. "Strauss and the Greeks." In *Nature in Music and Other Studies in Tone-Poetry of Today,* 111–132. Freeport, NY: Books for Libraries Press, Inc., 1966.

Hofmannsthal, Hugo von. *Elektra.* Libretto included with sound recording, trans. Boosey & Hawkes, Inc. London OSA1269, 1966–1967.

Kramer, Lawrence. "*Fin-de-siècle* fantasies: *Elektra,* degeneration and sexual science." *Cambridge Opera Journal* 5, no. 2 (July 1993): 141–165.

Mann, William. *Richard Strauss: A Critical Study of the Operas.* New York: Oxford University Press, 1966.

Marek, George R. "Cry of Anguish." *Opera News* 49 (December 8, 1984): 16–18.

Marx, Robert. "Act Two." *Opera News* 63, no. 9 (March 1999): 18–21.

Opel, Adolf. "The Legacies of Dissolution." Introduction to *The Sacred Spring: The Arts in Vienna 1898–1918,* by Nicolas Powell. London: Studio Vista, 1974.

Puffett, Derrick, ed. *Richard Strauss: Elektra.* Cambridge Opera Handbooks. Cambridge: Cambridge University Press, 1989.

Schorske, Carl E. *Fin-de-Siècle Vienna: Politics and Culture.* New York: Vintage Books, 1981.

Simon, John. "Daughter of Death." *Opera News* 56, no. 15 (April 11, 1992): 14–16, 18.

Smith, Patrick J. *The Tenth Muse: A Historical Study of the Opera Libretto.* New York: Schirmer Books, 1970.

Strauss, Richard. *Elektra,* Op. 58. London: Boosey & Hawkes, 1996.

# Index